ISLINGTON

Please return this item on or before the last date stamped below or you may be liable to overdue charges. To renew an item call the number below, or access the online catalogue at www.islington.gov.uk/libraries. You will need your library membership number and PIN number.

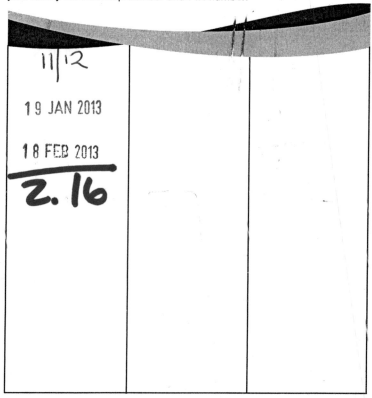

11/12

1 9 JAN 2013

1 8 FEB 2013

2.16

Islington Libraries

020 7527 6900   **www.islington.gov.uk/libraries**

First published February 2008.

This revised second edition published July 2012.

Every effort has been made to ensure the accuracy of the information given but the author and the publisher accept no responsibility for any injury, loss or inconvenience sustained by anyone using this guide. If you have any comments, information or photographs which would be useful to include in future editions of *The Motorcaravanning Handbook*, please send them to:
Books Division, Haynes Publishing,
Sparkford, Yeovil, Somerset BA22 7JJ.

ISBN 978 1 84425 428 6

British Library Cataloguing in Publication Data
A catalogue record for this book is available from the British Library

Haynes Publishing
Sparkford, Yeovil, Somerset BA22 7JJ
Telephone: **01963 442030**
Fax: **01963 440001**
E-mail: **sales@haynes.co.uk**
Web site: **www.haynes.co.uk**

Haynes North America Inc.,
861 Lawrence Drive, Newbury Park, California 91320, USA

Designed and typeset by Rod Teasdale.

Printed and bound in the USA by Odcombe Press LP,
1299 Bridgestone Parkway, La Vergne, TN 37086.

the
MOTORCARAVANNING
handbook
BUYING • OWNING • ENJOYING

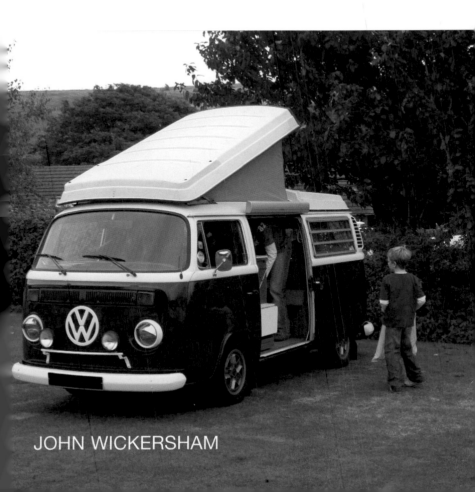

JOHN WICKERSHAM

CONTENTS

CHAPTER ONE

FREEDOM
TO ROAM

Fresh milk is all that's needed before my motorcaravan is ready for action. The parked vehicle is always equipped with clothes, a basic supply of food, clean bedding, outdoor chairs and wellies. To escape for a break it's merely a matter of climbing aboard, starting the engine and turning right when leaving the drive. That's one of the benefits of owning a motorcaravan – holidays can be taken with minimum fuss.

An increasing number of motorcaravans are purchased every year.

Launched in the 1950s, VW 'camper vans' have gained iconic status.

Motorcaravan statistics

The Society of Motor Manufacturers and Traders (SMMT) records that the annual sales of new motorcaravans and recent registration totals have sometimes exceeded 11,000 vehicles during a 12-monthly period. In addition, the National Caravan Council (NCC) keeps records of new registrations and there have been several significant increases in annual sales figures during the last 10 years.

Notwithstanding data about new products, you might wonder how many people currently own a motorcaravan in the UK. In a Press Release circulated in 2006, the NCC put the figure at 120,000 vehicles. In reality, this is unlikely to tell the whole story because some motorcaravans are not included in the records. A surprising number of people purchase a van and convert it themselves, and self-built motorcaravans are often overlooked when reports are compiled.

More and more people have realised that a motorcaravan offers the freedom to roam. It is just what you need to 'get up and go' and it's scarcely surprising that motorcaravanning is growing in popularity in many European countries.

In the UK, sales of new and pre-owned motorcaravans continue to rise, even during periods when money is tight. Whether this trend reflects people's discontent with airport delays, or their disappointments when hotels don't attain expected standards, is anyone's guess. But one thing is clear: more and more people confess that they'd love to own a motorcaravan.

Of course, an interest in motorcaravans isn't new. In the 1950s, many were intrigued when Volkswagen introduced rear-engined light vans, which turned out to be ideal for converting into camping vehicles. Over the years the 'V-Dub' became an icon, and people of all ages still display a fond affection for these basic, but rather cute, campers.

Name games

The previous few words highlight a problem of terminology. Is this book about campers, Dormobiles, caravanettes, coachbuilts, van conversions, motorcaravans, motorhomes or RVs? And what do these terms actually mean? It all sounds rather confusing. Furthermore, if you chuck an old mattress in the back of a van, together with a camp table and a couple of folding chairs, could this be regarded as a motorcaravan?

The accompanying panel clarifies what constitutes a motorcaravan as far as 'officialdom' is concerned. Chapter Two, takes this further and draws attention to the different types of leisure vehicle. After all, motorcaravans come in many shapes and sizes, and you'll come across terms such as van conversions, coachbuilts, A-class models, dismountables, and American Recreational Vehicles (RVs). So variations on the theme are described in more detail later and their respective merits are compared.

Reviewing the different types of leisure vehicle is important because the whole point of this book is to help readers find out more about this leisure pursuit. For the most part, the vehicles will be referred to as motorcaravans or motorhomes, since both terms are commonly used in this country. In addition, the term 'camper' is a popular term, so this is also used to describe small van conversions. However, I won't refer to campers or camper vans as 'caravanettes' – a term that has virtually disappeared. Nor will you see the word 'Dormobiles'. Dormobile was one of the early van converters whose trading name slipped into popular usage some 50 years ago. Even today a few people still describe van conversions as Dormobiles, just as many householders refer to any vacuum cleaner as a Hoover.

Choosing the right model isn't as easy as you might imagine.

Choosing wisely

No doubt you'll have already detected the author's enthusiasm for motorcaravanning. Having tested dozens for magazine reports, and having built three motorcaravans from scratch, I know the pleasures they can offer.

On the other hand, it's not easy for intending motorcaravanners to make an informed purchase.

What is a motorcaravan?

In legal publications, the term used for this kind of leisure vehicle is 'motor caravan' rather than 'motorhome'. If you check European Type Approval documents you'll also find that a motor caravan is 'a special purpose M1 category vehicle constructed to include living accommodation which contains at least the following equipment: seats and table, sleeping accommodation (which may be converted from the seats), cooking facilities, storage facilities.' The statement also adds: 'This equipment shall be rigidly fixed to the living compartment; however, the table may be designed to be easily removable.'

Whilst the term 'motorhome', and the single word 'motorcaravan' are used both in this book and specialist magazines, these terms don't normally get used in documents of a legal nature. For instance, in the 'D5 Body Type' section in a UK Vehicle Registration Certificate, (often called the 'log book'), the entry normally reads: MOTOR CARAVAN.

Later in this book, the more complex issues about 'M1 vehicles' and elements like Vehicle Excise Duty will be discussed further. For the moment, it's quite clear that a panel van with a mattress in the back is not deemed to be a motor caravan.

Some owners use a motorcaravan to support their hobbies and leisure activities.

In fact, a worrying number of first-time owners confess they've bought the wrong kind of model, and change it remarkably quickly. This can be an expensive mistake.

In truth, there are many points to consider. For instance, what kind of vehicle best suits your particular needs? Would you mainly use it for warm weather trips, or would it be used in cold weather too? Where would you keep it? Are there licensing issues to check? And are you aware of height limits at car parks?

Learning the ropes

Once you have made the right purchase, there is still a lot to learn. For instance, a kitchen appliance like a leisure refrigerator is surprisingly different from the fridges we use in our homes. Similarly, a motorhome toilet has unique features. Heating appliances often need periodic servicing checks, and during cold winter spells, water systems usually need draining-down too.

It might be presumed that user guidance relating to appliances would be covered in the owner's manual supplied by the motorhome manufacturer. But be warned – some so-called 'manuals' consist of nothing more than a folder filled with leaflets published by appliance suppliers. Even if there is a model-specific booklet, purchasers of second-hand models often discover that the original owner's manual has been lost.

Even the best handbooks that are supplied with new models aren't always easy for a first-time owner to understand. Illustrations are not always clear, and getting things to work can be as frustrating as when coping with a new digital camera, desktop computer or multi-function washing machine. Mindful of this, some manufacturers have started to include quick-start guides to supplement their main instruction manual. However, quick-start guides are more commonly supplied with touring caravans; curiously, they're seldom included with motorhomes.

Sometimes parking places prohibit tall vehicles.

Guidance, hints and tips

Explaining how to get appliances and supply systems to operate is one of the many aims in this book, and separate chapters provide hints and tips relating to gas, water and electrical supplies. This guidance is useful, but equally important is the advice about supplementary accessories, different types of campsites, and things to consider when touring abroad.

Of course, this book isn't your only source of help. To keep abreast of the latest models, changing legislation, new campsites, ferry operations and so on, readers are strongly recommended to look at magazines that specialise in motorcaravanning. Similarly, some websites provide guidance through movie clips, such as www.wickyworld.co.uk

There are also TV programmes that offer guidance, such as *The Caravan Channel*, which encompasses motorcaravans too.

When looking at the many aspects of this pastime, don't forget that some people buy a motorcaravan to pursue leisure activities, and others prefer more relaxed breaks. Equally, some owners are young, while others are elderly. Many motorhome owners have children or grandchildren, and a number have dogs that share the trips too. Also bear in mind that several motorcaravan manufacturers specialise in adapting vehicles for users with physical disabilities. All motorcaravanners' needs are different.

Bearing these points in mind, manufacturers produce a huge variety of motorcaravan types. In fact, a 'Buyers Guide', included with *Practical Motorhome* (March 2012) listed 332 British-built models, 744 European imports and 11 American RV importing specialists. Add to these all the second-hand models on sale and it shows the vast number of motorcaravans available. What's more, you need to make certain that you buy one that meets your particular requirements. The pages that follow will help you make an informed choice.

Many motorcaravanners enjoy social get-togethers and local clubs arrange regular meetings.

Some motorcaravanners want to tow a trailer and not all vehicles are able to do this.

Many owners have children or grandchildren and some layouts inside are more suitable than others.

Dogs and other pets are often accommodated in a motorcaravan, which also influences the choice of vehicle.

CHAPTER **TWO**

DIFFERENT TYPES OF MOTORCARAVAN

The previous chapter explained that there are many contrasting types of motorcaravan, and different models are built to satisfy different needs, so you'll have to choose your options with care. Here's a way to narrow your search.

With so many products on sale, it's hard to decide on a model you like.

One variety of motorcaravan starts life as a panel van, a window van or a multi-purpose car.

Motorcaravans usually fall into one of two broad groups according to the way they're built. Admittedly there are a few products that defy classification, but the majority of leisure vehicles fall into one of these categories:

1. Van conversions. This type of motorcaravan starts life as a panel van, a multi-purpose vehicle, or a van equipped with factory-fitted side windows. When fitted-out with domestic appliances, furniture and comfort items, the resulting motorcaravan is prosaically referred to as a van conversion. Others prefer to call it a 'camper van' or 'camper'.

2. Coachbuilt models. These motorcaravans use base vehicles that comprise an engine and chassis, which is explained in more detail in Chapter Three. All that needs to be said here is that some base vehicles used for coachbuilt models start life with a cab; others have no cab at all. In automotive language the former type is referred to as 'a chassis cab'; the latter is simply called a 'chassis cowl'. Either of these will provide a structure on which a 'coachbuilt' living enclosure can be mounted.

Coachbuilt motorcaravans are constructed either on a 'chassis cab' or 'chassis cowl'.

Having recognised these contrasting base vehicles, let's consider their respective merits and weaknesses.

Van conversions

Plus points – If you want a vehicle that drives
like a conventional car and is easy to park, a van
conversion is the answer. In most cases they aren't
as large as coachbuilt models and are easier to drive
through busy towns. Their manoeuvrability is no less
important when parking a vehicle at home; a few
small van conversions can even fit inside an ordinary
domestic garage, although height is often a problem.

Minus points – A panel van or a van fitted with
side windows doesn't lend itself to high output
production-line construction. For example, the
restricted space inside limits the number of people
who can work simultaneously during the fitting-out
operation. Moreover, the intricate shape inside a steel
shell means that furniture takes a considerable time
to install. These factors contribute to the surprisingly
high prices of most brand new models.

Coachbuilt motorcaravans

Plus points – By using prefabricated insulated panels
for the floor, roof and flat sides, production-line
assembly can be utilised. In fact, several caravan
and motorhome manufacturers install furniture and
appliances on an unenclosed floor panel, preserving

*Above left: Van
conversions are easy to
drive, easy to park, and a
large sliding door offers
generous side access too.*

*Above: Converting a van is
hindered by lack of space,
so not many people can
work inside at the same
time.*

*To achieve working space,
coachbuilt caravans and
motorhomes are often
assembled on a floor
panel – walls are added
much later.*

Coachbuilt motorcaravans like this Auto-Trail can be spacious inside and a variety of different layouts are offered.

Constructional differences

This chapter only looks at structural elements briefly; Chapter Four pursues the subject in greater depth. As regards base vehicles, these are also described more thoroughly in Chapter Three.

the fitters' freedom of movement by not adding the wall panels until later. This facilitates speedy construction, which in turn is reflected in the vehicle's price. If you compare similarly priced van conversion and coachbuilt models, the latter usually offer a lot more space for your money. Coachbuilt models built with flat sides also provide greater scope for layout variations in the living area.

Minus points – Since the body structure is usually constructed using separate panels, joints can't be avoided. In time, the joining points often become weak spots and water ingress then poses a threat.

The situation is made worse when dissimilar materials are used. For example, steel panels forming the cab, aluminium-skinned panels used for the walls and contoured plastic mouldings installed elsewhere all have different rates of expansion/contraction. So during periods of high temperatures, dissimilar thermal movements of adjacent panels challenge the flexibility of the joint sealant. In time it becomes brittle, and when it fails, the body's weather-resistance is challenged. Examples of coachbuilt models afflicted by damp are often reported in magazine articles.

Bearing in mind that we've identified two distinctly different types of motorcaravan, a purchaser needs to consider their respective merits extremely carefully to avoid disappointment later. For example, coachbuilt models may offer spacious and opulent interiors, but van conversions are much better when you're driving along narrow lanes or you've decided to explore remote highland terrain. These considerations are discussed in more detail in Chapter Five.

CONTRASTING TYPES OF VAN CONVERSION

Some micro caravans like this Romahome Duo Hylo are sufficiently small to be parked in a typical domestic garage.

Micro conversions

Not many micro-motorcaravans are currently being manufactured, and small-scale converters produce most examples. Some specialists are also noted for building micro camper vans to suit customers' individual requirements. Not all conversions include the installation of an elevating roof, although most owners prefer to have standing room inside. However, with a roof lowered in its road-ready state, the smallest vans can usually be stored in a domestic garage. For some owners this is a real bonus.

Recent examples

A well-respected designer, Barry Stimson of Design Developments, created models like the Provence. A similar conversion is now being sold by Lifestyle Vehicle Developments as La Parisienne, which is based on the Citroën Berlingo.

Another Micro specialist is JC Leisure, whose models have included the Porterhome, based on the Piaggio Porter, and the Rio, based on the Renault Kangoo.

When exhibited in 2000, the Romahome Duo Hylo also attracted attention. In addition to its garaging potential, the Hylo achieves an internal height of 1.83m when its roof is raised.

Plus points
- Usually the least expensive of all new models
- Easy to drive, park and store
- Good fuel economy
- Suitable as a daily commuting to work vehicle.

Minus points
- Little space for storing your gear
- Tidy, organised living is imperative in the space available
- Beds formed using cab seats aren't noted for comfort
- On-board toilet provision is usually very basic
- Lounging comforts are lacking.

In this small fixed roof van from Young Conversions, cooking has to be carried out from a seated position.

Plus points
- Easy to drive and park
- Good fuel economy
- Suitable for daily commuting to work
- Business versions built for mobile executives
- Some models can pass under car park height barriers.

Minus points
- Intolerable if you want to stand up to stretch your legs
- Not particularly pleasant for long holidays
- Storage space is minimal
- Heat is lost if single-glazed windows are fitted throughout
- If used, an MPV is a far more expensive base than a light van.

Although a small fixed-roof van has advantages, preparing and cooking meals in a seated position is not to everyone's taste.

Low fixed-roof conversions
Most motorcaravanners would expect to be able to stand up in the living space, but that's out of the question in some fixed-roof conversions. The idea of cooking and generally living in a seated position was often adopted in converted Volkswagen T2 vans in the 1950s. Today, a few van conversions are still built on short wheelbase vans with low rooflines.

Similarly, some manufacturers convert Multi Purpose Vehicles (MPVs) – especially to act as mobile offices for executives who work on the move, convene occasional meetings, and seldom expect the vehicle to provide overnight accommodation.

Recent examples
A well-constructed model, the Murvi Meteor, has been built using Fiat and Peugeot short wheelbase vans. However, versions bearing the Meteor name have also been built with elevating roofs. Fixed roof T4 Volkswagen vans have also been manufactured by Bilbo's Design and Young Conversions. Wheelhome, a company particularly noted for MPV conversions, has also fitted out vehicles like the fixed-roof Suzuki Wagon R.

Fixed-roof high-top van conversions

Some light commercial panel vans have a longer wheelbase and a high roof. For example, the Fiat Ducato long wheelbase (lwb) maxi van has an internal height of around 1.88m (74in). This is slightly reduced when insulation material and plywood is added to the floor and ceiling, but high-roof vans on the Fiat Ducato/Peugeot Boxer, Mercedes Sprinter and Renault Master have often been converted into motorcaravans. For example, the Fiat-based Murvi Morello has won awards for its noteworthy design and pleasing comforts.

Overall, this type of motorcaravan meets the needs of many people, but it may not be the best option for the very tall.

Recent examples

The Murvi Morello is particularly well-known and its converter in South Devon has won numerous trophies in 'design and drive' competitions. Although its price is high compared with many van conversions, this model is sold with a long list of ancillary items that are seldom included by other manufacturers. Bilbo's Design, a company well-known for VW conversions, has also developed the Fiat-based Cyclone in recent years. The Oregon from IH Motor Campers, based on a Renault Master, is another high fixed-roof model fitted with notably well-finished furniture.

As regards imported vehicles, the *la strada* Regent from Germany and the Adria Twin from Slovenia have been well received in Britain. Similarly, the early examples of Tribute models from Trigano were noted for their competitive price. Incidentally, Trigano is the parent company of Auto-Trail.

Manufactured in South Devon, the Morello has been one of Murvi's most successful models; it has won many awards since its launch in the 1990s.

Plus points
- Easy to drive
- Reasonable fuel economy
- No need for roof alterations during manufacture
- Good weather integrity
- Small enough to fit most servicing centres with ease
- A large sliding side door offers a wide point of entry.

Minus points
- Not suitable for really tall owners
- Costly when compared with large coachbuilts of similar price
- A sliding side door tends to limit the number of layouts possible inside.

Many innovative campervans are designed by Wheelhome and this Suzuki Wagon-R is fitted with a canvas-sided elevating roof.

Elevating (rising) roof conversions

Fitting elevating roofs on vans became a popular practice among converters of Volkswagen (VW) camper vans in the 1950s. As the years passed, different elevating systems were developed, and some models have been fitted with hinged wooden panels that fold upwards to form the sides of a box. The VW-based Trooper, made by Auto-Sleepers, is a well-known example; the Holdsworth Villa 3 was another example from the 1980s.

However, most elevating structures have canvas sides and a specially built roof panel of glass-reinforced plastic (GRP). Some hinge along the side, while others hinge from the front or rear. This is a clever way to create generous headroom, and once a vehicle is parked the elevated structure is sometimes equipped to support a high-level bed. This will often be a 'stretcher-bed' for young children but some manufacturers have managed to fit a sturdy double bed for adults.

Today's elevating roof mechanisms are cleverly engineered, but you cannot overlook the fact that even a well-designed canvas-sided enclosure is not good at retaining heat in the winter. It is also more likely to get very hot inside when parked in direct sunlight.

Recent examples

Auto-Sleepers builds the Trooper with fold-up panel sides, and the Villa from Holdsworth was similarly popular until the Company ceased building motorcaravans. Bilbo's Design also offers fabric-sided models like the VW-based Celex, Komba and Nexa. Danbury Motorcaravans offer slightly different products, as they have been converting replica Type 3 VWs made under licence in Brazil. These have also been fitted with elevating roofs.

Unusually, VW is one of the only vehicle manufacturers directly involved with motorcaravan conversions as well. The California Comfortline, SE, and Trendline are being built at the Hanover Plant in Germany. Each model features an elevating roof constructed on a VW T5 window van.

The former van converter, Richard Holdsworth, offered the Villa 3 with its solid-sided elevating roof.

Plus points
- Easy to drive and park
- Good fuel economy
- Suitable for daily commuting to work
- More comfortable indoors than a low fixed-roof van
- Good access via the wide sliding side door.

Minus points
- The interior can get cold in winter and hot in summer
- Packing away a damp roof leads to damage
- Useful high-level storage is seldom available
- Operating some mechanisms involves strenuous effort and is worth checking.

Small vans are often fitted with a GRP roof moulding to provide headroom – as with this high-top model.

High-tops

Arguably, the high fixed-roof conversions described earlier could be classified in the 'high-top' category. However, in the motorcaravan industry, the term is more often used for vans that have been retrospectively fitted with a GRP moulding in place of their original metal panel roof.

In high-quality conversions, a GRP (glass-reinforced plastic, often called 'fibre glass') moulding will perfectly match the colour of the parent van. Its surfaces will also be free of undulations and the moulding will look as if it has always been part of the original vehicle. High-top vans built by Auto-Sleepers are a case in point. Using roof mouldings manufactured by Cheltenham Laminations, Auto-Sleepers is well known for good body construction.

Of course, GRP roof mouldings can sometimes be added retrospectively and a number of manufacturers will cut away a steel roof panel for a client, install a robust reinforcing framework around the aperture and then mount a GRP high-top moulding in its place. Specialists like Concept-Multicar, Middlesex Motorcaravans, and Young Conversions are three of several small-scale converters who offer a first-class service. Vehicle manufacturers who approve roof modifications set down strict guidelines to ensure that any loss of rigidity from the removal of a panel and its strength struts is compensated for by the installation of a prescribed reinforcing framework.

It is therefore a matter of grave concern that there are some installers who do not fit the all-important reinforcement before adding a GRP moulding. Low prices attract clients, but there have been examples of flexing mouldings that have subsequently become detached from the parent vehicle. The dangers of this are obvious.

Inside a GRP moulded roof shell, it's important that bare surfaces are insulated, and this is usually done as part of a conversion operation. Some owners also want cubbyholes added so that small items can be stored in the enclosure.

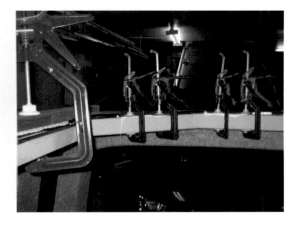

When a steel roof panel is removed in order to fit an elevating roof or a GRP high-top moulding, it is essential for a strengthening frame to be installed.

Recent examples

Many manufacturers of elevating roof motorcaravans also include high-top van conversions in their product line-ups. Auto-Sleepers builds high-tops using several base vehicles, eg the Duetto (Ford Transit panel van), Symbol (Peugeot panel van) and both the Topaz and Trident (VW T5 window van).

Models from Bilbo's Design are also well known. Concept Multi-Car imports Reimo roof mouldings from Germany for its Sportline and Ergoline high-tops. The Matrix and Motion II are well-finished products from Middlesex Motorcaravans, and Torbay Camper Conversions include the Nimbus and Sirius on VW T5 vehicles.

Many other converters manufacturing high-top models are also listed in the Buyers' Guides compiled by motorcaravan magazine publishers.

Plus points
- Driving characteristics are generally good
- Reasonable fuel economy
- Suitable for daily commuting to work
- More comfortable inside than a low fixed-roof van
- Good access via the wide sliding side door
- Some vehicles yield enough space for a toilet cubicle
- Small-scale converters might accommodate customer alterations.

Minus points
- Strong side winds can spoil the driving experience
- Some conversions can be surprisingly expensive
- Seldom the storage space found in similarly priced coachbuilt models
- Models based on window vans lose heat in winter and get hot in summer.

Although there is a capacious over-cab bed in this 2012 Bailey Approach SE 760, it is less attractive externally than low-line models in the Approach SE range.

COACHBUILT MODELS

Over-cab coachbuilts

Starting with a chassis cab, many manufacturers construct coachbuilt models that feature a large compartment built directly over the cab. Sometimes referred to as a 'Luton', this compartment is often used to house a permanent double bed.

An over-cab facility offers useful space in the living area, but externally it can detract from a vehicle's appearance. Moreover, some users dislike a high-level enclosed bed and opt to have cupboards fitted instead. Large 'pods' don't help a vehicle's aerodynamic properties either, and fuel economy can be detrimentally affected.

Underneath, a sturdy chassis supports the floor of the living space and this is either the original chassis supplied by the vehicle manufacturer or a lighter structure designed by AL-KO for motorcaravans. Further information about these chassis is given in Chapter Three.

Right: In some cases an over-cab space is used for storage as shown in this Auto-Trail Dakota.

To celebrate 50 years manufacturing motorcaravans, Auto-Sleepers produced a Limited Edition GRP monocoque coachbuilt model.

As regards the living enclosure, this is usually built using prefabricated, bonded and insulated panels, and purpose-made plastic mouldings. Alternatively, a few manufacturers use monocoque construction in which a one-piece shell of GRP is mounted on the chassis.

Monocoque GRP body shells are usually rather heavy but the benefits of a seam-free, one-piece shell are indisputable. The lack of joints means that the weatherproofing qualities are as good as those of a GRP boat. The material also enables a builder to create an attractive, curvaceous shell without the prosaic flat sides found on most coachbuilt models.

Recent examples

Many manufacturers specialise in the construction of coachbuilt motorcaravans. In Britain, manufacturers like Autocruise, Auto-Sleepers, Auto-Trail, the Explorer Group and the Swift Group have dozens of models on offer. In fact, the Swift Group presents models under the different badge names of Ace, Bessacarr and Swift. And since the involvement of Bailey, hitherto known solely as a touring caravan manufacturer, one of its first models launched in 2011 adopted an overcab bed with unusually good headroom. Huge numbers of over-cab coachbuilts are also produced by manufacturers in mainland Europe, and several British dealers specialise in selling models imported from abroad.

As regards monocoque examples, Auto-Sleepers commissioned a celebrated car designer, the late William Towns, to create a GRP monocoque living compartment. His creations were built by Cheltenham Laminations, and in 1980, Auto-Sleepers launched its first distinctive monocoque. Since then the product has been updated to reflect changes in vehicle design, and recent Auto-Sleepers monocoque coachbuilts include the Peugeot Boxer-based Executive, Mezan and Talisman, and the Ford-based Amethyst. To celebrate

Plus points
- Coachbuilt motorcaravans offer spacious accommodation
- An over-cab bed requires little preparation at bedtime
- Considering size and price, coachbuilt models are particularly good value.

Minus points
- Though easy to drive, a coachbuilt doesn't perform like a car
- Road-handling can be ponderous and punctuated by body roll
- Negotiating narrow lanes can be challenging
- Parking is sometimes difficult
- A typical coachbuilt isn't good for daily commuting
- If not checked at service intervals, some models can later suffer from damp.

The 2011 Burstner Ixeo introduced a subtle lift in the roofline without changing the overall benefits of a low-profile coachbuilt.

50 years building motorcaravans, Auto-Trail also offered a limited edition monocoque model in 2011.

Monocoque models from manufacturers in mainland Europe include the Mobilvetta Kimu and *la strada* Nova.

Low-profile coachbuilts

Most points relating to over-cab coachbuilts are applicable to low-profile models as well. The key difference is the omission of an over-cab 'Luton'.

Some owners find an over-cab bed too restrictive and it can easily become a dumping area for sun-loungers, camp tables and other possessions. The issue of aerodynamics and fuel economy also renders Luton designs questionable. In recognition of these points, low-profile models have been developed to offer a reduced height and a cleaner roofline. This style of motorcaravan gained initial impetus in mainland Europe, and UK manufacturers were less hasty in introducing their own products. But now a huge number is being built; over 400 from both Britain and abroad were listed in the 2012 Buyer's Guide mentioned in Chapter One.

Recent examples

Large-scale UK manufacturers like Auto-Sleepers, Auto-Trail, Elddis, Lunar and the Swift Group all include examples of low-profile models in their ranges. Bailey is also following the trend with its developing products.

Imported low-profile models from Continental manufacturers include examples from Adria, Burstner, Chausson, Dethleffs, Frankia, Hobby, Hymer, Knaus, Laika, Maess, Pilote, Rapido, TEC and many more. The Hobby range in particular is noted for its high proportion of low-profile models, all of which bear the company's distinctive design cues.

Plus points

- Low-profiles share most of the points applicable to over-cab coachbuilts
- The reduced height is helpful when driving near trees
- They are likely to achieve better fuel economy figures.

Minus points

- Most of the disadvantages of over-cab models also apply to low-profile models
- They offer reduced storage space
- Headroom may not be sufficient for tall users.

A-class

Many discerning enthusiasts aspire to own an A-class motorcaravan. There are undoubtedly smart examples, but some features aren't to everyone's liking.

Using terms introduced earlier, an A-class model is normally built using a chassis cowl as opposed to a chassis cab. In consequence, the manufacturer has to construct a body that is all-embracing – rather like a modern coach. Since a chassis cowl doesn't have a cab and is open to the elements, the body design integrates the driving zone with the living accommodation.

Building an A-class body is a major undertaking, and needs to include a windscreen, cab windows and a means of access for the driver. In the event, many manufacturers avoid the exacting task of building the kind of doors fitted to a normal cab. This means that the only way to reach the driving controls is by using the same door that provides entry to the living quarters. No other door is provided.

For many people, this is a poor arrangement, so Auto-Trail boldly fabricated hinged cab-like doors in the Grande Frontier A-class. These were made using GRP, and whilst they lack the rigidity of standard steel doors, the result is far better than having to rely on a single caravan door to gain entry.

Replicating steel automotive doors complete with electric windows isn't easy, so Belgian manufacturer Maess used another strategy. Recognising that a standard cab has all the attributes needed apart from being too narrow, the company found ways to widen its steel shell. By skilfully adding small panels and subsequently installing a wider, commercial, stock-sized windscreen, they produced a masterpiece of modification.

Of course, one of the many opportunities presented by a wider cab in A-class motorcaravans is the chance to install a drop-down bed. Even though seats

This Hymer A-class motorcaravan is built using a chassis cowl that supports a body embracing both the driving and living areas.

Plus points
- The body design lends itself to clean, attractive lines
- An elevating bed in the cab can be left with its bedding in place
- Most models have well-appointed interiors
- The storage capacity is usually generous.

Minus points
- A cab bereft of doors is not to everyone's liking
- Replacement windscreens can be very expensive
- Large models are not suitable for use on narrow lanes
- Parking is often a problem
- Fuel economy on large models is usually disappointing
- If a large side panel gets damaged, repairs are often costly
- Some campsites are unable to accept large vehicles
- Keeping a vehicle of this kind clean is not an easy task.

in the living area can normally be converted into beds, the one above the cab seats can be folded away with its bedding still in place. Clever geometry and gas spring assistance means that an elevating mechanism requires little effort by the operator.

Apart from this feature, A-class interiors aren't a great deal different from chassis cab coachbuilts – unless you include those grandiose monsters built on truck chassis that command six-figure prices.

Recent examples
Few British manufacturers have built A-class models, and at the time of writing, there are no UK volume manufacturers making any. The compact Autoking produced by Elddis in the 1980s achieved disappointing sales. The 1998 Bel-Air manufactured by Swift wasn't a big seller either and was withdrawn after four years. Auto-Sleepers introduced the Luxor in 2002, but this was essentially a reworked version of the Italian-built Mirage. Finally, Auto-Trail introduced the Grande Frontier in 2005; this British-built model received much praise but production ended in 2007.

In contrast, manufacturers in mainland Europe produce an incredible number of A-class models. The German company Concorde has 48 A-class models; Frankia currently lists 41; Dethleffs lists 38; and Hymer 25. The Pilote range from France numbers 38, and there are Laika models manufactured in Italy. According to *Practical Motorhome's Buyer's Guide* (2012), the current total of models in mainland Europe amounts to over 330.

Among the really large vehicles, marques like Carthago and ClouLINER, are undoubtedly impressive. So are models built in North Wales by MCL. Fitted-out to customer specifications, MCL's beautiful creations cost around £250,000 and the company's strategy is to focus on quality rather than quantity.

By skilfully widening a standard chassis cab, Maess has offered A-class models with sturdy doors and wind-down windows.

American RVs

A significant number of big American recreational vehicles or RVs are also purchased in this country. However, whether driving an inter-state leviathan on European roads is appropriate is a matter often debated. Furthermore, some campsite owners cannot accommodate vehicles of this size and weight.

Surprisingly, American RVs are not as expensive to purchase as many people imagine. New models are hardly cheap, but if you calculate floor area and take account of all the standard equipment, you get an awful lot for your money. However, the purchase price is only one issue: servicing this type of vehicle and filling its fuel tanks is an aspect you mustn't ignore.

Another point to note relates to the build quality inside. The design of American furniture won't meet everyone's taste and buyers should look at it closely. Sometimes you'll find cabinets that have been assembled in haste and the craftsmanship of furniture constructors can be dreadfully disappointing. In contrast, other constructional elements display much better build quality.

Recent examples

Motorcaravan magazines list several UK importers who specialise in the sale and servicing of RVs. It's probably best to purchase through a specialist dealer because electrical items and water components are usually totally different from equivalent European products. Dealers in the UK include American RV Imports, Anglo American RV, Castle Motors, Dreams RV Centre, Dudleys of Oxfordshire, Freedom Motor Homes, Itchy Feet, Oakwell, Stingray RV, Signature Motorhomes, and Travelworld.

There are also active clubs whose members are usually eager to offer advice, and also a mail order RV parts specialist – ABP Accessories in Leicestershire.

American RV models with their slide-out sides can be purchased in the UK from several import specialists.

Plus points
- Storage space aplenty
- A veritable home on wheels
- Models offer items like hip baths, huge TVs, settees, on board generators and so on.

Minus points
- Some campsites cannot accommodate large vehicles
- Fuel and maintenance costs are high
- Their size limits touring possibilities; winter storage might also be difficult
- Few specialists have space for repairs, servicing and MoT tests
- Non-standard parts may have to be fitted; spares might be hard to obtain
- Build quality inside is sometimes disappointing.

Anyone who owns a pickup truck like this powerful Nissan has an opportunity to use it with a 'living pod' for holidays, too.

OTHER MODELS

It was pointed out earlier that a few products defy classification. That isn't to say that they aren't important options, although neither of the types described here are as popular in Europe as they are in North America. However, if pickup trucks become more common in Europe, then both products listed below are likely to become popular here as well.

Dismountables

The amount of internal space in a dismountable 'pod' is surprisingly good, and once it has been detached, the base vehicle is ready for driving off-site.

Recent examples

Apollo, based in Lancashire, has manufactured dismountable units for more than a decade, with versions for both single and crew-cab pickup trucks. Ranger Motorhomes, from the same county, also manufactures dismountables. American products, including folding-roof versions, are imported by Niche Marketing.

Plus points
- If you own a pickup truck, a pod is an inexpensive extra
- Detaching the pod releases the base vehicle for solo use.

Minus points
- Cab space doesn't contribute to the living area
- With a top-heavy rig, dismountables can roll badly on twisting roads.

This dismountable unit manufactured by Ranger in Lancashire offers a surprising amount of living space.

Fifth wheelers

These articulated products require a pickup truck for towing. Not that it's like towing a caravan. Forget a poorly matched caravan's problem of snaking, and the difficulties of reversing an outfit. Fifth-wheelers are far easier to control, and deserve more acclaim in this country.

Of course, some of the American juggernauts are very large for Britain's small roads but they offer an excellent way to travel.

Recent examples

Products made by the Fifth Wheel Co in North Wales are built to extremely high standards and this has been recognised in The Caravan Club's Award contests. Arguably the original Celtic Rambler GRP monocoque is rather large for many of Britain's roads, but smaller versions are now also available. All models from the Fifth Wheel Co feature slide-out sides, which significantly increase the space inside. These leisure vehicles are sold with or without a Nissan pickup and customer requirements can be built-in to order.

A few American Fifth Wheel products are also imported by specialists in the UK such as Nene Overland and Niche Marketing.

So is a fifth wheeler a caravan or a motorhome? Classification uncertainty is not the fault of the products, which have many points in their favour. But so do other models – as this chapter has already shown.

The fixtures and fittings inside the Fifth Wheel Company's models are built to a very high standard.

Plus points
- Surprisingly easy to tow, reverse and manoeuvre on-site
- Prices are not as high as many presume
- An ideal addition for owners of suitable pickup trucks
- A permanent bed fits into the half-height front section
- Usually spacious inside.

Minus points
- There's a need for even smaller models – one-off micro models have been built in the past
- Fifth wheelers might be difficult to sell-on later.

These high quality products made in North Wales by The Fifth Wheel Company are specifically built to meet European standards.

CHAPTER THREE

BASE VEHICLES

Although it can be tempting to choose a motorcaravan solely on the basis of its living accommodation, that would be a mistake. From an early stage in the decision making process you need to consider its road-going characteristics and confirm that it's pleasant to drive. This means you'll need to compare different types of base vehicle and decide which one meets your particular needs. Products that look good in a showroom can be quite dull on the road.

33

Motorcaravan driving courses are run by The Camping and Caravanning Club.

Courses to improve your driving skills are run by both The Camping and Caravanning Club and The Caravan Club.

The drivers of today's cars are pretty versatile. The range of vehicles currently on sale means that one moment you might be driving a small town car, and the next an off-road vehicle, perched on a seat high above the ground. Anyone with a range of experiences like these will find driving most types of motorcaravan relatively easy. If not, both The Camping and Caravanning Club and The Caravan Club run short training courses for prospective motorhome drivers.

Also bear in mind that the majority of motorcaravans are constructed using light commercial vehicles (LCVs), and modern examples are surprisingly car-like to drive. This is why many people feel confident to take the wheel of a small or medium-sized motorhome. On the other hand, if your licence permits and you're eager to purchase an American RV or one of Europe's larger conversions, heavy goods vehicles (HGVs) are *not* car-like, and appropriate training is recommended.

 Technical Tip

Terminology

Throughout this book, the term 'base vehicle' is used to describe the automotive product on which a motorcaravan is built. Just to clear up potential confusion, note that when some people comment that they'd have liked their motorcaravan to have been built 'on a different chassis', what they actually mean is 'on a different base vehicle'.

When the word 'chassis' is used in this book it refers specifically to the structure that supports a coachbuilt motorcaravan body. To be pedantic, a panel van or side-window van doesn't have a traditional chassis; in fact it's like a modern car, which is built with a floorpan. Strengthened brackets that form part of this steel base accept items of running gear such as axles and suspension components.

Converted MPVs

In recent years the distinctions between cars, multi-purpose vehicles (MPVs) and vans have become increasingly blurred. In fact a few companies have specialised in the conversion of MPVs, into campervans, and Wheelhome is especially prominent in this field. Of course, these are fitted with a lining and finished inside like a car at the point of sale. In consequence converted MPVs are considerably more expensive than campervans based on light commercial vans.

In the previous chapter, the point was also made that most motorhomes are either 'fitted-out' vans or coachbuilt models that have a purpose-made living space fixed to a commercial chassis. However, there are a few coachbuilt models built on a third type of commercial base structure known as a 'platform cab'. Not surprisingly, these different products influence the driving experience.

Driving most motorcaravans is much like driving a car. However, that's not true of large vehicles such as American RVs.

Left: Van conversions have a pre-constructed enclosure and a base panel referred to as a floor pan.

Above: A 'platform cab' uses a reinforced floor assembly that vehicle manufacturers design and construct.

Left: This commercial cab is connected to a lightweight chassis manufactured by AL-KO Kober.

Tall drivers often find that seats heightened by retrofitted swivels cause their eye-line to meet the top of the screen.

GENERAL MATTERS

Since many potential owners haven't had experience driving different types of light commercial vehicles (LCVs), they are unfamiliar with several of their unusual characteristics. For example, taller drivers often find that in some LCVs the screen is too low for comfort. This occurs if seats in the cab have been retrofitted with 360° swivel systems; a swivelling turntable often adds height to the seat squab and tall people then find their line of vision is too close to the top of the screen.

Shorter people might decide that high seats won't present a problem for them. This is certainly true where the screen is concerned, but instead they may have an issue with the floor height. Letters published in motorcaravan magazines often reveal that many people sitting in the passenger seat find their feet barely touch the floor. The responses also report how owners solve this by using things like typists' foot-support platforms, hassocks from churches and homemade plinths.

Details such as this can prove irritating and might come as a surprise to new motorcaravanners. This is why potential owners are advised to hire a motorcaravan for a short period to gain first-hand experience of its driving and habitation characteristics. Admittedly hiring can be costly during high season, but it's less costly outside of peak periods.

Some dealers also run 'hire before you buy' schemes. Having hired one of their vehicles, clients often have the fee reimbursed if they subsequently buy a model from the dealer within a certain time.

So far this chapter has been concerned with matters of detail so now let's look at the larger picture.

Useful Tip

Arrange a test drive

- There are far too many cases of new owners changing their motorcaravan a very short time after purchasing it. One reason for dissatisfaction concerns the driving experience and the base vehicle's features.
- It appears that many people don't insist on a test drive before making a purchase. That is certainly an oversight.
- If a dealer isn't prepared to arrange a test drive, it would be better to go elsewhere.

Seat height

Recognising that retrofitted seat swivel mechanisms often render the height of cab seats unsuitable, when Fiat launched its revised Ducato in 2006 one of its improvements involved a redesigned seating arrangement that addressed this.

Owners of earlier models can sometimes remedy the problem by fitting lower profile plinths sold by independent specialists such as TEK Seating. These fit in place of the original items and bring the seat squabs closer to the floor.

37

POINTS TO CONSIDER

In addition to idiosyncrasies like seat heights, potential owners need to give due consideration to matters such as:

- Right- or left-hand drive?
- Engine capacity
- Choice of fuel – diesel or petrol?
- Emission levels
- Fuel economy
- Transmission – front-, rear- or four-wheel drive?
- Gears – manual gearbox, automatic or 'sprint shift'?
- Suspension – leaf spring, coil spring, torsion bars or air bellows?
- Chassis – vehicle manufacturer's or AL-KO Kober's products?
- Potential for towing
- Option lists – ABS, airbags, stability controls, GPS systems, upgraded stereos, central locking, electric windows, high output alternator, upgraded payload capacity and so on.

From their 2006 models on, Fiat offered optional lower bases and swivelling turntables so that the final seat heights are more acceptable.

Many motorcaravans can't be fitted with a towbar, which is something to check if you intend to tow a trailer.

Many coachbuilt models have been paired with Fiat's 2.8 turbo diesel engine, which is pleasingly powerful.

Right- or left-hand drive?

Some imported motorcaravans are only available in left-hand drive form. These can be difficult to sell at a later date and typically command a lower price during a trade-in transaction. This usually deters potential owners from buying what is affectionately known as a 'left-hooker'.

On the other hand, some retired owners spend a considerable amount of time in the warmer parts of mainland Europe, especially during the winter months. If such trips are going to constitute a significant proportion of your own motorcaravanning activities, the purchase of a left-hand drive model might make good sense.

Engine capacity

There are considerable differences between the performance characteristics of the engines of base vehicles. Drivers' expectations differ as well. Some of us drive cautiously and are happy to potter along country lanes, while others prefer a brisker pace and wish to drive along motorways with purposeful zest.

Once again, first-hand experience is the best way to compare the performance of vehicles, as the author found out himself. A campervan he owned for 10 years was notable for its lively driving. Then the editor of a motorcaravan magazine commissioned a report on a coachbuilt model and this produced some surprises. The vehicle was a 1995 Swift Royale over-cab model based on a Fiat Ducato with a 1.9 non-turbo diesel engine. Driving across France on motorways was one of the dullest drives imaginable. Even with the pedal pressed to the floor, speeds exceeding 60mph were only achieved with a struggle. Information like this is important for anyone planning to purchase an older vehicle, although performance characteristics improved a lot in subsequent years.

The greater use of turbo engines played an important part and when a 1999 Fiat Ducato coachbuilt fitted with a 2.8-litre turbo diesel engine was tested for a

magazine report; the differences were hard to believe. Acceleration, general pulling power, top speeds and a reasonable economy delivered the performance characteristics that many owners expect. The use of large capacity engines continued, and in 2005, a number of motorcaravan manufacturers also built on Renault Master base vehicles, some of which had a 3.0-litre turbo diesel engine. Having extra power in reserve is appealing; especially when you recognise that from an aerodynamic viewpoint the body shape of coachbuilt motorcaravans is little more streamlined than a house brick.

The Fiat 2.3 litre 120 Multijet engine in this 2007 Adria Twin is both lively and economical.

In the latter part of the decade, engine efficiency grew apace, and this was particularly evident in 2006 after the Fiat Multijet engines were introduced. In fact, the 130 Multijet (2287cc engine) was particularly designed for use in motorcaravans. Of course, engines have to be chosen to suit the size of motorhome, and in 2012, many coachbuilt models built using Fiat base vehicles included the following alternatives:

Multijet 130: Engine size 2287cc: Max. Power output: 130bhp @ 3600rpm: Peak torque 320Nm @ 1800rpm

Multijet 150: Engine size 2287cc: Max. Power output: 148bhp @ 3600rpm: Peak torque 350Nm @ 1500rpm

Multijet 180: Engine size 2999cc: Max. Power output: 177bhp @ 3600rpm: Peak torque 400Nm @ 1400rpm

Of course, technical specification data might be of little interest to many potential owners and 'proof of the pudding' is best found by test-driving a vehicle before making a purchase. Personal requirements are different too, and several readers might not share the author's expectations with regard to acceleration, speed, emissions and fuel economy. However, individual preferences aside, do be aware that engine performances do vary a lot and huge changes have occurred over the last 20 years. Anyone purchasing an older model should bear this in mind when taking test drives.

Some engines are more fuel-efficient than others, but large over-cab constructions also affect fuel economy.

Choice of fuel

The majority of today's motorcaravans are driven by turbo diesel engines, and the pedestrian performance of non-turbo diesels has already been described. It's also worth noting that non-turbo models are unlikely to offer improved fuel economy.

In recent years there have been significant improvements in diesel engine design, and compared with petrol-driven units, they've achieved remarkable levels of efficiency. Therefore it's a shame that fuel forecourt prices in the UK have been unfavourable to owners of diesel vehicles, whereas in much of mainland Europe, the cost of diesel is much lower.

Petrol-driven motorcaravans are far less common but they still have points in their favour. The initial purchase price of a petrol-engined vehicle is often less, the performance is good and a power unit is less noisy. At present, petrol-driven vehicles aren't subject to the fees payable in low emission zones either.

However, most commercial vehicles traditionally have diesel engines because they're more robustly built and typically achieve a longer working life than petrol units, and since motorcaravans are normally built on LCVs, this helps account for the predominance of turbo diesel models. Recent models are certainly good to drive and they're a giant's leap away from the smelly, smoky, plodding power units that once gave diesel engines a bad name.

Emission levels

On another fuel-related issue, there are also restrictions imposed within low emission zones, which are now being introduced in cities all over Europe. For instance, London's low emission zone, which came into force in January 2012, imposes three-figure daily payments for all but the more recent diesel vehicles. In broad terms, diesel motorcaravans in standard form that were manufactured before 2006 do not meet the criteria, so fees have to be paid to drive within the zone. Further information on this subject is given in Chapter Six.

Rear-wheel-drive vehicles have a prop shaft under the floor and this can present problems when fitting underfloor tanks.

Economy

As well as thinking about fuel economy based on the type of base vehicle, there are also issues related to conversion elements to remember. Both the weight and shape of motorcaravans are key contributors to fuel economy. There's little doubt that a modern van conversion is going to stand a better chance of achieving good fuel economy than a coachbuilt model with an identical engine. Large over-cab lumps certainly don't enhance aerodynamic performance, although these disadvantages might not become significant until you attain higher speeds.

Work on alternative fuels is also being carried out with increasing vigour. It is possible to convert engines to run on LPG, but this is only catching on in Britain slowly. Biologically produced versions of diesel fuel are also gaining a foothold and are worth keeping an eye on.

Transmission

Like so many modern cars, LCVs have become predominantly front-wheel driven. However, Ford has only recently followed this trend on some Transit models, while the Mercedes Sprinter has remained wedded to its rear-wheel drive configuration. As for four-wheel drive, only a few models have offered this, including some VW Transporters and vans from Mazda and Toyota.

Whatever the benefits of rear-wheel drive, the long propshaft fitted to vehicles with a front-mounted engine and driven back axle can make it harder for a motorcaravan manufacturer to install components below floor level. It also precludes replacing a short chassis on a pre-converted chassis cab with a longer chassis made by AL-KO Kober. This is one reason why the Mercedes Sprinter hasn't been used more often by motorcaravan manufacturers.

The fifth gear ratio on some Fiats is too high for heavy vehicles but it's not expensive to alter the gearing.

Gears

LCVs have been fitted with manual gearboxes for many years. Models offering five gears gained ground in the 1990s, but many of these have now been superseded by six-gear versions.

Fiat won much acclaim when the Ducato was launched in 1993 with its cable-operated, fascia-mounted gear lever. Improved access to the living area was noted at once, and a decade later this had become the norm in all but a few base vehicles. However, in some post-2000 Ducatos, the fifth gear ratio proved too high when the vehicle was heavily laden, and a number of owners had a surprisingly inexpensive conversion carried out to achieve a lower ratio.

Automatic gearboxes have been unusual on vans but the latest Volkswagen T5 includes this option.

Rear leaf springs are quite common on light commercial vehicles, but ride comfort isn't always pleasing.

Below: Motorhomes built on the distinctive lightweight chassis from AL-KO Kober benefit from torsion bar rear suspension.

Below: To enjoy first class comfort and an automatic self-levelling system, some vehicles have full 'air suspension'.

Below right: Adding 'air assisters' can boost tired springs but don't confuse this with air suspension, which replaces steel springs.

For many years automatic transmissions were seldom available in LCVs, although some firms installed retrospective electronic systems. The Sprintshift (Mercedes) and the Durashift (Ford) were among the first to appear, and now other manufacturers also offer several types of automatic systems, including Volkswagen on the new T5. There's clearly a need for such options, especially for elderly and partly disabled drivers.

Suspension

Although Volkswagen has been noted for its use of rear coil springs, this is an unusual feature. Most commercial vehicles use leaf springs at the rear, which is fine when carrying industrial loads, but isn't the most comfortable suspension for people-carrying vehicles. However, on base vehicles fitted with an AL-KO Kober motorhome chassis, the rear axle offers the benefits of torsion bar suspension.

A few motorcaravans also have the original leaf spring system removed and replaced by a computer-controlled, load-levelling *'air suspension'* system. In recent years, VB Air suspension systems have become increasingly fitted on light commercial vehicles. AL-KO has developed air suspension components, too.

This mustn't be confused with systems in which leaf springs are augmented by inflatable bellows. This retrofit strategy is correctly known as *'air assistance'*, in which the installation of air inflatable units helps compensate for tired springs. However, these products do not help to raise the permitted loading limits of a vehicle. It's also somewhat

The chassis supplied with a base vehicle is a robust structure and many leisure vehicle manufacturers use this for their motorcaravans.

misleading when some suppliers wrongly describe modified arrangements in which inflatable units are added to help weak steel springs as 'air suspension'. Retrofit 'air assistance' conversions do not offer the same benefits as a full 'air suspension' installation, and several advertisements placed in motorcaravan magazines do not make these distinctions clear.

Chassis

Some coachbuilt motorcaravans are constructed on the vehicle manufacturer's original chassis and suspension. These structures are sound, but until Fiat introduced its 2006 chassis-cab range, original chassis have not been designed specifically for motorcaravans. This is why some motorcaravan manufacturers have preferred to use AL-KO Kober's purpose-made, lightweight motorcaravan chassis instead. These also have torsion bar suspension for improved comfort.

The AL-KO AMC product, to use its full title, offers several additional benefits, including an opportunity to create a lower floor height in the living quarters.

Lightweight AL-KO chassis are sometimes fitted as a replacement. This example offers a lower floor height.

This AL-KO chassis is specified by motorhome builders that want a double floor. Tanks and services use the lower section.

On some models, such as this 2004 model Bessacarr, the body extends too far rearwards of chassis members to safely use an AL-KO towbar.

Alternatively, some motorcaravans are produced with a double floor so that water tanks, services and storage lockers can be placed in a dry area, which may even receive ducted heat from the living space.

The AL-KO chassis is also made to receive easy-fit add-on items such as a scooter rack or a towbar. However, these products cannot be fitted where a coachbuilt manufacturer extends the rear part of the body enclosure beyond the last cross member on the chassis. For instance, several older models from the Swift Group – including some in the Bessacarr range – cannot accommodate these accessories because the body extends beyond the AL-KO chassis more than the requisite distance. That was changed in 2008 models.

More information on chassis alternatives is provided in Chapter Four of the *Motorcaravan Manual* (3rd edition, 2012), also published by Haynes.

Potential for towing

If it is your intention to tow a trailer, you need to check very carefully that it's possible to have a towbar fitted to your choice of motorcaravan. Many vans appear in catalogues listing model-specific towbars, but on closer inspection you'll find these can't be installed once the vehicle has been converted into a motorcaravan. Items such as under-floor water tanks often obscure fixing points for towbar brackets. There are also instances where an AL-KO towbar can't be installed because the coachbuilt body extends too far rearwards of the AL-KO chassis attachment points. In consequence, a towball will not be able to project far enough beyond the rear body panels to allow a trailer to achieve the articulation it needs when sharp bends are negotiated.

Option lists

Consistent with the growing sophistication of commercial vehicles, the latest motorcaravans are often supplied with ABS braking, airbags, central locking, electric windows, high-quality sound systems, satellite navigation and computerised

Independent specialist PWS designs and installs tailor-made towbars – but not all vehicles can be thus equipped.

stability control devices, just like many cars. Decide which features you consider important and check specification details with care.

Less well-known is that you have the chance to specify a high output alternator, which clearly copes better with the task of running 12V components both on the base vehicle *and* inside the living area.

EXAMPLES OF BASE VEHICLES

Citroën
Small van conversions sometimes use the Citroën Berlingo, which is the base vehicle for three models in the 2012 Romahome line-up. In addition, the Citroën Dispatch is used by Nu Venture motorhomes, but this is essentially a 'badge-engineered' Fiat Scudo. With regard to larger conversions, the badge-engineered Citroën Relay van is built by Fiat, and these vans are currently used by East Neuk Campervans for the short, medium and long wheelbase models.

Daihatsu
For several years, the tiny Hijet van was converted by Devon and JC Leisure to create micro campervans. However, poor roadholding, susceptibility to crosswinds and minimal protection from front impact didn't help the number of sales. The Piaggio Porter, based on the Daihatsu, has also been made under licence.

Fiat Ducato
The first model was introduced in 1981 and over 900,000 were built. In 1991 it was subject to a restyle, but this revamped model was short-lived. The Mark 2 Ducato was launched in 1993 and its fascia-mounted, cable-driven gear selector was seen as a ground-breaking feature. Without the intrusion of a floor-mounted gear stick it became easy to move into the living area from the cab.

When Fiat launched a new Ducato in 2006, the company introduced a motorhome-specific chassis and cab complete with accessories such as swivelling seats.

A facelift model appeared in 2002 with cab improvements and changes to the engine, but no automatic transmission versions for right-hand drive vehicles. Similarly, four-wheel drive versions were not available in the UK.

In recent years the Fiat Ducato has been the base vehicle for over half of all UK-built motorcaravans, and in order to retain this dominance, a completely new model was introduced in 2006. Until then, most vehicle manufacturers regarded motorcaravan applications as a relatively insignificant segment of the market. The majority went to commercial users and few design/specification features were available for motorcaravan converters.

But Fiat changed its stance in 2006 by introducing vehicles specifically designed for conversion into motorhomes. These included anti-roll bars and a wider rear axle to create a track of 1.98m as opposed to the standard 1.79m. The top of the chassis members is also 145mm lower (around 5¾in).

The ratings for spring and shock absorbers have also been amended to suit passengers and there is a 3.8m long chassis version. Moreover, running the brake cables to one side of the chassis, instead of adopting a central route, has facilitated the installation of such items as under-floor tanks.

Cab changes include structural reinforcements and roofs that are pre-cut in the factory, improved B pillars for integration with a coachbuilt body, and swivelling cab seats, which attain the appropriate height.

A range of Multijet engines has also been improved, both in terms of power and pulling performance ('torque'). Matched with this are significant reductions in exhaust emissions and improvements in fuel efficiency. Meanwhile, a six-speed gearbox provides ratios especially suitable for motorhome driving.

Comparisons are certainly not easy to make with earlier models, and it's generally agreed that the Multijet engine is a vast improvement. For instance, the

Below: The Fiat Multi-jet range of engines introduced in 2006 offers good economy, reduced emissions and improved performance.

motorhome-only 2.3-litre 130 Multijet has greater power than the 2.8JTD engine used in previous generation vehicles (the 130 achieves in excess of 127bhp), greater torque (320Nm against 300) and a predicted 23% improvement in fuel economy. The larger capacity 3.0-litre 160 Multijet is more powerful still.

Initially the revised bulbous front on 2006 Fiat Ducatos received many critical comments, but as time passed, motorists became more accustomed to the overall shape.

Ford Transit

The Ford Transit has been in production in various 'generations' for over 40 years. It is also worthy of note that it has been by far the best-selling light commercial vehicle in Britain. Enthusiasts point out there have been three generations but five 'series' of Transits since it was launched in 1965. Originally, all but one model in the 1965 range had petrol engines. Today that situation has been totally reversed and diesel is almost universal.

But the Transit hasn't been popular in a motorcaravan context, one reason is that most versions have been rear-wheel drive. As we've already seen, the existence of a prop-shaft running down the centre of a vehicle to drive the back axle can pose problems when installing under-floor items such as water tanks. A further disincentive has been the long-standing use of floor-mounted gear sticks. However, in September 2000, the Transit range broke with tradition when some models became available in front-wheel drive form.

In the general absence of automatic gear change systems in LCVs, it should be added that some Transits have been fitted with what Ford calls the 'Durashift' automatic gearbox.

In 2007 further revisions were made to Transits, including cosmetic features such as headlamp and grille alterations. In the cab, dash-mounted gear stick and car-type instrumentation were noteworthy. Under the bonnet, a range of new TDCi common-rail diesel engines was introduced, and a revised electronic

Several specialists have imported pre-owned Mazda Bongo vehicles from Japan and converted them into campervans.

automatic transmission later replaced the Durashift system. These changes immediately prompted the manufacturer of Orian motorcaravans to use the Transit as the base for its Dorado and Gemini models, which were previously built using Peugeot vehicles. Today, all the 2012 fixed roof vehicles made by Auto Campers are Ford Transit based. All but one model in the 2012 range from Horizons Unlimited is based on the Ford Transit, too.

Iveco
The large Daily van has been popular with a number of Italian converters and includes models with prodigious payloads. However, Iveco vehicles are more 'van-like' to drive than many models and some owners haven't found this to their liking.

Mazda Bongo Friendee
On account of the strict test regimes in Japan, many vehicles are replaced when comparatively new. This has led to a blossoming import strategy in the UK whereby pre-owned models like the Mazda Bongo are used for converting into motorcaravans. Not only is there a price attraction, but these base vehicles are usually well-equipped with numerous optional extras, including four-wheel drive. Wellhouse Leisure, near Huddersfield, is one of several specialists that convert these imports to suit the individual requirements of customers.

Mercedes Vito and Sprinter
Though used by some converters, the Vito van hasn't been as popular in the motorcaravan industry as the Fiat Ducato and VW Transporter, and has been described in some reports as having heavier controls and less pleasurable drive characteristics.

The Sprinter has been more popular and is sometimes chosen as the base vehicle for A-class motorcaravans. Many models in the 2012 Frankia range are built using Sprinters. However, rear-wheel drive vans have been used in conversions too.

Depending on the model, the Sprinter has sometimes been supplied with an automatic gearbox using the Mercedes 'Sprintshift' system. This is a hybrid model in the form of a clutchless manual/automatic.

Further changes occurred in 2007 following collaboration with Volkswagen. The Sprinter was launched with a number of wheelbase options and a Gross Vehicle Weight limit of between 3,000kg and 5,000kg depending on model. New engine options also appeared and diesel versions have a six-speed gearbox as standard. The 'not always popular' Sprintshift system was replaced by a hybrid torque-converter/automated manual transmission that has been acclaimed when used in some Mercedes cars.

Peugeot
These are 'badge-engineered' products. For instance, the Partner is virtually a Fiat Berlingo, the Expert is a Fiat Scudo/Citroën Dispatch and the Boxer is a Fiat Ducato/Citroën Relay.

Renault
In spite of their capabilities, Renaults were rarely used as base vehicles, although this began to change around 2005. Moreover, some small campervans have been built using the Kangoo, which has been available with petrol and diesel

The rear-wheel-drive Mercedes Sprinter has been a popular base vehicle with A-Class motorcaravan manufacturers.

Below left: Many models from the Fiat Ducato range are also available bearing Citroën Relay and Peugeot Boxer badges.

Below: In spite of the Peugeot badge, the engine and major features of this vehicle will have been assembled in Fiat's factory.

Recent Renault Masters have some lively engine options and this 2005 Knaus Sun Ti was constructed on a Renault base vehicle.

engines, automatic transmission options and four-wheel drive.

Recent versions of the Trafic (shared with Vauxhall as the Vivaro) have also been used by a number of converters. The latest Master is certainly becoming extremely popular too, and is likely to gain increasing prominence. In the UK, the 2012 range of Bentley Motorhomes is exclusively based on Trafic and Master base vehicles.

Toyota Hiace van and Hilux pickup

The mid-sized Hiace van is a rear-wheel drive vehicle. The Hilux four-wheel drive pickup truck is a good base for dismountable motorcaravans.

Volkswagen Transporter, LT and Crafter

Van conversions have been based on Volkswagen vehicles for many years – but very few coachbuilt motorcaravans. Other models in the VW range have included the car-like Caddy and the LT. The latter, however, hasn't been a popular base vehicle due to its truck-like features, including a floor-mounted gear shift.

Historically, the 'split-screen' Transporter of the 1950s and the later 'bay window' model of the 1960s and 1970s undoubtedly popularised motorcaravanning in Europe. Many regard it as an icon in its own right.

The VW Crafter replaced the VW LT van in 2006, but few UK campervan manufacturers are converting it.

Compared with the Transporter, VW's LT van has never been a popular base for motorcaravans. This model finally ran its course around 2006, and was replaced by the VW Crafter. This shares components with the Mercedes Sprinter and exemplifies the continuing links forged between different vehicle manufacturers. Engines, however, are not shared, and VW offers the Crafter with its car-type five-cylinder power units. Very few van converters have used it, although models have been built in Germany by CS-Reisemobil, Robel and Seitz. In the UK, the 2012 Murvi Morello can be built on a VW Crafter too, if requested.

Updated versions of traditional VW 'window vans' are being manufactured under licence in Brazil and imported into the UK by Danbury.

Summary

The base vehicle is undoubtedly an important part of any motorcaravan 'package', and whilst it's often claimed that there are very few poor vehicles being manufactured today, that isn't to say that some suit certain owners more than others. That's why it is so important to arrange a test drive before making a purchase.

Many different base vehicles are now available and potential owners should take a test drive before making a purchase.

CHAPTER **FOUR**

DESIGN AND
CONSTRUCTION

Many potential owners are not
particularly interested in the design and
construction of motorcaravans and might
skip this chapter. However, that could be
a mistake; if you acquire a rudimentary
knowledge about constructional details,
you'll soon be able to recognise good and
bad workmanship. Similarly, if something
goes wrong, you'll be better informed
about remedial work when discussing
repairs with a dealer.

53

*Designers are faced with
the task of fitting a lot into
the available space and
not many converted vans
have a convenience room
like this Murvi Morello.*

If a motorcaravan is to provide comfortable living irrespective of season, good insulation is essential.

Is it really necessary to know how motorcaravans are designed and constructed? As long as everything is working properly, why would you need to know anything about the construction, roof design or choice of components like windows?

Let's compare this with the purchase of a house. Does a potential buyer need to enquire if a property has double glazing? Does it really matter if rain creates large puddles on a flat roof? Is there any need to know the strengths and weaknesses of different types of central heating system and the fuel they use? Of course there is! And such things are equally important when you're purchasing a motorcaravan. Thermal insulation, for example, determines whether a vehicle can provide comfortable accommodation in cold weather. Some motorcaravans are far better insulated than others and this also affects comfort levels in summer. Park a vehicle with poor insulation in direct sunlight and it becomes like an oven inside.

Practical issues like this need to be taken into account. To give another example, you'd be surprised how many coachbuilt models have poorly designed roofs. This might not be apparent during the first few years of ownership, but when sealants lose their effectiveness, a roof starts to leak.

LEARNING THE ROPES

Although the intention here is to look mainly at structural considerations, let's start with some day-to-day issues. Here are three practical features that should concern a discerning purchaser.

Exotic interiors are impressive but may not be the best answer for families with young children.

Soft furnishings

For several years, the majority of British manufacturers equipped their motorcaravans with fitted carpets. This is a homely floor covering, but designers seemed unaware that campsites often get muddy. Moreover, fixed carpeting is hardly the best covering for parents of young children, those with active outdoor hobbies, or dog owners. On the other hand, owners with passive leisure interests often regard carpeting as an essential comfort feature.

When you compare British products with motorhomes manufactured abroad you'll notice that many models from mainland Europe have vinyl floor coverings. This is more practical than carpet, but a plasticised sheeting is not very warm for the feet.

A much better idea is to have a vinyl base layer topped by tailor-made removable carpet sections. This combination was fitted in the author's first self-built van in the mid-1980s, and its versatility was soon apparent. Regrettably, it took more than a decade for British manufacturers to adopt this alternative arrangement and you'll still come across recent models fitted with non-removable carpet.

Light upholstery fabric with suede trims might not be wise for owners with dogs.

(i) Useful Tip

Consider the floor covering in relationship to your leisure interests. Similarly, look at the upholstery and consider whether it would show dirty marks too easily. Some motorcaravans, though wonderfully exotic inside, are wholly impractical for many people's needs.

ⓘ Useful Tip

Don't be immediately enamoured by the attractiveness of a kitchen. Picture what it would be like to use. Is there sufficient worktop space? What's the draining board like? Where would you temporarily dispose of a tin, a teabag or bacon rinds?

Remember, too, that if you plan to purchase an imported motorcaravan, their kitchens are often much smaller than those in British models, for one very good reason: their owners prefer to dine in bars and restaurants. Furthermore, only a few people on mainland Europe have discovered the pleasure of toast, so the fitted hobs seldom include a grill.

56

Like many German-built kitchens, the facility in this Knaus Sport Ti has very little worktop space.

Poor kitchen design meant that rubbish had to be put into a plastic bag in this award-winning model.

Kitchen design elements

Practicalities are important, and an important feature often absent in a British-built motorcaravan has been the provision of a waste bin in the kitchen. In contrast, this was normally a standard fitment in German and Italian motorhomes. Frankly, it's hardly a major design challenge to create a kitchen that includes a compact waste bin, but for many years, most UK manufacturers fitted nothing at all.

In the absence of a simple waste bin, many owners dangled a plastic carrier bag from their oven door-handle – hardly a dignified practice in a motorhome costing thousands of pounds. One manufacturer even complained that I'd voiced this criticism in magazine reports, and potential customers were now asking for a bin to be fitted! Eventually, the message got through, and today a bin is normally provided in UK motorcaravans. Meanwhile in Germany, some models now have three bins, differentiated by colour to accept different types of recyclable waste.

Another kitchen matter relates to space on a worktop and the types of appliances fitted. Kitchens in imported vans are sometimes rather disappointing and there is a good reason for this. See the accompanying Useful Tip panel for more details.

External omissions

A third oversight noted during live-in tests for magazine reports is the fact that manufacturers of coachbuilt models seldom fit rear mudflaps. In consequence, the underside of floor panels behind the rear wheels become bespattered with thick mud. Electric cables to the road lights soon get coated with road dirt, and the mechanisms of wastewater drain-down taps may prematurely fail as well.

The lack of mudflaps on this 2006 Swift Kon-Tiki Vogue meant the drain-down tap control was caked in mud.

It is true that manufacturers have to monitor build-costs very closely, but since commercial mudflaps from lorry component suppliers sell for less than £6 apiece there's really no excuse. In truth, some manufacturers have noted these critical comments, and in 2005 both Auto-Sleepers and Auto-Trail acted accordingly, and mud flaps were fitted. Regrettably, numerous other reputable manufacturers have yet to respond.

These examples focus on just three areas of attention that purchasers often overlook. Design and specification shortcomings might not become apparent when looking at a van in a showroom but they are truly annoying when you are using your motorhome. Of course, some weaknesses can be resolved retrospectively, but that isn't always the case. So check the accompanying Useful Tip panel for further items to check.

Below: The 2006 Mobilvetta Top Driver S71 was fitted with mudflaps, as are models from Auto-Sleepers and Auto-Trail.

Useful Tip

Make a general inspection of external features and remember to look under the floor. Locate the waste water drain-down control, consider its location and check its operation. Also look at pipe runs on the underside. Check there are no uphill sections and downturns in the waste-pipe where water would collect and then freeze in winter.

Check if there's a step to assist entry into a high commercial cab and check how easy it is to access the living area from outside. Also check for a light near the door so that you can find the keyhole when it's dark.

This Auto Cruise Starmist has a poorly secured drain-down hose and there are better emptying systems.

Check waste pipes under motorcaravans – look for consistent gradients rather than rises and falls in pipe runs.

This Dethleffs Esprit has a useful step created by the converter to improve access to the cab.

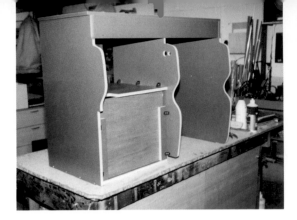

Contoured furniture for Bilbo's conversions is assembled on a bench and fitted in the van later.

VAN CONVERSIONS AND COACHBUILT MODELS

It was stated in the previous chapter that most motorcaravans are either created by converting a light van or by constructing a coachbuilt body that's mounted on a vehicle's chassis. When comparing the two types of vehicle you'll find that some elements are broadly the same. For example, electricity and gas supply systems are similarly constructed in campervans and coachbuilts in accordance with British Standards (BS) and European Norms (ENs). Appliances like space heaters and refrigerators are also similar. The main differences between conversions and coachbuilt models concern their body structures.

Body detailing in van conversions

In a van conversion, the body of the original base vehicle should provide full weather resistance from the outset. When a converter fits additional windows and ventilators, or an elevating roof, their success depends on: a) the quality of the product; and b) the installation itself.

Fitting-out work inside is the real challenge. It's much harder than fitting furniture and installing domestic appliances in a coachbuilt structure, in which the living area is normally assembled using flat, preformed wall boards. In contrast, a light commercial panel van is full of curved panels, composite angles and strengthening members.

Insulation will also need to be added all around a van enclosure; in contrast, the majority of coachbuilt models are created using composite boards that already include a bonded layer of rigid foam in the core. Constructing items of furniture that faithfully match a commercial van's internal shape can also be a time-consuming operation.

As explained in Chapter Two, these issues help to explain why van conversions are often surprisingly costly. Fitting-out operations can take a long time. When furniture units are built and installed they're either

constructed in situ or assembled on a bench and offered-up for installation later.

Larger manufacturers such as Auto-Sleepers, Bilbo's and Murvi normally favour the second approach. Once the standard patterns have been created for a particular layout, items of furniture can then be replicated and assembled on a bench to achieve speedier completion.

The production of modular units away from the assembly area also frees-up space inside a van's enclosure, thereby allowing other operations to be carried out. It's only in one-off bespoke conversions that items of furniture are created inside a vehicle and not on a bench.

Also be aware that in many van conversions, modular furniture is constructed using light, but surprisingly substantial (15mm), plywood. This usually has factory-bonded plastic laminate facings. In coachbuilt models you're more likely to find furniture constructed using frameworks that are subsequently clad using 3mm faced plywood. This approach leads to much lighter assemblies than furniture built using 15mm ply, and if units are well designed, their rigidity is still assured.

Body detailing in coachbuilt models

The chassis of a coachbuilt model is the key foundation on which its habitation area is built, and different types of structure were outlined in Chapter Three.

There are also two main types of body construction. Chapter Two made reference to moulded monocoque ('one-piece') shells made with materials such as glass-reinforced plastic (GRP). As pointed out earlier, shell construction adopts similar practices as those employed in the building of small GRP boats. Furthermore, their water-resistance is second to none.

A GRP monocoque 'shell' can also be visually attractive because curving profiles can be made to match the curves of the steel cab.

Aesthetically, the end product is a far cry from the flat-sided boxes that typify so many coachbuilt models. Repairs to damaged sections are much

Designed and manufactured in Italy, Wingamm single-piece, seam-free, monocoque motorhomes faithfully follow the curves of the cab.

Although there are flat 'slab sides' on this Auto-Sleepers Sandhurst, GRP mouldings enhance its appearance.

easier to carry out too. But there are snags. To achieve the appropriate strength, monocoque shells are usually heavy. And fine though the curves are to a critical eye, fitting-out a shapely interior involves the same time-consuming challenges already mentioned in respect of van conversion projects.

This is why the majority of coachbuilts are constructed using the assembly methods used for touring caravans. For instance, both touring and motorcaravans are generally built using prefabricated, bonded and insulated panels. However, to prevent a finished vehicle from looking too much like a commercial box-van with windows, more expensive versions have a GRP moulded panel over the cab, a moulded panel for the rear wall, and the roof is sometimes constructed using GRP too.

Bonded panels

'Sandwich construction' methods, in which prefabricated bonded panels are used, were first introduced around 1980. Individually the three components forming the 'sandwich' are light and surprisingly weak. However, when the components have been coated with industrial adhesive and bonded in a huge press they assume remarkable strength.

Floor panels

When making a bonded floor, two layers of treated plywood (around 5mm or $^3/_{16}$in thick) are bonded on either side of rigid Styrofoam insulation panels (around 30mm or 1¼in thick). Timber battens are also bonded into the core of the sandwich to add further strength, although in Bailey Motorhomes, plasticised battens are used on account of their better weather-resistance.

- **Advantage** – The resulting product is light, rigid, and well-insulated.
- **Disadvantage** – If part of the adhesive agent fails, areas of plywood can lose their bond with the middle layer of foam. This problem, referred to as 'delamination', leads to a huge reduction in a floor panel's strength. If you are purchasing a pre-owned

coachbuilt motorcaravan and notice that the floor is creaky in certain places, it is a common sign that delamination is taking place. For more information on this, and illustrations showing how a dealer repairs a delaminating floor, see pages 56–57 of the *Motorcaravan Manual* (3rd edition, 2012), also published by Haynes.

Composite floors are assembled using styrofoam, battens and ply panels, which are subsequently bonded in a press.

Wall panels

In sandwich-constructed wall panels the components are typically:

1 A 3mm decorative-faced plywood for the interior finish.

(i) Technical Tip

The level of insulation in motorcaravans varies, and some models only have 25mm boards in the walls. This can be revealed by either opening a window or the entrance door and checking wall thickness at the aperture. Models from Auto-Trail are much better, having been built with 35mm insulation in the walls and floor. At 116mm (4½in) overall, the insulation boards in the Italian Genetics 2007 models from GiottiLine are even thicker. Remember that efficient insulation not only retains heat inside during winter trips, it also keeps out excessive heat when a motorhome is parked in direct sunlight.

Some models have an aluminium trim strip along the junction where wall and roof panels meet. This will be bedded on a non-setting

mastic and fastened in place with screws. In time, however, mastics dry out, become brittle, and fracture. Then rain can find its way into a structure via the screw holes. Bearing this in mind, a much better way to finish the junction between adjacent panels is to bond plastic angle trim over it. If trims are secured with adhesive sealant, screws won't be needed and there won't be any holes in the structure.

Some models only have 25mm (1in) bonded side walls, but this Auto-Trail floor sample is considerably thicker.

To cope with the severities of winter, the walls of GiottiLine Genetics A-class models are incredibly thick.

External corners on this 2005 Pilote Reference have bonded cover sections, which are so much better than screwed trim strips.

All the plastic mouldings around the lighting units on this Dethleffs Esprit are made in acrylic-capped ABS.

2 Block foam insulation such as Styrofoam. (Polystyrene foam is occasionally used, which is sometimes as thin as 25mm or 1in.) Wood strengthening battens are usually fitted around the perimeters and apertures for windows and doors, although Bailey has started using plasticised imitation wood instead.

3 Exterior cladding, using either pre-painted aluminium sheet, or a scratch and damage-resistant GRP sheet.

Diversity of body materials

Although bonded panels are important components in the construction of a coachbuilt, these are only one of a surprising number of materials used externally. For example, other materials might include:

- Painted steel panels (on the cab)
- GRP mouldings (sometimes installed over the cab)
- ABS mouldings (sometimes used for wheel arch embellishment)
- Moulded aluminium panels (sometimes used for side skirts)
- Pre-painted smooth aluminium sheet (external cladding)
- Pre-painted textured aluminium sheet (external cladding)
- Pigmented (ie pre-coloured) layer of thin GRP sheet (alternative external cladding)
- Various types of plastic used for ventilators and grilles (such as refrigerator vents)
- Extruded aluminium strips (for body trim).

This type of pimpled textured cladding is extremely difficult to 'patch repair', whereas a smooth aluminium surface with minor damage is much easier to deal with.

An important point here is the difference between mouldings made in GRP as opposed to mouldings made in ABS plastic. Whereas many body repair specialists know how to repair GRP, far fewer are trained in the repair of ABS plastic. This has implications if a vehicle gets damaged so check the comments made in the following section.

Identifying ABS and GRP

• GRP stands for glass-reinforced plastic, which is often misleadingly referred to as fibreglass. Some GRP contains a colourising pigment that's added when the polyester resin is being prepared. Other GRP mouldings contain no added pigment and are subsequently sprayed with an etching primer followed by automotive paint.

• ABS stands for acrylonitrile-butadiene-styrene. If it's acrylic-capped ABS it will have a further surface coating in order to give it a high gloss finish. An ABS moulding is usually pre-coloured during manufacture.

Terminology

• The word 'mould' refers to a master shape in which a component is cast.

• The word 'moulding' refers to the finished product that was originally made in a mould.

The moulded section here is made in GRP – the rough surface on the reverse confirms that it isn't ABS plastic.

ⓘ Technical Tip

External damage is an ever-present possibility and freak hailstorms can inflict awful surface damage. Fortunately, some body repairs are easy and inexpensive to carry out. Others are extremely costly, and if spare parts are needed, they can take a long time to obtain. Sales staff seldom mention 'reparability' issues and you can get a better insight into the reality of repair work by consulting model-specific owners' clubs, whose addresses are published in magazines.

On an aluminium-skinned bonded wall, the repair strategy usually involves carrying out structural repairs first, followed by a re-skinning operation in which the entire side has a new panel of aluminium sheet bonded on top of the original. Re-skinning operations like this are more complicated if thin GRP sheet has been used for cladding instead of aluminium. On the other hand, skilled body-shop specialists often carry out patch repairs that are undetectable on GRP materials.

With regards to ABS mouldings, these are usually replaced, but this poses problems on older vehicles, as spare parts are not held in stock forever. Fortunately, there are companies, such as V&G near Peterborough and GFL panels near Preston, which reassemble cracked ABS components and then make a copy mould in GRP. This new mould is then used to produce a GRP moulding replicating the shape of the original ABS component.

When a replacement ABS bowl was no longer available, V&G staff made this copy mould in order to create a GRP replica.

This rear skirt made from acrylic-capped ABS plastic hit a kerbstone. Although repairs are possible, most repairers would replace this.

These distinctive types of moulded plastic body panels are easy to identify. The rear face of a GRP moulding is normally rough and you'll often be able to see the strands of glass used as a reinforcing binder to give strength to the polyester resin.

In contrast, the rear face of an ABS moulding is smooth, and this material is often used for vehicle bumpers, albeit with a textured outer face. Acrylic-capped ABS is shiny on both faces and is often used for items such as fairings on motorcycles, wings on cars and external detailing on motorcaravans.

Both materials can be repaired when cracked or split, but although the process is similar, the chemicals involved are different. That's why you need to establish whether a damaged moulding is made from GRP or ABS. And be warned: though many repair specialists in both automotive and marine workshops successfully repair cracked or split GRP mouldings, motorcaravan service specialists prefer to order replacement components, which are often surprisingly costly. No less disconcerting is the fact that obtaining replacement ABS components often takes several weeks.

A new rear lamp housing is being fitted on a Bessacarr after the original one got cracked when it brushed against a wall.

Rainwater that ponded badly on the roof of this Knaus Sun Ti Sport was adjacent to some mastic-filled joining seams.

DESIGN AND CONSTRUCTIONAL POINTS TO CHECK

Keeping all the above in mind, let's consider some individual details.

The roof

Even when there's an access ladder to reach the roof of a motorcaravan, few prospective buyers bother to inspect this all-important part of the vehicle. Some products are well designed and carefully constructed, whereas others reveal disturbing features that could later result in water ingress.

Even a recent award-winning model that impressed the competition judges with its smart upholstery and fine internal fittings had a poorly finished roof. The judges obviously didn't bother to inspect this important element of construction.

Features to check

Remember that a well-designed roof is no less important than a well-equipped kitchen or a thoughtful interior layout. Look for the following features:

- A design that facilitates the swift discharge of rainwater whenever a vehicle is parked on a level pitch
- Specifically constructed outlets so that water will be released in a planned manner and at appropriate points
- A slope (or slopes) so that puddles don't form on the roof when the vehicle's parked on level ground

The draining outlets are a good feature on the roof of the 2006 Orian Gemini. Some designers don't include this facility.

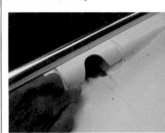

The one-piece GRP roofs on recent Auto-Trail models have well-designed and discreet channels for discharging rainwater.

• A one-piece roof panel. This is more likely to offer weather resistance than a roof assembled in separate panels as its junctions are sealed using flexible mastics.

In an outdoor setting a roof gathers dust and dirt and is hard to keep clean. When it rains you don't want accumulated dust dispersing all over the sides. It's better to have a couple of outlets so that any post-rainfall discharge is confined to one or two areas.

It is also important to recognise that a substantial quantity of discharging rainwater shouldn't challenge vulnerable components mounted on the sides. Some lockers, for example, are susceptible to leaks, especially when subjected to torrents of water. Equally, you wouldn't want copious quantities of roof water to head towards a 230V mains input socket.

Now let's look at some examples.

Roofs under scrutiny

One manufacturer that has put time and effort into designing good roofs is Auto-Trail. On recent models you'll notice there is usually a single-piece GRP roof moulding, which means there are neither joins nor gaps through which water might seep when sealant starts to lose its effectiveness.

Moreover, when a model like the 2004 Auto-Trail Cheyenne was tested, it was noted that when the vehicle was parked level, its roof sloped gently to the rear. Less conspicuous – unless you check the roof more closely – are the rainwater channels also found on either side. Good design means that rain drains away and doesn't form in puddles.

More manufacturers are now designing roofs with outlets, but with varying success. It's not unusual to find that when the structure was assembled an outlet point was blocked by excessive sealant. And

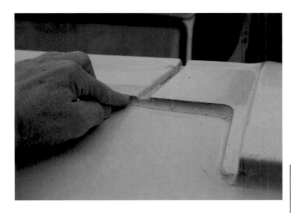

don't be surprised to find a junction of adjacent panels that introduces a step, thereby impeding the outflow of water.

Motorcaravans look impressive in a covered showroom but weaknesses are certainly more evident when vehicles are parked outdoors on a forecourt. An inspection of these may reveal examples of 'ponding', and it's worth looking for dirty patches even if recent rain puddles have dried up. Then check if there's a sealant-filled seam in the vicinity of the spot where water appears to settle. One day, that is where leaks might start.

Roof fittings

If you do have an opportunity to check a roof, also look carefully at the installation of roof windows, vents and fixed roof rails. On a well-designed model, roof windows will be mounted on a raised section of the roof. This means that any rainwater resting on the surface won't threaten the join around the perimeter of the component. On a GRP roof, a good designer will have created raised plinths on which to mount the skylights.

Below: Since a roof takes the worst of the weather, sealant between panels must be good. The join on this new Swift Kon-Tiki was poorly finished.

Above: When components such as racks are screwed through a roof, sealant is important. It wasn't applied well on this Mobilvetta Kimu.

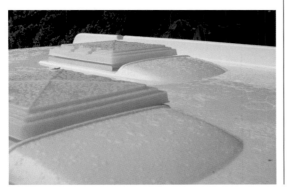

Left: Good roof design on this Auto-Sleepers Sandhurst. The GRP roof has moulded plinths that elevate the 'skylight' mounting points above the overall roof level where rain accumulates. Also note the wind deflectors at the forward edges.

Not all roofs are meant to be walked on but that's not the case on this TEC Freetec. Note the use of abrasive surface strips.

Also check if there's a deflector on the forward side of skylights. When you're proceeding briskly along a motorway in driving rain, water can easily challenge the forward edge where these fittings are mounted. Bedding sealant around a rooflight flange takes the brunt of the weather and a deflector adds further protection.

Structural capacity

Many owners like to use a roof to carry equipment, either by fitting a rack or by installing roof boxes. However, you should check the feasibility of this with the manufacturer. For instance, some A-class vehicles, such as the 2002 Niesmann+Bischoff Arto 69 GL Lux, are fitted with side roof rack rails and a ladder. However, in response to a critical observation relating to this vehicle's roof published in *Which Motorcaravan* (Dec 2002), a marketing specialist for the company advised that, 'the roof is not actually designed to be walked on.' His statement came as a surprise and one is left wondering how a canoe or surfboard could be secured to the rack if you're not permitted to walk beyond the top rung of an access ladder. It also begs the question: why was a ladder fitted in the first place?

Clearly you need to seek guidance on such matters prior to purchase, especially if you plan to fit a roof box or purpose-made rack to transport equipment. Remember, too, that some side rails are merely cosmetic appendages.

On models where it is acceptable to use a roof for access and storage, abrasive strips are undoubtedly an excellent safety feature – as shown on this TEC Freetec.

Windows

In the commercial vehicles used for motorcaravans, single-glazed safety glass is fitted in the cab. If a

A single glazed panel over the cab of this Knaus model is fine in warm weather, but condensation is bad in some conditions.

van with side windows is used for conversion, safety glass will again be evident. Double-glazed units are sometimes fitted in high-quality coaches, but these are extremely heavy, and are only installed in very expensive motorcaravans.

Automotive glass is certainly resistant to scratches, which is a great benefit if you brush against a hedge or encounter overhanging brambles. Unfortunately it doesn't offer effective thermal insulation so condensation problems are commonplace.

To reduce heat loss in converted vans and coachbuilt models, manufacturers normally fit double-glazed acrylic plastic windows instead. There are two types of plastic window and, predictably, the costlier version is certainly the better product. The less expensive type doesn't have a frame and weatherproofing is provided by a rubber sealing-strip fitted around the aperture cut in the motorcaravan's

Double-glazed acrylic windows such as this aren't made with a separate frame.

With frameless windows, the seal around apertures is important. It didn't fit well on this 2007 Swift Bolero.

wall panel. Understandably, a frameless window has to achieve a close register with the rubber strip and its catches need to hold it securely in place. After several seasons, a deteriorating rubber surround or failing catches sometimes lead to the ingress of rain.

The installation of frameless units certainly helps keep down the price of a finished vehicle. However, it's generally agreed that framed windows, although more expensive, are not only better performers but also easier to install. Accordingly, they're normally fitted in high specification motorcaravans, although you'll find them in many van conversions too.

Seitz units are the best known and comprise an outer frame that secures the acrylic pane, together with an inner frame complete with blind and fly-screen. When these interlocking frames are fastened together, a van's wall panel is sandwiched tightly between their flanges to provide noteworthy weather-resistance.

It's inevitable that windows sometimes get scratched or even damaged beyond repair. When it comes to replacing standard automotive glass, main dealers or specialist windscreen companies can usually help. It's seldom a problem if a motorcaravan

Framed windows fitted on this Auto-Sleepers Sandhurst are smartly finished with matching white frames.

Seitz S4 framed windows comprise an outer frame that houses hinged or sliding plastic panes. This couples tightly to the white or cream inner frame that houses a roller blind and fly screen.

is constructed using a light commercial vehicle.

However, replacing a windscreen or side screen in an A-class motorcaravan may present a problem: usually it's a job for a dealer specialising in that particular model, or its UK importer. A replacement windscreen is often costly, too. That isn't to say that acrylic double-glazed windows are particularly cheap to replace; nor are they easy to obtain. On recent models, the most common way to get a replacement unit is to order it through a dealer-workshop. However, awaiting its delivery calls for patience – letters published in magazines report delays of over six weeks. One mail order specialist that deals direct with owners and makes bespoke replacements is EECO (the Exhaust Ejector Co). Even at the height of a summer season, EECO is usually able to manufacture and dispatch a replica window in less than four weeks.

This shows the outer frame of a Seitz S4 window. Its plastic pane is easy to replace.

 **Useful Tip**

Most vehicle windscreen specialists are able to fit replacement glass in light commercial vehicles, and units are usually obtained without difficulty. However, some owners of A-class vehicles have reported problems. In several cases a replacement has been extremely costly and there can be a long wait. These may be exceptional cases but it would be wise for anyone planning to purchase an A-class vehicle to enquire about windscreen costs and delivery dates.

Conclusion

Inevitably this chapter has only focussed on a selection of issues relating to the design and construction of motorcaravans. However, if it has drawn attention to points that purchasers hadn't previously thought to check, it will have achieved its objective.

CHAPTER **FIVE**

BUYING **ADVICE**

There are so many contrasting types of motorcaravan being manufactured that deciding which one to buy is far from easy. There are also many different ways to make a purchase, and the advice that follows compares the various options. Incidentally, if you haven't spent long in a motorcaravan before, then hiring one for several days is a practical way to find out what suits you best.

For first-time buyers, a forecourt offers a bewildering choice of models.

'Just Go' is one of many UK motorcaravan hire specialists.

Preceding chapters drew attention to a number of important issues. Between the extremes of a compact campervan and an American RV are leisure vehicles of all shapes and sizes. The people who use them are different as well. There's no such thing as a 'typical motorcaravanner', and your needs are likely to be different from those of other people you'll meet.

That is why it's so important to look closely at as many motorcaravans as possible before you buy one. You should also talk to existing owners, and read the reports in magazines. Hire one for a few days to find what a vehicle's like on both the road and the campsite. Then compile a personal checklist to help you focus your needs more clearly. Note: Check the advice in the Tip panel on hiring a motorcaravan that appears later in this chapter on page 80.

MODEL CHOICE

Although it's important to choose your preferred inside layout, many people make the mistake of basing a purchase on that factor alone. So check the issues raised in earlier chapters. For instance,

Few spare wheels are as easy to reach as this one fitted on the 2011 Auto-Trail Tracker EK.

Some owners decide to build their own motorcaravan to obtain unusual features that may be related to their hobbies.

the importance of choosing the right base vehicle was discussed in Chapter Three. Then there are practical issues such as how easy it is to withdraw a spare wheel, to check a leisure battery, or to drain the waste water tank. There are also constructional matters to appreciate, as explained in Chapter Four.

Throughout the search process, don't expect perfection! Unless you have a bespoke vehicle constructed by a specialist builder, or embark on a self-build project, you won't find a model that meets all your criteria.

On the subject of layouts and interior detailing, the illustrations here will serve as a reminder about some of the options. Firstly, there are practical issues to keep in mind. Secondly, there are decisions to be made about things like kitchens, beds and toilets. The following guidelines will help.

General practical issues

• Will your motorcaravan have to be small enough to park outside your house? Are there covenants that restrict the parking of large vehicles on a housing estate? Is there sufficient space and height to manoeuvre it onto its parking place?

Parking space at home determines many owners' choice of vehicle.

Right: Children often spill their food so look for easy-to-clean surfaces.

Far right: Some important switches are harder to reach than this one.

Right: In some models you can erect a portable cot, like this one from Graco.

Far right: When using a motorhome with children, storage facilities are especially important.

- If a family includes children or grandchildren, will surfaces be easy to clean if there's a spillage? Can they operate switches? Is there room for a travel cot? Is there plenty of storage?
- Are the users' leisure interests active or passive? Outdoor sports participants will often track mud inside, so check that floor covering materials can be easily cleaned. Fixed carpet is hardly the best choice in this situation.
- With ever-changing legislation regarding seatbelt provision in motorcaravans, how many seats in the living space are designated as 'travel seats'? Are the belted bench seats suitable for children's portable seats and booster bases? Seating units in the living area are often too soft to provide good support for a child-seat, as when you're turning a corner, their foam can compress, the inertia reel belt pays out more strap, and the child-seat can tip over.

Below: Check how many seats in the living area are designated as 'travel seats'.

Below right: Child-seats can be unstable on a soft cushion base, and on corners they sometimes turn over.

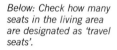

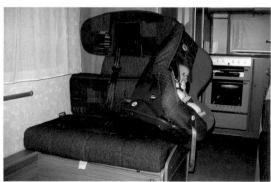

- Will you be travelling abroad? The beams on some of the latest high output headlamps can't be redirected merely by applying adhesive tape. Instead, the lights have to be realigned at a workshop for driving on the right, and the bill can be surprisingly high.
- To maximise space, it is always useful if the cab seats can be rotated to provide extra room in the living area. However, in some models it is only the passenger seat that can be rotated to face the rear. There are also many models in which neither the driver's seat nor the passenger seat can be rotated like this.
- Don't overlook the fact that some motorcaravans, both van conversions and coachbuilt models, cannot be fitted with a towbar.

Contrasting interior designs

- Cooking facilities vary enormously. Some kitchens have large worktop areas, whereas others are desperately small. The kitchen will certainly be an important feature for many UK owners and a full complement of appliances is often required. Other motorcaravanners are content with more rudimentary facilities and it was mentioned in the opening pages of the previous chapter that kitchens in some imported models are often surprisingly compact and can be poorly equipped.

Above: Some headlamps can't be adjusted like this for driving abroad and have to be realigned in a workshop.

Above: These cab seats can be swivelled so that you can make use of the cab when you're parked. That isn't possible on some layouts.

Above: A surprising number of motorcaravans can't be fitted with a towing bracket.

There's generous worktop space in this Auto-Trail Miami 740D.

Small van conversions need a privacy curtain for their toilet because there's insufficient space for a fixed cubicle.

• A washroom and a shower are often omitted from small camper vans, and if a portable toilet has to be pulled from a drawer for use indoors, a temporary privacy curtain is needed. At the other extreme, larger motorcaravans sometimes have grandly appointed dressing rooms complete with washbasin and shower cubicle, duly adorned with opulent fittings. It is true that many German coachbuilt motorcaravans have more spacious washrooms than you normally find in UK models.

Right: The daytime bench seats in the lounge of this Auto-Sleepers Sandhurst convert into beds.

Far right: This Romahome offers two singles, but many small vans have to fold the cab seats flat to achieve a good length.

Right: Not everyone wants to climb a ladder to reach a bed and children need safety-net sides.

Far right: Many owners want a fixed double bed like this example in an Auto-Trail Chieftain.

Right: A recent trend in coachbuilts such as this Cheyenne 840 Lo is to create a bedroom with permanent single beds.

Far right: A-Class motorcaravans have sufficient width in their cabs to accommodate a drop-down double bed.

Erecting beds

Potential purchasers viewing motorcaravans at a dealer's showroom should always ask sales staff to demonstrate how *all* the beds are erected. Experienced sales specialists who know the product should be able to do this in minutes.

Always get a sales person to demonstrate how all the beds are set up.

On this Lunar coachbuilt motorcaravan a clever base provides bed and seat versatility.

- Beds come in all shapes and sizes, as the panel alongside shows. Where a couple are to be the sole users of a motorcaravan, a fixed double or a pair of single beds situated in a purpose-made bedroom has become a popular arrangement. However, that area becomes a redundant space during daytime. Larger families often prefer sleeping arrangements with daytime bench seats that are converted into beds at night.
- Tables vary too, and several German manufacturers fit robust units mounted on concertina pillars that cannot be removed. Some rattle when you're driving. Freestanding tables that can be moved outside for picnics are useful. Incidentally, tables used as bed bases will usually cause damp to form on the underside of a bed mattress unless a purpose-made ventilation underlay is used. An example of this is shown in Chapter Seven.

A number of German motorcaravans have a fixed table with a rise-and-fall mechanism.

Whether a layout works efficiently is really only apparent when you put a van into use. This is why hiring a motorhome is useful to highlight some of the issues you need to keep in mind.

Hiring a motorcaravan

This is an ideal way to evaluate a motorcaravan, and a report in the April 2006 issue of *Which Motorcaravan* included a table listing no fewer than 126 hire specialists located around the UK. Regarding hire prices, these are considerably higher for peak season than in winter. Hiring in winter will show the effectiveness of heating systems and internal lighting during dark evenings, so it's a good time of year to evaluate a vehicle. Insurance can be high, however, and regrettably there are age restrictions that often preclude hiring by people under 25 and over 70 years of age. Penalty points on driving licences may also pose a problem.

Personal checklist

It's impossible to draw up a 'definitive tick list' when everyone's needs and preferences are different. You are therefore advised to create your own list of personal 'must-haves'. The contrived one that follows represents the requirements of an imaginary couple with a young child who want to purchase a new van conversion.

Base vehicle

☐ Any colour except white, preferably a metallic paint
☐ Turbo diesel engine but not one that is underpowered
☐ Manual gearbox preferred
☐ Front-wheel drive
☐ Fitted with a high-top roof
☐ Optional higher output alternator if available
☐ Headlights that are easy to convert for driving in France
☐ Panel van rather than a window van with its single glazing
☐ Double-glazed plastic windows installed in the living section
☐ Able to be fitted with a towbar
☐ Electric windows in the cab preferred
☐ Generous payload potential – it's likely to be carrying plenty of gear
☐ Mustn't be longer than 5.5m (18ft) in order to park by the house
☐ Generous-sized driving mirrors with electric adjustment

External conversion features

☐ Easy-to-operate drain-down valve for wastewater tank
☐ Good colour matching of GRP high-top roof
☐ Colour co-ordinated painted Dometic fridge vents preferred
☐ Medium-sized roof window in the high-top
☐ Towbar with bolt-on towball and electric socket
☐ Reversing camera with integral LED lighting for night use
☐ External shower rose coupling point for cleaning boots
☐ Small rear rack to stow a toilet/ shower tent for external use

Internal conversion features

☐ Swivelling cab seats
☐ Facility for two small gas cylinders in a sealed locker
☐ Easy-to-reach leisure battery; preferably room for a 120Ah unit
☐ Bench seat in rear to make into a double bed
☐ Occasional bed for child in the high-top
☐ Small absorption fridge
☐ Provision for stowing a portable toilet
☐ Oil-fired compact locker-type space heater
☐ Water heater not a high priority item
☐ Hob and grill essential but no need for an oven
☐ Roller blinds for windows but curtains not needed
☐ LED lighting – generous provision including reading lights
☐ Two double and one single mains sockets (minimum)
☐ One of the sockets near small table for laptop/phone charging
☐ Semi-rigid push-fit plumbing pipe rather than hose and clips
☐ Vinyl floor with some edge-bound removable carpet pieces
☐ Dark-coloured upholstery that doesn't show dirt easily
☐ Combined charger/mains supply and 12V fused control unit
☐ 12V socket for TV

Remember that this is a hypothetical checklist for a couple with a young child. Setting this out helps to narrow down the choice of vehicles, but don't expect to find a model that matches everything on your wish-list.

An increasing number of motorcaravanners prefer an external coupling for a shower head, although this is typically used for boot cleaning chores.

Magazine tests

A good way to find out more about new or pre-owned motorcaravans is to read magazine reports. Specialist magazines have teams of experienced journalists who put products under the microscope for several days and then compile their candid reports. In some instances manufacturers and importers lend models to magazine editorial staff for six-month periods; reports are then compiled using a number of different user-perspectives.

Magazine award competitions

Both *Practical Motorhome* (Haymarket Publishers) and *Motorcaravan, Motorhome Monthly* (*MMM*) (in conjunction with *Which Motorhome*) (Warners Group Publishers) run annual award schemes. The results are normally announced by the organising magazines in one of the late winter/early spring editions and the respective reports give detailed descriptions of products under scrutiny. Arguably

 Buyers' tip

Many new motorcaravans bear the National Caravan Council (NCC) approval badge which confirms compliance with: European and UK requirements, national regulations and industry Codes of Practice.

To gain an approval badge, a prototype model is inspected by NCC engineers and the process involves checks on over 400 elements including an evaluation of its Owner's Manual. This onerous task which typically takes up to seven hours gives prospective purchasers sound reassurance about a product's overall integrity and fitness for purpose.

Some imported motorcaravans like this 2007 Adria Twin bear an NCC approval badge.

The Renault-based Bentley Indigo was the overall winner of the 2011 Design and Drive Competition.

this information is mainly of interest to purchasers who are in a position to order a brand new current model. Moreover, the entry list only represents a small sample of models, and there are many good products available from small converters that are seldom entered into competitions like these. On the other hand, these events undoubtedly help a newcomer gain broad impressions about motorcaravan products.

Design and Drive competition

The Caravan Club conducts an annual 'Design and Drive' competition. In the 2011 event, for example, 51 models were placed in six different categories. The classification took price into account and three types of vehicle were identified: van conversions, coachbuilts, and A-class models. A rigorous checking schedule includes scrutinising vehicle weights, evaluating performance on the road, and appraising a wide range of design elements.

Imports as well as home-built models are put under the judges' critical eyes. The first contest was introduced in 1996, although it initially did not include an opportunity to drive vehicles. This was soon included and although honours have been widely shared, it is noteworthy that Murvi, a small-scale van converter based in Devon, has won approaching 20 Caravan Club Awards in different classes.

Warranty terms and conditions

When comparing new models in a shortlist, don't forget to check the warranties too. These differ in various ways, especially with regard to the period over which a motorcaravan's external fabric is insured against leaks that are caused by faulty construction.

MAKING A PURCHASE

The Marquis branch near Newbury always has a wide stock of models to inspect.

There are many ways to purchase a motorcaravan, irrespective of whether you're buying new or buying a pre-owned model. Here are some of the options.

Buying new

Choosing a dealer
This isn't quite as simple as you might imagine. For example, an impressive discount from a motorcaravan specialist based a long way from your home carries with it a problem that doesn't arise when you buy a

---

 Tip

Pre-delivery inspection (PDI)
A motorcaravan should leave the factory in a clean state and in full working order, although large manufacturers require their dealers to arrange a final PDI. Some dealers carry this out in their own workshops; others commission a nearby service specialist to perform the final cleaning and operational checks. Many dealers take this very seriously and supply vehicles to customers in tip-top condition. Others are less meticulous and owners collecting new vehicles often comment about loose screws rattling in drawers, sawdust left around installed appliances, and faults such as blinds that don't work properly. Small-scale converters who sell direct to customers are seldom the subject of critical reports.

The PDI had been poorly carried out here, with odd screws and sawdust on the floor of some lockers.

Many people order a new motorcaravan from a manufacturer's stand at an indoor exhibition.

car: in the event of a warranty repair being needed on a conversion element (eg a collapsing bed) you usually have to take your motorcaravan back to its original supplier. If the dealer's workshop is a long way from your home and it's a job likely to take more than a day, you may have to arrange overnight accommodation. That isn't the case with the base vehicle, of course, for which warranty work relating to original automotive elements can be carried out at any franchise dealership.

Buying at an exhibition

Caravan and motorhome exhibitions don't follow the pattern of motor shows, where manufacturers are solely in attendance to display the latest models. In contrast, motorcaravanning exhibitors usually take orders on products as well. This is because major motorhome manufacturers share their stands with staff from a selection of their approved dealers from around the country.

First-time visitors can find this confusing. For example, if you start looking at new models, suited sales staff will often offer help and might endeavour to conduct a sale. Let's say, by way of example, that the factory making the motorcaravans is based in the East Yorkshire/North Lincolnshire area, whereas some sales staff on the stand represent a dealership located in the West Country. If you return to the stand some hours later for a second look you might be made a competing offer from a dealer who comes from Surrey. This can get rather confusing, and if, in this example, your home is in Shropshire, that's when you need to be careful. Money-saving bargains lose their benefit if warranty work on the conversion itself has to be repaired a long way from your home.

Outdoor shows held at racecourses (between race meetings) and agricultural showgrounds offer

Barons had many vehicles on sale at this outdoor show held on Peterborough's Agricultural Showground.

similar buying opportunities, except that they are also attended by some of the direct-selling, small-volume manufacturers. That is because the pitches cost far less than those at indoor events. *Note: Many small-scale manufacturers sell direct to the public, whereas large-scale manufacturers, such as Bailey, Elddis, and the Swift Group, only sell products through their dealer networks.*

In practice, many satisfactory deals are negotiated at indoor and outdoor exhibitions, but letters sent to motorcaravanning magazines also report the ones that go wrong. To reinforce earlier advice, we would emphasise once again that magazine letters are helpful to read.

Delivery and sales calendars

Having chosen a motorcaravan in a brochure, there's often a long time lapse between placing an order and obtaining the vehicle. Magazine reports often relate tales of woe in which promised handover dates are later revised. Some owners order at Easter, book a ferry and campsites for a July holiday and then find delivery is delayed until August.

Experienced motorcaravanners are more familiar with the annual cycle in this seasonal industry. For instance, next year's models are usually unveiled around September. Experience also shows that a motorcaravan ordered in late autumn is likely to be delivered in time for a trip the following Easter. However, the waiting period can by much longer if you place an order in early spring – which is when the season gets frenetically busy.

Difficulties are unlikely to occur if you buy a new model direct from a dealer's forecourt, but many purchasers want an array of factory-fitted accessories as well. In fact, Auto-Trail has stated that every motorcaravan passing along its production line is

 Tip

Buyers' Guides
Most monthly magazines include 'Buyers' Guides' in which key information is tabulated for easy analysis. This allows you to identify new models which meet your needs using criteria such as price, weight, payload, dimensions, berths, belted seats, heating provision and many other factors. Magazines also give manufacturer/importer addresses, thereby enabling you to send for brochures. In addition a growing number of manufacturers also have websites.

When a new-look Fiat arrived in 2007 previous models were sold with generous discounts.

Tip

Test drive
When you reach the final stage of making a purchase, you should always request a short test drive. It's amazing that many owners don't arrange a drive prior to purchase and some dealers don't encourage this either. Naturally, a dealer doesn't want to add miles to an odometer on a new vehicle, but if you're intending to purchase a motorcaravan that costs thousands of pounds a brief test drive is really important.

In autumn, dealers offer big discounts to clear their forecourts in readiness for the next year's models.

a one-off model that has been pre-ordered by a particular customer. Consistent with this claim, Auto-Trail promotes its 'create your own motorhome' concept at exhibitions and explains that any person placing an order has included a list of the options they want. For instance, the current option list from Auto-Trail includes the type of engine, the choice of upholstery, the body profile, the internal layout and a choice of different accessory 'packs'. The opportunity to buy a model that suits your particular needs is praiseworthy – though it inevitably means that delivery of your self-specified vehicle won't happen overnight.

Similar time delays occur if you want to purchase a bespoke van conversion built by a small-scale specialist; good manufacturers are never short of work. For example, Young Conversions advises potential clients that when an order is placed for a new base vehicle with a particular specification of

Lowdham Leisureworld in Nottinghamshire always has a good selection of pre-owned motorcaravans.

extras, there's usually a wait of at least two to three months, depending on the model. When the requested base vehicle has eventually been delivered, you then have to arrange a date for the commencement of the conversion itself. Inevitably there are seasonal variations, and Young Conversions' work programme typically involves a wait of several more months as well.

On a different seasonal note, bear in mind that from late August onwards, dealers need to clear their forecourts to make way for the following year's models. That's when the sale period starts with a vengeance, and reductions in price can be stunningly good. Similar reductions arise when a base vehicle manufacturer introduces a new or facelifted model – during the transition period dealers are left with stocks of motorcaravans built on the outgoing model, and these are often sharply reduced in price.

BUYING SECOND-HAND

Purchasing privately

Specialist magazines contain a classified advertisements section devoted to motorcaravans. In addition, vehicles are also changing hands at ever-increasing pace as a result of websites like E-Bay. There are certainly some good products for sale, but do not forget the expression caveat emptor – 'buyer beware!'

In truth, every transaction has to be evaluated individually and it's quite impossible to give any more than a few guidelines. Suggestions include the following:

ⓘ Technical Tip

HPI check

Working closely with the UK motorcaravan industry, HPI has created a joint venture called 'Minder' to protect against theft and fraud.

The HPI website states: 'Motorhomes sold since 2001 carry a unique motorhome identification number (MIN), a vehicle identification number (VIN) and their vehicle registration mark (VRM).' Vehicles built in the UK since this date also have a hidden electronic tag and the MIN number is etched on the window.

Requesting an HPI check can establish whether a motorcaravan is stolen, written-off by an insurer or still subject to further payments under a loan agreement. Securing the check involves payment of a fee, but it's a wise measure when buying a motorcaravan of unknown provenance and from an uncertain source. To find out more, contact HPI on 01722 422422 or use the website, www.hpicheck.com, where you can see a sample HPI check report.

- Follow the usual procedures when buying a road-going vehicle. For instance, establish whether the vehicle is currently taxed. Is it insured for use on the road? Ask to see the current MoT certificate (if applicable). Check information in Chapter Seven concerning registration documents (once called the 'log book').
- Establish when a motorcaravan last received vehicle and habitation services and ask to see the signed/dated service schedules. Has the base vehicle got a full service history?
- Ask if there are recent approval certificates to verify that the gas and electrical systems have been checked and deemed safe.
- Enquire when the last professional damp check was carried out, and ask to see the workshop certificate.
- Have an HPI check carried out.
- Always inspect a private sale at the vendor's home, and not at a public car park.
- Ask the vendor if they would object to the vehicle being checked at the buyer's expense by a mechanical engineer appointed through the AA or RAC.
- The habitation element can also be checked by an independent specialist such as Autovan Services, based in Wimborne, Dorset (01202 848414).
- Enquire if both the base vehicle owner's manual and the motorcaravan manufacturer's manual are available for inspection.
- Insist on arranging a test drive – tall drivers sometimes experience poor lines of vision, and some models are known for jumping out of fifth gear. There have also been problems with some post-2005 Fiat/Peugeot base vehicles in which pronounced transmission vibrations occurred when reversed up

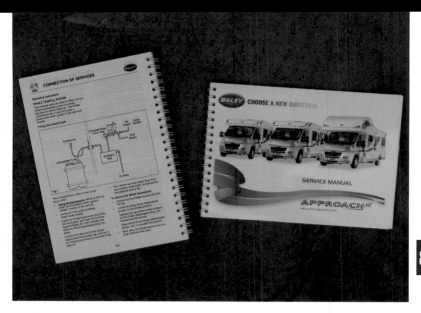

a slope. Measures were later available to solve this, but it would be wise to conduct a brief reversing manoeuvre during a test drive.

Notwithstanding the points made above, you often find that service documentation and owner manuals are missing and you then have to decide for yourself whether the motorcaravan has been well looked after. If the price is attractive and you're prepared to get servicing and checking work carried out yourself, it's a gamble you might decide to take.

Without doubt, there are examples of well cared for motorcaravans for sale that have been lovingly cherished and maintained. Some are advertised with a touch of personal sadness too. Ill health or a bereavement sometimes prompts their sale, and low mileage models are often advertised in motorcaravan magazines. When an owner is no longer in a position to continue motorcaravanning, dealers are disinclined to trade-in a vehicle if they won't be selling the client a replacement, and the owner may then endeavour to sell the vehicle privately – often at an attractive price.

Dealer pre-owned models
Obviously there are inherent risks when purchasing privately, whereas buying a pre-owned motorcaravan from a dealer generally includes support in the event of subsequent problems. Admittedly the degree of cover offered by a warranty on a second-hand motorcaravan varies from dealer to dealer but there's far more likelihood of after-sale assistance. The asking price is usually higher than in a private transaction, but this secures you additional peace of mind.

Naturally there's a higher likelihood of redress if you have problems with a van bought through a dealer.

If the owner's handbook and servicing manual is missing from a pre-owned motorcaravan, replacements are very hard to obtain.

Sales of caravans and motorhomes are conducted by British Car Auctions; events are regularly held at BCA's Measham branch in the Midlands.

You might also negotiate for a new MoT test to be arranged (where applicable) with the vendor as a condition of purchase.

Motorcaravan auctions

British Car Auctions (BCA) organises regular sales of caravans and motorhomes throughout the year, particularly at its centres in Measham and Nottingham. Full advice is given in BCA literature on procedures for bidding and making a purchase. Indoor and outdoor compounds are used and there are plenty of opportunities to check vehicles prior to the start of each sale.

If you want to purchase a light commercial vehicle with a view to having it converted, BCA also conducts auctions of commercial vehicles at many of its centres. Dates of sales and other information is given on the BCA website: www.british-car-auctions.co.uk

One of the problems buying this way is that you'll be expected to produce the full payment in a day or so. Moreover, you really need to know how to spot a sound vehicle.

Imported models

A growing number of people import motorcaravans themselves, with models coming from both Europe and North America. On the face of it there's a lot of money to be saved, but there are also numerous things that need to be done. For example, a vehicle has to gain a UK registration, which involves completing a V55/5 form issued by the DVLA. And with regard to insurance, companies sometimes set higher premiums for imported models.

Some potential purchasers also overlook the fact that an imported vehicle usually has to be altered in a number of ways before it can be legally used on Britain's roads. For instance, a vehicle has to comply with the UK's Construction and Use regulations as well as legislation relating to road vehicle lighting. This may mean that headlamp units may need to be changed and other road lights might need to be added.

Items such as the mirrors must provide the required field of vision appropriate for driving on the left. Speedometers also have to show speeds in mph rather than kph.

In the living space, electrical sockets will need changing, and older foreign vehicles often have gas appliances that run at a different pressure from their British counterparts.

Making alterations can be quite involved and it's certainly easier to buy an imported, pre-owned model through a specialist company. A number of dealers import pre-owned vans from Japan, such as the Mazda Bongo and the Toyota Regius; these are popular for conversion projects because Japanese vehicles have a right-hand drive like ours.

Pre-owned Mazda and Toyota vehicles are often imported from Japan by UK van converters, all of which are right-hand drive models.

VAT concessions for the disabled
HM Revenue and Customs (HMRC) operates VAT relief to assist motorhome owners with disabilities. However, strict criteria have to be met and these are set out in HMRC Notice 701/59. You can also receive guidance by telephoning 0845 109000, although only general advice is given because applications are evaluated on an individual basis according to needs.

A very substantial wheelchair hoist and a converted toilet room were built on this Benimar coachbuilt.

As a rule, someone wholly wheelchair-dependent who wants to purchase a motorhome with permanent adaptations is normally able to claim full VAT relief on the vehicle. The administrative process is carried out at the supplying dealers and the disabled person has to complete a self-certifying form. At one time, this concession was only applicable if the user had to remain seated in the wheelchair within the vehicle, but that's no longer the case. There are other points of detail too. For instance, if a trailer and towbar are considered necessary, these fall outside the vehicle's VAT-free concession arrangement.

VAT relief is also available for those with less severe disabilities. This includes owners who aren't wheelchair-bound but who need the benefit of equipment such as support rails and other adaptations. In this instance, VAT relief usually only applies to individual fittings and not the vehicle as a whole. Moreover, some retrospective alterations, such as having an automatic gearbox fitted, do not qualify for concessionary treatment.

For further advice, *Motorcaravan and Motorhome Monthly* magazine publishes an annual 'Mobility Supplement', which contains a wealth of information and plenty of addresses of specialist manufacturers and retailers. This notable publication was first introduced in 1993 and is an invaluable guide.

Final handover

When a new owner collects a motorcaravan, the level of attention during the handover process varies from dealer to dealer. Some suppliers are extremely busy during the height of the season and don't always provide the level of help a buyer deserves. Furthermore, today's motorhomes are sophisticated products and a complete beginner can be easily bewildered by a multitude of technical issues.

Conversions by Middlesex Motorcaravans using new or pre-owned vans are popular with new owners.

However, it is not always like that. At a Marquis branch near Portsmouth many years ago, the author was given an excellent introduction to a Swift motorhome that had been hired for a fortnight. Equally, when a bespoke camper van was handed over to a complete beginner recently, the manufacturer provided three hours of explanation and several mugs of coffee when describing how everything works. That is the sort of service a customer needs and the accompanying photos record that particular occasion.

The co-owner of the company spent three hours giving a thorough explanation of how everything worked.

Although built to suit the purchaser's needs, there was still a lot of equipment to demonstrate at handover time.

Early apprehensions were soon cast aside, thanks to the attention given by this family-owned manufacturer.

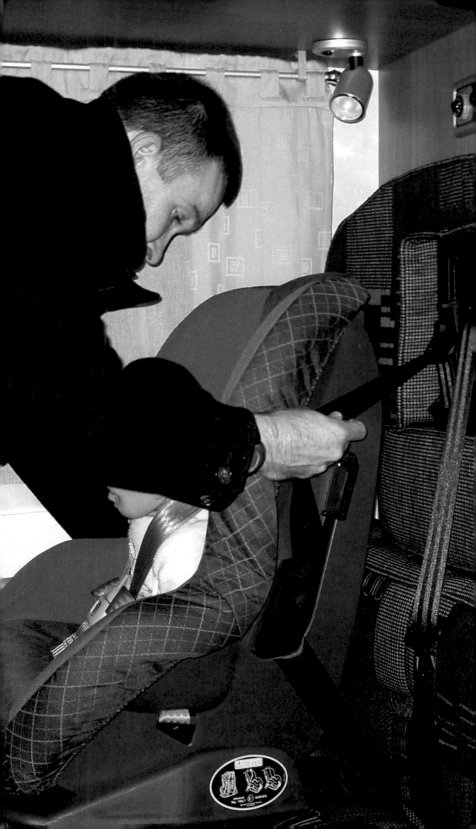

CHAPTER SIX

LEGAL
CONSIDERATIONS

The fact that some motorcaravans are compact 'campervans', whereas others are very much larger, inevitably means that legal requirements vary. For instance, dissimilar rulings apply on the basis of a vehicle's weight; a driver's age and qualifications may also have an effect. Then there are issues such as Vehicle Excise Duty, MoT testing, Type Approval and seat belt requirements, all of which serve to complicate the situation. This chapter provides an introduction to such issues.

95

Seat belts in motorcaravans are a matter of recent concern.

Charges for entry into London's Low Emission Zone might discourage visitors from using the city's caravan and motorhome sites.

Of the 17 chapters in this book, this is the one that will need updating the most often; laws relating to the classification of vehicles, Road Tax categories, Driving Licences and seat belt requirements are constantly under review.

To illustrate how things can change, the panel below describes past and pending modifications to the design of approved towbars. This is just one of many motorcaravan-related issues that has recently been discussed in high places.

So here's the problem. Whilst it's important to describe key issues relating to motorcaravans, laws change with such frequency that you'll need to confirm the latest directives and mandatory requirements by

Towbars and motorcaravans

For many years, most motorcaravans used for towing were fitted with a bespoke towbar, whereas the towbars fitted to virtually all recent cars (first registered on or after 1 August 1998) must be Type Approved products that comply with European Directive 94/20/EC. On vehicles where the installation of a Type Approved towbar is not mandatory, it is highly desirable to fit a product that complies with British Standard BS ISO 1103.

From 29 April 2012, new motorcaravans have to be Type Approved – and some manufacturers voluntarily chose to achieve Type Approval for their models ahead of that date. This has a particular relevance for towbar installations. Any motorcaravan which is Type Approved can legally only be fitted with a Type Approved towbar that conforms with European Directive 94/20/EC. The Type Approved status of a vehicle can be checked in its documentation papers or on the vehicle plate. Look on the plate for a lengthy number that begins with an 'e'. If you still have any doubt, confirm its status by seeking advice from the manufacturer or dealer.

For many years, specialists have been permitted to design and fit bespoke towbars. This is no longer the case on motorcaravans that are Type Approved models.

The AL-KO towbar designed to couple directly to an AL-KO vehicle chassis is an example of a Type Approved bracket that has been specifically designed for motorcaravans.

Info

London's Low Emission Zone

Eagerness to improve air quality in Europe has led to the establishment of Low Emission Zones (LEZs) in which the pollution from vehicle exhausts is required to fall within specified limits. In technical terms, the amount of 'particulate matter' discharged by an exhaust defines whether a vehicle falls within the permitted pollution level or not.

In this country, Transport for London (TfL) discourages non-compliant vehicles from entering the Capital's LEZ by imposing a daily tariff. In broad terms, this zone falls roughly within the boundary of the M25. (For more precise information, a map defining the exact LEZ boundary is shown on the website www.tfl.gov.uk/lezlondon).

As regards entry into a low emission zone, different criteria exist throughout Europe, and the situation in London is based on a vehicle's gross weight and the level of its engine emissions. Since this matter started to gather momentum, diesel engines have been classified using the terms Euro III, Euro IV and Euro V. In practice, many owners are unaware of their motorcaravan's engine classification, but it is possible to find out in advance whether entry into London's LEZ will necessitate payment of the tariff by using the website www.tfl.gov.uk/roadusers/lez/17700.aspx

When a vehicle's registration number is entered on the website, the database reveals whether the tariff is chargeable.

In London, the introduction of enforceable tariffs is being implemented in phases, and cameras within the zone read registration plates and check them with the databases held by DVLA and VOSA. The minimum daily charge currently payable for a non-compliant vehicle to drive within London's LEZ is £100 and ignoring the payment carries a fine of £500. With fees at this level, few owners of non-compliant motorcaravans will want to enter the zone, and the tariff is a disastrous blow to owners of non-compliant motorcaravans *who already live within the zone* and park their vehicle at home.

The phased introduction of the scheme commenced on 4 February 2008 and applied to commercial vehicles over 12 tonnes GVW. As regards motorcaravans, those with a GVW in excess of 3,500kg (3.5t) are required to meet the Euro 4 standard. However, since vehicles with these engines were not introduced until late 2006, a motorcaravan with a GVW above 3,500kg that was registered new before 1 October 2006 is unlikely to meet the Euro IV standard. A fee must therefore be paid before its entry into the zone.

On 3 January 2012 the next phase came into effect. Motorcaravans with a GVW over 2,500kg (2.5t) and up to 3,500kg (3.5t) are required to meet a minimum emission standard of Euro III to avoid the daily charge. As a guide, this generally means that diesel vehicles registered before 1 January 2002 are unlikely to comply unless they have had expensive modifications. Moreover, if an approved emissions filter is fitted, VOSA must be notified in order to record this on the database. In addition, the filter has to be submitted every 12 months for an emissions test. Current supply and installation costs for an exhaust filter are from around £1,850 to £3,500. At the time of writing, an annual emissions test of an exhaust filter costs £32. *Note: Manufacturers of approved modification kits are listed on the TfL website.*

For more information, see Transport for London website: tfl.gov.uk/lezlondon or telephone the helpline: 0845 676 9489.

checking official literature or website information issued by appropriate Government agencies. Also bear in mind that these sources sometimes lack explicit guidance concerning commercial vehicles that have been converted into private leisure accommodation vehicles, ie motorcaravans.

Some administrators seem to overlook the fact that leisure vehicles are built on a light commercial base vehicle. That's where there is particular concern about London's Low Emission Zone (LEZ) charge rates.

Transport for London (TfL) has imposed three-figure sums that are payable by drivers of light commercial lorries entering the LEZ, but these, by definition, also apply to most diesel-powered motorcaravans.

Arguably, not many motorcaravanners would want to drive directly to attractions situated in the heart of this busy capital, but significant zone charges still have to be paid if you want to use one of The Caravan Club's excellent sites at Abbey Wood or Crystal Palace. Similarly, there are some pleasant private sites that fall within the designated area. Naturally, these zone fees are also a discouragement to visiting tourists who drive motorcaravans, many of whom are from mainland Europe

Concerted efforts by motorcaravanners and clubs have strongly encouraged TfL to reconsider its inclusion of motorcaravans within the scheme, but to date, these requests have not been successful. More information on this matter is given in the accompanying panel.

With so many congestion problems on roads in Europe, changes to legislation are frequent, and many low emission zones are being introduced in other European cities. For detailed information on this, visit www.lowemissionzones.eu/

However, when you check other updated legislation, be aware that when some vehicle-related laws are introduced, they are not always applied retrospectively – in other words, existing vehicles don't always have to be updated to comply with new requirements. Hence, there are many classic cars being legally used on our roads that are not fitted with seat belts. That is because seat belt laws don't carry retrospective enforcement. The position is the same regarding seat belts in motorcaravans, which is discussed later.

What is a motorcaravan?

In Chapter One, the definition of a motorcaravan stated that it is 'a special-purpose M1 category vehicle constructed to include living accommodation.' The same chapter also explains some of the issues that differentiate its status from that of commercial road-going vehicles, in spite of the fact that their base units are often the same. In addition, the definition is normally made explicit on a vehicle's registration certificate.

However, different interpretations occur when it comes to Vehicle Excise Duty (VED – often referred to as 'Road Tax'). For example, the M1 Status of motorcaravans means that these vehicles normally fall into the same category as cars. Yet in the context of VED, most motorcaravans are paradoxically treated as either Private Light Goods vehicles or Heavy Private Goods vehicles.

Unsuccessful attempts have been made in the past by independent specialists such as The Motorhome

Information Service (which has since disbanded) to gain a discrete classification for motorcaravans, thereby permitting greater clarity for legislators, owners and the Police. Without doubt, it is unhelpfully confusing when in one context, a motorcaravan is treated like a car, whereas in another, it comes under rulings applicable to goods vehicles.

The Department for Transport (DfT) also appears to be experiencing some difficulties differentiating between motorcaravans, which are fully-equipped leisure vehicles, and 'living vans', which are commercial vehicles equipped with a facility enabling a driver to sleep inside. Many long-distance lorries, for example, have a sleeping compartment over the cab. As explained in the next section, that's why the words 'motor caravan' should be entered in section D.3 (headed 'Body Type') on the V5C Registration Certificate.

When a commercial panel van is subsequently converted into a motorcaravan, the change must be recorded in Section D.3 (Body Type) on the Registration Certificate.

The Registration Certificate

This document, once referred to as the 'log book', has undergone several changes. For example, the V5 'Registration Document' was replaced by a V5C 'registration certificate' so that all member states of the European Union adopted a common format. Furthermore, at the time of writing, a revised red V5C certificate is currently being sent out nationwide with the aim to replace all the older *blue* versions by November 2012.

Owners should also note that they have a legal obligation to notify the DVLA if details on a V5C Registration Certificate need alteration. For example, notification must be given if a different engine is installed, the body colour is changed, or alterations have been made that place it in a new revenue category. A change might occur, for example, when a Private/Light Goods (PLG) vehicle, hitherto driven as a panel van for delivering goods, is later converted into a motorcaravan. The term 'motor caravan' must then be officially recorded in section D.3 ('Body Type'). Formal recognition of its status as a leisure vehicle as opposed to a goods-carrying vehicle also has implications for matters such as speed limits.

Should you find inaccurate statements, the certificate should be returned to DVLA, Swansea, SA99 1BA, with an explanatory letter, preferably including photographs of the interier and exterior of the vehicle if it needs to be reclassified as a motor caravan. *Note: Very recent DVLA advice appears to suggest that any changes can also be recorded by one of the local offices of DVLA. However, the Government has also announced its intention to close these offices by the end of 2013, subject to the outcome of ongoing consultation. It therefore remains to be seen how the recording of V5C changes will be carried out in the future.*

Having the correct information is also important when a new vehicle excise licence (*ie* 'tax disc') is due. If, for some reason, you don't receive a V11 Licence Renewal form in the post, you have to produce your registration certificate at a licence-issuing post office or DVLA local office. Naturally, it should contain up-to-date information.

Statutory Off Road Notification (SORN)

Like owners of classic cars and self-built kit cars, some motorcaravanners only use their vehicles during the warmer months of the year. In consequence, they only pay VED (road tax) for a six-month period and then provide Statutory Off Road Notification (SORN) when the vehicle is removed from public roads and put into storage. Once the declaration has been made, the DVLA sends a notification letter verifying that this request has been officially recorded.

When an owner subsequently wants to re-licence a vehicle for use on the road, it is necessary to complete and then submit Vehicle Licence Application form V10 to a licence-issuing post office or DVLA local office, and this must be accompanied by the V5C registration certificate, a certificate of insurance, and a valid MoT certificate (if applicable).

Although it is better from a mechanical viewpoint for a vehicle to be used regularly throughout the year, some motorcaravan owners work abroad for long spells and are forced to lay-up their vehicle for extended periods. In this case, SORN is something to be aware of. You are no longer permitted to allow payment of Vehicle Excise Duty to lapse – you're legally required to declare SORN and to remove your motorcaravan from public roads.

Detailed guidance on SORN is available from licensing post offices, DVLA local offices and on the internet (www.direct.gov.uk/motoring). Note that you can also declare SORN via the internet, and the website explains this procedure.

MOTORCARAVAN WEIGHTS

Different categories recorded on a driving licence indicate the size and types of vehicle the holder is permitted to drive.

It might seem curious to find a section dealing with vehicle weight in a chapter concerned with legal issues. However, the reason for this is simple: driving licence categories and speed limits are related to vehicle weights.

Loading terms

Weight is currently expressed in kilograms (1kg = roughly 2.2lb). An imperial ton is 20cwt, *ie* 2,240lb. A metric ton, properly called a 'tonne', is 1,000kg, or 2,204.62lb. For rough-and-ready reference, an imperial ton is not hugely different from a tonne; it's approximately 36lb greater.

- **Maximum technically permissible laden mass** (MTPLM): This refers to a vehicle's total allowable legal weight, as defined by the base vehicle manufacturer. It has previously been called the 'maximum laden weight' (MLW), 'maximum authorised mass' (MAM), 'gross vehicle weight' (GVW), and 'maximum authorised weight' (MAW). Incidentally, the DVLA uses the term MAM, whereas the Caravan and Motorhome industries refer to it as MTPLM. The term GVW continues to be popular, too, and is also used elsewhere in this chapter.
- **Actual laden weight** (ALW): This is the actual weight of a motorcaravan including all its contents, its passengers, and its fuel. A check on a weighbridge will reveal whether the ALW exceeds a vehicle's 'maximum technically permissible laden mass' or MTPLM. (Using a weighbridge is explained later.)
- **Mass in running order** (MIRO): This refers to the minimum practical usable condition of a vehicle.

The term Gross Train Weight refers to the maximum permitted weight of a laden towing vehicle, together with its trailer and the load being carried.

The most common interpretation of MIRO consists of a total of a vehicle's unladen ('ex works') weight, a tank of fuel, fresh water tank and gas cylinder all filled to 90%, all essential liquids, the weight of a driver (taken as 75kg) and a driver's personal effects. Most manufacturers adopt this interpretation because it aligns with the EC Masses and Dimensions Directive requirements for Type Approval. However, there is an alternative interpretation that complies with UK legislation in which the driver is excluded from the MIRO figure.

ⓘ Technical Note

Payload

In the past, there have been several alterations to the way that 'payload' and the components it includes have been classified. Recent practice has been to identify the following three elements.

1. Essential equipment, such as gas cylinders and toilet chemicals.
2. Optional equipment, such as solar panels, bike rack and air conditioning system.
3. Personal effects, such as clothing, food and holiday gear.

Together, these items add up to the 'payload', and working within the MTPLM limit some motorcaravans can carry much more equipment than others. So ask about the weight of optional equipment that you might want to purchase – particularly heavy products such as an onboard generator. This should be related to your payload potential. Also compare any addition with the equivalent weight of shoes, socks, shirts and cold-weather wear. Adding accessory items will mean that fewer personal effects can be packed.

Personal effects form part of your permitted payload and families with children often carry a surprising variety of holiday items.

- **Maximum user payload** (MUP): This refers to a vehicle's maximum carrying capacity and is calculated by deducting a vehicle's mass in running order from its maximum technically permissible laden mass.
- **Maximum axle weights** (MAW): Front and rear axles have maximum weights too, and these figures must not be exceeded. Their respective loading can normally be checked on a weighbridge by driving one axle at a time onto the weighing plate.
- **Gross train weight** (GTW): This refers to the maximum weight permitted for the vehicle together with a trailer and the combined loads being carried. It is important to work within this limit and to conduct checks before towing heavy items such as a support car. GTW is sometimes referred to as 'Combined Weight'.

Interpretation difficulties

Data relating to the MTPLM, Axle Weight limits, and GTW is displayed on an information plate or adhesive label that is usually permanently fixed in the engine bay or on a door surround. It is an offence to exceed these clearly stated limits.

However, as regards terms like MIRO and payload, some manufacturers have calculated these differently in the past – as old catalogues reveal. Much-needed clarification was welcomed in 1999, after which all new motorcaravans covered by BS EN 1646-2 adopted a standard approach to the way that weights and payloads were expressed. That was helpful for everyone, but at the time of writing, further alterations are now anticipated in order to conform to new Type Approval requirements.

A further issue that sometimes leads to misunderstandings is the fact that some models are sold with a 'deluxe' package that can include items such as a rollout sunblind, a satellite TV system and alloy wheels. The addition of accessories like these inevitably means that a catalogue's published payload figure, which relates strictly to a basic model, may need adjustment. In effect, the

In three out of the four pictures on pages 103 and 104, the vehicle's Type Approval 'e' number is clearly visible.

Below left: Many plates are permanently fixed in engine compartments.

Below: A few plates are mounted on door surrounds.

Right: This is the Fiat base vehicle data plate in the engine compartment of a 2011 Auto-Trail Tracker.

Below: The manufacturer of the motorcaravan has also added a plate after the conversion's completed and this gives an amended GTW limit of 4,750kg.

additional deluxe pack installations have now taken up some of the payload that might otherwise have been earmarked for clothing and food. To make this clearer to purchasers, recent catalogues have started to reveal the weight of all accessories in a manufacturer's 'optional extra' list.

Keeping things simple

Notwithstanding the potential for ambiguities and misinterpretation, there is no argument about a vehicle's maximum weight limit, which is shown on its data plate. Not only could it be dangerous to exceed this limit: it is also a serious offence. However, on recent motorcaravans, you might find more than one plate giving weight information. This arises because vehicles like coachbuilt models are built in two or three stages using: 1) a base vehicle, 2) possibly a chassis extension structure, and 3) the living enclosure. In the accompanying illustration showing two separate plates in a 2011 Auto-Trail Tracker EK, there is Fiat's plate together with the plate of the converter, namely Auto-Trail. In effect the two plates only differ when it comes to the gross train weight (GTW) and the maximum figure relating to the finished motorhome has been reduced by the converter from 6,000kg to 4,750kg.

Having noted the weight limits for a fully laden vehicle (complete with driver and passengers) you then need to establish weight details before you start loading up for a holiday, or before you get a heavy accessory installed. Having learnt from bitter experience that some manufacturers' claimed payload figures are misleading, the author had concluded that sometimes you cannot rely solely on catalogue information. For this reason, when testing motorcaravans for magazine reports, an empty vehicle is filled to the brim with fuel and then checked on a weighbridge. A calculation duly reveals if a claimed payload figure is accurate or optimistically exaggerated. In truth, inaccuracies are not unusual.

This has also been noted by The Caravan Club when vehicles are entered for the annual 'Design and Drive' competition. As a matter of routine, each model is taken to a weighbridge for checking before the judges commence their searching evaluations.

Roadside inspections conducted by the Police have also revealed examples of gross overloading, and whereas towed caravans used to be the main subject of scrutiny, attention is presently turning to motorcaravans.

Anyway to keep this simple, you need to get a vehicle weighed before you start loading it up. Then you subtract this information from the figures given on the weight limit plates. The result reveals the weight of the load you can carry – not forgetting to include all the occupants, too. To be even more precise, a vehicle fully loaded for a typical trip can later be weighed again just in case you added too much when packing the gear.

So taking weight checks is important and it's disappointing that many owners never bother to check their motorcaravan. It is also no secret that when many owners finally act on this advice, they get the shock of their lives. A remarkable number of vehicles are badly overladen.

On that note, let's describe how the weight checks are done.

Finding a weighbridge

All motorcaravan owners should get the weight of their vehicle checked, and local authorities usually have a list of weighbridges in the immediate area. Nowadays, there are fewer local-authority-maintained 'public weighbridges' than there used to be but some County Council offices also keep lists of privately owned weighbridges in their Weights and Measures Department. This department often comes under Trading Standards Services and it's usually possible to get a copy of the address list with phone numbers of weighbridges nearby. A telephone call then establishes whether a company is willing to weigh private motorcaravans. You may come across weighbridges that are only established to weigh the vehicles of the company. Similarly, agricultural weighbridges are less likely to help around harvest time when lorries filled with grain keep the staff busy.

When telephoning a weighbridge operator, enquire if an appointment is needed and ask if there are any

The motorhome is driven onto the weighing plate and the driver usually alights before the reading is taken.

busy periods you should avoid. Also ask about fees. As a rough guide, each measured weight currently costs around £8–£12 and a printed, dated form showing a vehicle's registration plate provides a customer with a record of the weight information. *Note: There are several websites that give weighbridge addresses – both commercial and non-commercial. One that provides comprehensive information is: http://chrishodgetrucks.co.uk/useful-info/weighbridges.htm*

Procedure at a weighbridge

On arrival, a vehicle is driven on to the weighing plate, the driver alights and the weight is recorded. Then you drive forwards to vacate the plate. Having done that, you then reverse so that only the rear wheels rest on the platform. Disembark once again, and the rear axle loading is recorded.

You could repeat this operation placing just the front wheels on the plate, but to save money, most people simply subtract the rear axle reading from the total vehicle weight to calculate the front axle load.

Collect the dated certificate giving the weights, and make notes to record if your vehicle was carrying gas cylinders, drinking water and items such as a toolkit at the time the weighbridge was used.

Back at home you can then add the combined weight of the passengers and driver to find out what payload remains for accessories and personal possessions. Alternatively, you could return to the weighbridge with your vehicle loaded-up for a typical holiday, thereby confirming beyond doubt that it is not illegally overweight. You shouldn't need to do this prior to every holiday, but be mindful of weight constraints when loading-up for your trips.

When you've gathered this information you can then rest in the knowledge that your loaded vehicle isn't exceeding its MTPLM. But don't forget that individual axle loadings must not exceed the limits stated on your vehicle's data plate. For instance, a loaded

Driving just the rear wheels onto the plate enables the operator to take a back axle load weight.

motorcaravan might fall within its MTPLM, but if too many heavy items are positioned at the back, this could exceed the rear axle's limit and lead to prosecution.

Note: Weighing procedures may vary and some weighbridges do not permit a driver to disembark for health and safety reasons. If that is the case, deduct your personal weight from the vehicle's data.

Upgrading the MTPLM

Some commercial vehicle specialists, such as SVTech in Leyland, Lancashire, are equipped and authorised to advise if the MTPLM of a vehicle can be upgraded.

For example, it is sometimes possible to upgrade and re-plate a light commercial vehicle from 3,500kg to 3,850kg. However, this can be costly, because the operation might necessitate fitting up-rated tyres, strengthening the rear axle tube, altering the suspension, improving brake specifications and so on.

There are also disadvantages in running a vehicle that is plated with an MTPLM greater than 3,500kg.

For example:
- Since January 1997 new Category B Driving Licence holders in the UK are limited to driving vehicles up to 3,500kg (or 4,250kg with a trailer).
- Many motoring organisations in the UK will not recover motorhomes weighing over 3,500kg.

Information is recorded on an electronic device that's linked to a printer.

You'll be given a dated printout with the registration details of your vehicle and the weights recorded.

The weight limit on the back axle of a vehicle carrying heavy items at the rear might be exceeded. Motorcaravans with twin rear axles are able to carry much greater loads.

Above: SVTech has access to a large body of data that enables calculations to be made and alterations prescribed if a vehicle's permissible weights need revision.

Right: This modified motorcaravan bears a revised data plate after its MTPLM was raised from 3,500kg to 3,850kg.

Throughout Europe, it's often apparent that 3,500kg (3.5 tonnes) represents a significant recognised legal break point in respect of weight limits and legal issues applying to vehicles.

- In the UK, the minimum age to drive a vehicle not exceeding 3,500kg is 17; and for vehicles weighing over 3,500kg, it is 18.
- When a driver over 70 years of age applies to renew a licence, and wishes to drive a vehicle in the UK with an MTPLM over 3,500kg, additional eyesight and health tests are required.
- Drivers with certain medical conditions are not permitted to drive vehicles plated at more than 3,500kg. This includes diabetics who control their condition using insulin injections. Limitations applicable to diabetics have recently become more stringent and further advice is available from the charity Diabetes UK.
- In some countries, particularly Germany, a vehicle over 3,500kg is classified as a Goods Vehicle and is subject to lower speed limits, different overtaking rules, and restrictions of vehicle use at weekends.
- In Switzerland, a motorcaravan exceeding 3,500kg has to pay a Heavy Goods Vehicle tax supplement at the border in order to use motorways.

As explained above, keeping the MTPLM below 3,500kg has several points in its favour.

Down-rating strategies

Mindful of restrictions like those mentioned above, some owners adopt the reverse strategy and get an approved specialist to reduce the MTPLM of their motorcaravan and to fit an official replacement plate. Several dealers can carry out this service. Just remember that if you lower the MTPLM, you may have to reduce the amount of gear that you previously used to take on trips.

Down-rating a vehicle is normally straightforward and a magazine reader reported recently that having just turned 70, he decided to have his motorcaravan's MTPLM of 3,850kg down-rated to 3,500kg. The fact that he no longer used a motorcycle previously carried on a rear carrier meant that this wouldn't involve any hardship. Having completed form VTG10, he reported that it took only two weeks for VOSA to verify that the MTPLM had been amended to the lower figure. Of course, this strategy calls for a stricter approach when packing personal gear, but there are several benefits too, particularly in respect of driving licence classifications.

DRIVING LICENCES

Drivers under the age of 70
If you passed your test prior to 1 January 1997
A Category B Driving Licence obtained before 1 January 1997 permits you to drive a motorcaravan without a trailer as long as its MTPLM doesn't exceed 7,500kg. If you want to drive a large RV with a weight exceeding 7,500kg, the position is less clear. It has been suggested that a B Licence is probably deemed acceptable for a pre-1997 licence holder on the grounds that there is no higher rate category without moving into licences covering commercial vehicle drivers. (This matter is certainly defined more precisely if your category B licence was gained after 1 January 1997.)

If you want to tow a trailer, you are permitted to do this as long as the GTW of the trailer and the motorcaravan doesn't exceed 8,250kg. This is because the standard licence includes the B+E category.

If you gained your Category B licence on or after 1 January 1997
You are permitted to drive vehicles with an MTPLM up to 3,500kg. However, if you successfully pass an LGV test (category C1) you're then qualified to drive a motorcaravan with an MTPLM up to 7,500kg. If you want to tow a small trailer behind your motorcaravan, no further test has to be passed, as long as its laden weight doesn't exceed 750kg and the combined MTPLM of the motorcaravan and

Some owners would like to own a large RV but before considering a purchase look very carefully at the entitlements in your driving licence.

trailer doesn't exceed 4,250kg. However, if the laden weight of the trailer does exceed 750kg, towing is permitted as long as the combined MTPLM of both the motorcaravan and the trailer doesn't exceed 3,500kg. In the event of the combined MTPLM of the motorcaravan and trailer exceeding 3,500kg, then an additional test (B+E) must be passed.

As regards owners wanting to tow a trailer heavier than 750kg behind a motorcaravan whose MTPLM exceeds 3,500kg, it is then necessary to pass both a C1 Test and an E Test. For more information consult the website:
http://www.direct.gov.uk/en/Motoring/DriverLicensing/WhatCanYouDriveAndYourObligations/DG 4022547

If you wish to drive a motorcaravan that exceeds 7,500kg MTPLM you will have to pass a C Test.

Drivers aged 70 or more
If you passed your test prior to 1 January 1997
Provided the MTPLM of your motorcaravan is no more than 3,500kg, the driving entitlement for both Category B and combined Category B+E is normally retained when you reapply for a licence that will run for three years on reaching the age of 70. If the MTPLM of your motorcaravan is greater than 3,500kg you'll also have to submit a D4 medical form completed by a GP. This includes an eyesight test to verify that your vision achieves the required standard at 20.5m (67ft) and other medical checks. Further information on medical requirements is given on the DVLA website: http://www.direct.gov.uk/en/Motoring/DriverLicensing/NeedANewOrUpdatedLicence/DG 4022086

If you passed your test on or after 1 January 1997
As long as your medical condition is sound, you are permitted to drive a vehicle on your B licence

provided its MTPLM is no more than 3,500kg. However, if your motorcaravan's MTPLM exceeds this weight but is no greater than 7,500kg, you'll have to take a further test to gain a C1 licence – this is the qualification needed by drivers of 'medium commercial vehicles'. Alternatively, you can arrange for the MTPLM shown on the vehicle's plate to be down-rated, as explained earlier.

If you wish to drive a motorcaravan that exceeds 7,500kg MTPLM you'll have to pass a C Test.

For further information see DVLA Booklet D100 entitled 'What you need to know about Driving Licences', available from post offices. Unfortunately some editions of this booklet appear not to give a great deal of advice on aspects relating to medical certification for the over-70s.

SPEED LIMITS IN THE UK

As stated earlier, it is important that the words 'motor caravan' are entered in section D3 ('Body Type') of the V5C Registration Certificate. This differentiates your vehicle from those first registered after 2001 that have an MTPLM over 3,500kg and carry either passengers or goods for 'hire or reward'. Under recent legislation such vehicles have to be fitted with speed limiters and are restricted to 62mph when carrying passengers, and 56.6mph when carrying goods. Moreover, they are not permitted to be used in the outside lane of a motorway with three or more lanes. Clearly, these are not motorcaravans, and speed limiters are not required on privately-owned

111

Speed Limiters

Motorcaravans do not have to be fitted with speed limiters provided certain criteria are met. Key issues relating to this topic are explained in the text alongside.

This 2007 Knaus Sport is subject to the same speed limits as cars because its unladen weight of 2,820kg falls well below the 3,050kg defining limit.

leisure vehicles. However, a commercial vehicle built with such a limiter (or a tachograph), can have these devices removed if they are converted into a motorcaravan.

So what speeds are applicable to private motorcaravans? This isn't straightforward, because it's partly governed by the *unladen* weight of the vehicle. This figure isn't normally given in official documents, although it should be recorded in literature supplied by motorcaravan converters.

Motorcaravans with an unladen weight not exceeding 3,050kg

Note that the figure 3,050kg given here (which goes back to the old 3.0 imperial tons) is not a misprint and mustn't be confused with the more usually encountered weight 'milestone' of 3,500kg. As long as an unladen motorcaravan doesn't exceed 3,050kg and is listed as a 'motor caravan' in the V5C registration certificate it is subject to the same speed limits as cars. As a reminder, these are:

- 60mph on single carriageway roads unless a lower limit is in force
- 70mph on dual carriageway roads unless a lower limit is in force
- 70mph on motorways unless a lower limit is in force.

Motorcaravans less than 12m long with an unladen weight exceeding 3,050kg

This category includes a very large proportion of coachbuilt models. Speed limits are:

- 50mph on single carriageway roads unless a lower limit is in force
- 60mph on dual carriageway roads unless a lower limit is in force
- 70mph on motorways unless a lower limit is in force.

Motorcaravans more than 12m long

- 50mph on single carriageway roads unless a lower limit is in force
- 60mph on dual carriageway roads unless a lower limit is in force
- 60mph on motorways unless a lower limit is in force.

Speed limits when towing a trailer

- 50mph on single carriageway roads unless a lower limit is in force
- 60mph on dual carriageway roads unless a lower limit is in force
- 60mph on motorways unless a lower limit is in force.

If a motorcaravan is used to tow a trailer, different speed limits apply.

In addition, when you're towing you are not permitted to use the right-hand lane of a motorway with three or more lanes unless signs or roadworks indicate otherwise.

It is unfortunate that speed limits given in *The Highway Code* don't make mention of the limits applicable to motorcaravans. These are given instead in Section 86 (1) and Schedule 6 of The Road Traffic Regulation Act 1984.

Speed limits abroad

There are several differences between UK speed limits and those imposed abroad. There are also intriguing rulings, such as the autoroute limits applicable in France, where a lower speed is enforced in wet weather. Presumably a driver has to evaluate the situation and decide when a light drizzle calls for adherence to the lower limits.

The 3,500kg MTPLM weight is often significant too. For instance, in Germany vehicles that have been upgraded to a higher MTPLM are not permitted to be driven faster than 100kph (approx 60mph) on an autobahn, while in Austria they have to be fitted with a so-called 'GO-box' – this is available for a small fee from many of the country's service and petrol stations and is used for road-toll charging. (Information on the system can be found on www. austria.info and on http://www.asfinag.at/go-box-vehicles-over-3.5t-gross-weight.)

As these few examples indicate, it's obviously important for any motorcaravanner driving abroad to find out what speed limits and other driving requirements apply in the countries being visited. Books such as *Driving Abroad* by Robert Davies, also published by Haynes, provide useful advice.

MOT TESTING AND MOTORCARAVANS

When your motorcaravan is due for an MoT test, the inspection is referred to as a Class IV test. Although *goods vehicles* classified between 3,000 and 3,500kg have to be submitted for a Class VII test, this is not the case for motorcaravans. In this instance they fall under the same classification and test procedures as a car, irrespective of their weight.

This is fine, except for the fact that many MoT stations that conduct Class IV tests for car owners simply don't have good enough access or the height to accommodate a large coachbuilt motorcaravan.

Many Class IV MoT stations don't have enough space to test large motorcaravans.

This MoT test station didn't have an elevating ramp but an inspection pit gave alternative access underneath.

Equipment such as the elevating ramp might not have the lifting capacity to cope with a very large model either, and the rolling road for brake testing might not be suitable.

For this reason, many owners take their vehicles to a goods vehicle test station, which is fine – provided the management is familiar with car testing protocols.

Matters relating to MoT testing are dealt with by the Vehicle and Operator Services Agency (VOSA), and further information can be obtained from www.vosa.gov.uk. If you want to check the MoT status of a vehicle, this can be done by visiting www.motinfo.gov.uk or by telephoning 0870 33 00 444. You will need the vehicle's registration mark and either the reference number on its V5C registration certificate or the test number from a new-style VT20 MoT test certificate.

Since 1 January 2012, a towbar fitted to a motorcaravan, together with the towball, are subject to a visual inspection as part of the MoT test. All visible fixing points are checked to ensure that their

An analysis of exhaust emissions forms part of a standard Class IV MoT for cars, and currently many motorcaravans also qualify for Class IV testing.

connection to the host vehicle is sound and free of corrosion. The towball is also inspected to establish that there is no sign of undue wear. In addition, if a motorcaravan is fitted with a 13pin socket to operate a trailer's road lights, its general condition and the correct operation of the pins is verified using an approved tester. However, no test is carried out if a motorcaravan is fitted with a 7pin 12N socket.

Nowadays an MoT test result is recorded on VOSA's database and this, rather than a VT20 paper certificate, is used for legal purposes to verify that a vehicle has achieved a pass.

Although the rear axle tube had been extended on this motorcaravan, it just fitted into the rollers used for testing vehicles' brakes.

VEHICLE EXCISE DUTY

Although terms such as 'road fund licence', 'tax disc' and 'road tax' are used in everyday conversation, the term currently applicable in official documents is 'vehicle excise duty', or VED for short.

The amount payable for a motorcaravan varies in accordance with its base vehicle. This raises many questions and sometimes highlights complexities. For example, some campervans, such as the Starcraft, are converted saloon cars, while others, such as several models from Wheelhome, are converted MPVs. Then there are converted 'window vans', such as Bilbo's models built on Volkswagen T5s. Other motorcaravans are constructed on either light or heavy goods vehicles. These dissimilarities have various implications for the amount of VED payable.

There have also been challenges regarding the placement of some vehicles, particularly the VW California T5 conversion that, unusually, is carried out by its base vehicle manufacturer in a factory at Hanover, Germany. In the UK, these imported vehicles

The words 'motor caravan' should appear in section D.3 of a V5C Registration Certificate, together with the vehicle's taxation class.

have been classified as diesel cars and the VED payable after the 2008 budget was £400. That was considered extremely harsh when similar motorhomes were classified as PLG vehicles and charged a VED of £185. The anomaly led VW Commercial Vehicle division to open discussions with DVLA, after which changes were made to the V5C registration certificates fee levels, and refunds have since been made to owners that Volkswagen UK were able to trace.

In exceptional circumstances like this, reclassifications have occurred, although this area of administration is certainly not easy to grasp. It doesn't help either when the words 'motor caravan' should appear in section D.3 of a V5C registration certificate, whereas the issued tax disc normally uses the term 'Private/Light Goods' or PLG.

The rationale that governs the VED payable for different types of vehicle often seems obscure and

Technical Note

Vehicle Licensing Classification

An official of the DVLA writing to *Motor Caravan Magazine* (November 2007) explained the classification process applicable to vehicles registered after 1 March 2001. Since that date, 'VED rates for newly registered cars and light vans have been based firmly on the type approval information provided at first registration.' Thus a vehicle that is type approved as an M1 Passenger Vehicles is 'treated as a car and taxed according to carbon dioxide emissions and fuel type under the graduated VED provisions. Vans are type approved N1 and are taxed as light goods vehicles.' The type approval process for N1 vehicles does not include measurement of carbon dioxide emissions.

Also note that: 'Once a vehicle has been first registered and licensed in one of these taxation classes, its status for the purposes of payment of VED will not change irrespective of any subsequent alterations that may then be made to the vehicle.'

Since this statement was written, it would appear that in certain exceptional circumstances, changes can sometimes be made and the case of the VW California is reported in the main text.

criteria that govern VED charges also seem to change with surprising frequency. Without doubt, one of the most detailed reports on this topic can be found on the website: www.ukmotorhomes.net/motorhome-road-tax.shtml

In addition, current rates of duty for all taxation classes is given in DVLA leaflet V149, which can be downloaded from: www.dft.gov.uk/dvla/forms.aspx

TYPE APPROVAL

For some years, passenger cars have been subject to a certification process called Type Approval. The extension of this scheme now includes motorcaravans, and this took effect on 29 April 2012. However, manufacturers have also been permitted to gain Type Approval voluntarily for their motorcaravans since 29 April 2009. Accordingly, some have chosen to do this whenever new models were introduced.

Type Approved vehicles are required to comply with a wide range of technical and safety requirements, and stringent checks are carried out to ensure that this is not only the case for prototype models submitted for scrutiny. Compliance has to extend to all vehicles manufactured throughout a series production operation. Depending on the number of vehicles of a particular type that a manufacturer intends to produce, and whether it is intended to export any of the products elsewhere in Europe, three variations of this scheme have been devised:

1. **European community whole vehicle type approval**. Fulfilling the requirements of ECWVTA is an involved process which permits a vehicle to be offered for sale anywhere in Europe. To achieve this recognition, a vehicle must comply with a wide range of standards. For instance, the initial design will be thoroughly tested, documented, and the subsequent manufacturing process has to ensure that all vehicles produced to the approved design will comply fully with the agreed specification.
2. **National small series type approval**. The NSSTA scheme has been principally designed for manufacturers that do not intend to export any of its products. A reduced number of elements are subject to obligatory checks and the administration of the scheme is simplified, too.
3. **Individual vehicle approval**. The IVA scheme is a more recent version of the Single Vehicle Approval process that has been used for several

Vehicles like this 'one off' Toyota Regius Stimson Overlander conversion will have to be submitted for an Individual Type Approval (ITA) test.

years to legitimise the production of self-built kit cars in the UK. In the motorcaravan context, every single vehicle that is produced must be individually checked using what is popularly described as a 'super MoT Test'. The inspection is again considerably less elaborate than it is for the WVTA.

Both the NSSTA scheme and ITA validation are particularly helpful alternatives for small-scale manufacturers, some of whom specialise in the construction of bespoke vehicles for clients.

Vehicles that gain approval under these schemes can be considered safe and legal to use, although it is reasonable to presume that those meeting WVTA will attain the highest standard of proven design quality. The establishment of Type Approval as an obligatory requirement that manufacturers must embrace has been a challenging matter. It might also influence potential owners who intend importing a vehicle into the UK themselves because in some circumstances, an IVA test might be required. Similarly, if an owner wants to have a towbar fitted to a Type Approved motorcaravan, it is not permissible to install a non-Type Approved product. This matter was explained earlier in the chapter.

SEAT BELTS

Another difficult legal area for motorcaravanners relates to the use of seat belts. A well-established requirement states that when a seat belt has been fitted, it must be worn. That is certainly the case with regard to the cab seats. It is also the case in respect of seats equipped with belts in the living area, which a manufacturer describes as 'designated travel seats'. That aside, many experts assert that sideways-facing seats equipped with belts may cause

their occupants severe injuries to the torso in an accident. In consequence, these types of side-facing seats are seldom fitted with belts.

Bearing in mind the point made earlier that laws are not applied retrospectively, *ie* to older vehicles, it is required that as from October 2007, all seats intended for carrying passengers in new motorcaravans must be fitted with belts. These can then be designated and badged as 'travel seats'. Moreover, it is now illegal to use sideways-facing seats in new motorcaravans when a vehicle is being driven. A further change in legislation in 2009 requires passengers to use seats with belts if such seats are available. Once all the belted seats are full, additional passengers can then legally sit elsewhere, although the advisability for this for both their own safety and that of other occupants is highly questionable.

As regards the use of children's booster cushions and safety seats, the recent laws applicable to cars are also applicable to motorcaravans. The website www.thinkroadsafety.gov.uk gives advice about this, but the author has discovered a serious problem: children's car seats that fit safely and successfully on a standard vehicle seat are often wholly ineffective on the soft cushion bench seats in the rear of many motorcaravans. The accompanying photograph shows what can go wrong.

Stability is also much worse when a booster seat is placed on a motorhome bench seat. Doubtless the safety specialists will convene further debates.

On the mildest of bends, this child seat depressed the foam of a motorcaravan's bench seat, the recoil strap paid out more slack, and the child was then swinging upside down in the aisle.

SUMMARY

As stated at the beginning of this chapter, an attempt has been made here to unravel and explain a variety of legal issues relating to motorcaravans and their use. However, anything of this nature is subject to change, and readers are urged to seek updated information on all the topics that have been discussed.

CHAPTER **SEVEN**

OWNERSHIP
ISSUES

Before embarking on your first trip, several products will need to be purchased. For example, only a few models are sold with a complete complement of cutlery and crockery. You will also need bedding – some owners are content to use sleeping bags, whereas others prefer a duvet and fitted sheets. Finally, you'll want to keep the interior and exterior smart, which requires some specialist products.

Having purchased a motorcaravan, you'll want to look after it.

Fire Brigade demonstrations at motorcaravan shows reveal the folly of putting water on to a burning chip pan.

Mount a fire extinguisher away from a likely source of flames but make sure it's easy to reach.

When Carlight caravans were introduced more than 50 years ago, the company owner's wife enjoyed living in style and was particularly fond of Gordons Dry Gin. In consequence, these fine touring caravans came equipped with a bone china tea service as standard and a purpose-made cabinet holding a bottle of gin!

Regrettably, this quaint tradition came to an end a few years ago and today's caravans and motorhomes are seldom sold with items such as these. However, there are exceptions. Murvi van conversions, for instance, include portable items such as a First Aid kit, cutlery, crockery, a warning triangle, a spare bulb kit, a gas cylinder and a carbon monoxide detector. Models in the Auto-Sleepers and Orian ranges have also been sold with smart crockery as part of the 'package'.

But this is unusual, and new owners will normally have to purchase a variety of items before setting off on their first trip. Inevitably there's no such thing as a standard list of prerequisites, but this chapter provides some helpful reminders.

(i) Useful Tip

Fire extinguishers and safety alarms

When the fire brigade visits outdoor motorhome shows, they sometimes re-create the effect of putting water on a chip-pan fire in a purpose-built display vehicle. The resulting flames are a frightening sight, and it's probably a good thing that not many motorcaravan owners take fat-filled chip pans on holiday. On the other hand, if you do like a good fry-up occasionally, it's strongly recommended that you install a fire blanket that complies with EN 1869. In many vehicles a smoke alarm might also be fitted: so too might a carbon monoxide detector. A motorcaravan dealer can offer advice on suitable products.

As regards fire extinguishers, these are manufactured to deal with specific types of fire, and products have to meet the requirements set out in British Standards and European Norms. However, it would be impracticable to carry a range of extinguishers designed to deal with fires involving liquids, solid materials, flammable gases, electrical products and so on. Since the living area in a motorcaravan is quite small, a dry powder extinguisher is generally recommended for all-round use.

A fire extinguisher should be located where it is easily reached but shouldn't be situated too close to a likely fire source, such as the hob. Be familiar with its operating mechanism and keep a note of the date on its casing.

SOME ITEMS TO CONSIDER

1 Although this 2006 Orian Gemini was supplied with china cups and plates, the provision is rather unusual. Many owners will visit a dealer's accessory shop and choose a set of lightweight Melamine cups, saucers and plates.

1

2 Coat hangers will be needed but the type shown here don't hold clothing for very long, so items soon fall off when you're driving. Owners adopt a variety of solutions including pegging clothes in place and using elastic shock cord.

2

3 It's wise to have a tyre gauge in your glove box. Dial types are usually preferred, and to achieve optimum accuracy, the required pressure reading should fall midway in the range. This one is from the International Tool Co.

3

4 If you are a practical person who would normally fit a spare wheel yourself after a puncture, it's worth buying a telescopic wrench with sockets to suit the fixings used on light commercial vehicles. This type of wrench gives good leverage.

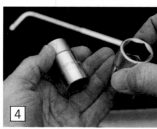

4

5 High-visibility jackets or waistcoats are inexpensive to purchase and in some countries it's now obligatory to carry one (or more) in your vehicle. It would certainly be unwise to attempt roadside repairs without wearing high visibility attire.

6 Some owners fill a fire bucket with water when stopping at a site. This might help in an emergency, but you should also have an appropriately mounted dry powder extinguisher and fire blanket indoors. These should be accessible, but not too close to possible sources of flames, like a gas hob.

5

6

Of course, this list isn't claimed to be exhaustive and Chapter Nine looks at many more accessories. Portable ramps for levelling a van on a sloping pitch, for example, are one of the many items mentioned. Also be aware that if you are planning to travel abroad, different countries have additional requirements, including an obligation to carry spare vehicle bulbs, First Aid kits, one – or sometimes two – breakdown warning triangles and a breathalyzer kit in France.

Among the best sources of information on European requirements are The Caravan Club's *Caravan Europe* site guides and touring handbooks; these present detailed general advice as well as country-specific requirements.

You will also need to decide which gas product you want to use. There are many suppliers of portable gas cylinders throughout Europe and some of the more common UK products are described in Chapter Fourteen.

Bags, bedding and related products

Bedding preferences are very much a personal matter. Some owners, for example, are content to use sleeping bags, and when space is limited – eg in small campervans – these can be pushed into compact stuff-sacks and stowed in small spaces.

However, when a large motorcaravan is equipped with a fixed double bed, many owners prefer to purchase fitted sheets and a duvet. Others like fitted sheets for single beds too. Recognising this trend, several specialists are now selling motorhome-specific products. The range from Jonic is particularly comprehensive.

Here are examples of useful items:

1 If you want a mattress protector under your base sheet, Jonic holds information on mattress sizes used in many popular makes of motorhome. Alternatively, if your vehicle isn't on their list, Jonic will make one to order.

2 Pillows are another bedding item about which people have strong personal preferences. Some prefer feather pillows; others like synthetic foam. The pillows shown here are just a selection of the types frequently sold at caravan and motorhome exhibitions.

3 If a mattress is supported by a solid plywood base as opposed to a slatted surface, it's a good idea to purchase a breathable underlay. Some are made using natural coir, others are synthetic, eg Vent Air mat, but both allow air to circulate underneath, thereby preventing damp from condensation.

4 Where young children are assigned a high-level bunk or bed it's important that there's no likelihood of them falling out. These safety nets from Seitz, which is part of the Dometic Group, are often fitted as standard, but they can usually be installed at a later date.

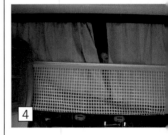

CLEANING

Like any vehicle, a motorhome deserves to be cleaned when it's dirty. However, before looking at cleaning products, let's spend a moment checking equipment that makes the work easier.

Cleaning equipment

If you have a large motorhome you'll need some means of access to reach the roof. After all, not many motorcaravanners own the types of mobile platforms and steps that dealers use.

This is why brush and squeegee products mounted on a telescopic pole are so useful. Examples are sold at most major exhibitions – but don't buy the cheapest one in the racks.

Get one that's robust, because these make light work of cleaning. Of course, there's not a lot of point in cleaning the sides of a motorcaravan if you omit to clean the roof. One shower of rain will prove the folly of that misguided strategy, so you'll also need

Above: Few owners will have the access equipment used by dealers.

Soft brushes mounted on telescopic poles are sold at most exhibitions.

a robust set of steps or trestles, together with a telescopic brush, to reach the top.

As regards high-pressure jet hoses, these can achieve good results in the hands of an experienced user – in fact dealers often use them to clean their forecourt models.

However, indiscriminate use without making appropriate reductions in pressure can cause a surprising amount of damage. On coachbuilt models in particular, a high-pressure hose directed at joining seams can soon blast away fragments of hardening sealant. The effect of this might not become apparent immediately, but after a few heavy rain showers the resultant water ingress can start to wreak havoc.

High-pressure hoses are used by workshop staff but can cause damage in the hands of inexperienced owners.

It might seem easy to clean a vehicle using a high-pressure washer and there are certainly some good machines on the market. On the other hand, other approaches (which usually take longer) are less likely to cause damage.

Cleaning products

One of the problems with most models is that there are so many different types of material to be treated. Frankly, it's impossible to formulate a single product that can clean materials as dissimilar as glass reinforced plastic (GRP) mouldings and acrylic windowpanes; or painted aluminium sheet and rubber tyres. Each material needs its own purpose-formulated cleaning compound, although some products do go some way towards achieving multifunctional effectiveness.

Avoid chemical reactions

Never mix different makes of cleaning compound together because their chemical constituents may react unfavourably. Also be aware that there's an ever-present possibility of damaging a motorcaravan's materials through a chemical reaction with an inappropriate cleaning product. For example, methylated spirits is often put into vehicles' windscreen washer bottles; not only does this reduce the likelihood of windscreen water freezing in cold weather, 'meths' also cleans automotive glass with pleasing results. Under no circumstances, however, should it be used on the acrylic 'plastic' windows often fitted in the living area. Initially, meths will give a plastic window a shiny appearance, but after several days, the entire surface develops a mass of tiny, hairline cracks. This is a condition called 'crazing', for which there is no cure.

So the careful choice of reputable products is important, and if you're not confident when using a new cleaning compound, try it out first on a small and inconspicuous area. You might leave it several days before deciding whether to put the product into full use.

Acrylic 'plastic' windows

Double-glazed acrylic windows supplied by specialists such as Polyplastic BV and Seitz are often fitted in the living quarters of motorcaravans – both in converted panel vans and coachbuilt models. Normal care instructions recommend that they're cleaned using warm, soapy water, followed by clean, fresh water. However, there are several proprietary products that can also be used to good effect. For example, Autoglym 'Fast Glass' is good on both safety glass and acrylic plastic windows. You can also use Autoglym's general purpose 'Caravan and Motorhome Cleaner'. The following sequence shows some of the stages.

Never use methylated spirits to clean the acrylic plastic windows often fitted on motorcaravans; it can lead to serious damage.

127

1 If a window is badly coated with grime and dry dust, apply fresh water. However, windows are sometimes not dirty enough to warrant this preliminary dousing. Whatever the decision, follow it up with a spray of 'Caravan and Motorhome Cleaner'.

2 Agitate the area using a soft sponge. If windows are hard to reach, you can use a very soft brush to activate the cleaner. However, its bristles should first be thoroughly cleansed with water to ensure there is no grit held in them.

3 Then remove the suds with clean water before drying the window off using a leather or synthetic cloth. If you choose to use Fast Glass, spray on the cleaner and then remove it using a sheet of absorbent kitchen paper.

4 Fast Glass is good on a vehicle's cab windows too. After being sprayed sparingly onto the surface, it can again be polished off using absorbent paper. Alternatively, some valet specialists are now using micro-fibre cloths, which also do the job.

Incidentally, if you find that an acrylic window has been scratched, Seitz scratch remover is often used in service workshops. There are also similar products from Farécla and from Fenwicks.

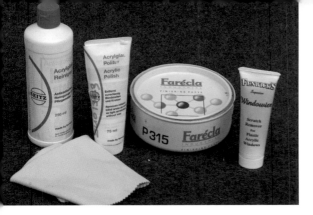

General cleaning

Many parts of a motorcaravan can be treated with products designed for cars, such as dark plastic bumper cleaners, vinyl cleaners, wheel cleaners and tyre cleaners. Shampoo additives are normally fine for a general wash-down and car polishes are often used. Polishes from Arnchem, Autoglym and Mer are examples of popular products.

However, motorcaravans are also afflicted by black streaks that develop below some of the body fittings.

For instance, rainwater discharging past a refrigerator ventilator or window frame often trickles down leaving lines of black deposits that are surprisingly hard to shift. Mindful of this problem, the chemists at Autoglym's Letchworth laboratories formulated 'Caravan and Motorhome Cleaner'. This is applied as a spray directly from its plastic container, agitated with a sponge or brush, hosed off, and dried with a leather.

Although this is principally intended as a preliminary treatment preceding the application of polish, it is easy to apply and leaves a pleasing shine. Consequently, many owners use it for most cleaning operations, and only resort to applying polish when time permits.

Several products are sold for removing light scratches from acrylic windows.

129

Above: Rainwater trickling past external ventilators often leaves black streaks that are hard to shift.

Below left: Autoglym 'Caravan and Motorhome Cleaner' is sprayed on to a small area direct from the container.

Below: It is then agitated with a sponge or soft brush before hosing off.

Useful Tip

Mobile Cleaning and Valet Services

Cleaning a large motorhome can be an onerous job and some owners might not want to work on the roof of a tall vehicle. When Arnchem introduced its motorcaravanning cleaning products several years ago, the company also created a mobile clean and valet service. The team attend most of the outdoor motorcaravan shows throughout the season and undertakes valeting work on visitors' vehicles parked within a showground. In addition, the cleaning team can arrange private visits to carry out work for owners of all types of motorcaravans. Naturally the staff bring all the necessary access equipment, especially when commissioned to clean large RV motorhomes.

In addition to selling a wide range of motorcaravan cleaning products, Arnchem also undertakes cleaning and valeting work for owners.

Paint sealing products

A different approach to cleaning is to have a sealing product applied to painted areas and to self-coloured glass-reinforced plastic (GRP). For many years, sealing products were used solely on expensive cars, airliners, public service vehicles, cabin cruisers and trains, but such products are now being sold for use on caravans and motorhomes too.

The principle behind such systems recognises that a sealant provides body panels with a protective coating. It has to be applied to a pre-cleaned surface and the barrier it achieves will provide a good resistance to black streaks, bird lime, algae and other marks. Once a motorcaravan has been treated, a periodic wash reinstates a shining surface with the minimum of effort. Also, there is sometimes a self-cleansing effect on vertical panels when it rains.

Admittedly it often takes a full day to prepare a motorcaravan and apply a proprietary sealant, but the benefits are subsequently reaped for around three to five years before re-treatment is needed.

For the DIY enthusiast, A-Glaze is one example of a sealant-type product. The treatment pack includes a cleaner and a paint sealant that certainly should last for three years or more if applied carefully to a well-prepared vehicle. Paintseal Direct is another specialist that uses a product containing Teflon®.

This is professionally applied, and the full service also includes the application of treatments on upholstery items inside. When a dealer applies Paintseal on a new motorcaravan, the benefits are claimed to last around five years. If you own an older motorcaravan, Paintseal Direct can also arrange a thorough body refurbishment as a precursor to the application of its sealant system.

Once body panels have been treated with a sealant, post-cleaning products make light work of routine washing. The accompanying illustrations show what this entails.

A sealing operation undertaken by Paintseal Direct

1 On this older motorcaravan being prepared by Paintseal Direct, a full buffing and cleaning regime removes remnants of surface dirt and all previously applied polishing products.

2 Preparatory work on a medium-sized coachbuilt model may take around five hours to complete. Obviously an application of the sealant cannot achieve good results on a blemished surface.

3 A paint sealant compound is sparingly applied on painted surfaces and GRP mouldings using a rag and a microfibre cloth. Be aware that it might not be applied to certain types of textured plastic.

4 Finally, a damp cloth is used to ease the product over the surfaces. If work can't be carried out indoors the operation has to be undertaken in favourable weather conditions.

Indoor cleaning

Many treatments designed for interior car cleaning can be used in motorcaravans. The accompanying illustrations show examples of products in use.

1 Foam interior shampoo products are easy to use on vehicle seat fabrics. Many are equally successful on seating in the living area, but check this point carefully.

2 Paradoxically, products like this cleaning foam in the Autoglym range can be used on cookers as well as seating fabrics.

3 Microfibre cloths and pads are a useful addition to a valeting specialist's armoury. Avoid using old rags that contain lint; this is abrasive. Never use dyed linen cloths, as they might release their colour.

A completely different approach to keeping interior fabrics in good condition is to apply a barrier product. Examples are often used on new household settees and upholstered chairs, and Paintseal Direct has now introduced similar barrier treatments for the fabrics found in motorhomes.

Treating internal fabrics with a protective finish

4

4 Included as part of the Paintseal Direct exterior treatment process is an application of stain repellents on seating and other fabric surfaces.

5 The treatment product is applied in a mist spray from a pressure container and then gently distributed over the surface with the help of a sponge.

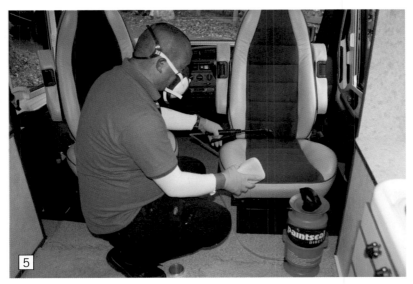

5

If your motorcaravan has clip-on embellishers it's worth anchoring them in place using cable ties.

CARE FOR YOUR WHEELS AND TYRES

When you own a motorcaravan, you often find that some types of wheel embellisher have a nasty habit of making a break for freedom. Fortunately, many light commercial vehicles now employ attachment systems that retain their embellishers much more effectively. Alloy wheels have also become a way of enhancing the appearance of a leisure vehicle, but if your model has clip-on embellishers it's worth anchoring them with some cable ties.

Another issue which is much more serious relates to the availability of tyres. Many coachbuilt motorcaravans are supplied with a 'camping' grade of tyre that has a ply structure designed to survive the heavy loadings typical on this type of vehicle. It is a reality that once a motorcaravan conversion is complete, the base vehicle never re-achieves its original light state, even when all personal effects are removed. So 'camping' grade tyres are normally

Some of the latest wheel embellisher trims are far more secure than cheap 'clip-on' products.

specified from the outset by motorhome converters, and vehicle manufacturers, such as Fiat, fit them as original equipment.

However, the base vehicle manufacturers' demand for uninterrupted supplies of 'camping' grade tyres sometimes means that owners encounter difficulty obtaining replacements. After an irreparable puncture, for example, the author learnt to his dismay that a six- to eight-week wait for replacement tyres is not unusual.

A national shortage of particular sizes of tyres undoubtedly poses problems when tread depths get low or sidewall walls show hairline cracks, especially when an MoT test is approaching. Safety and legality are important issues, and it is wise to keep an ongoing check on the availability of your particular size of tyres, especially if they are camping products.

That is one of many reasons why you need a spare wheel with a tyre in good condition and ready to bring into use. The idea adopted by some manufacturers to supply a Fix and Go puncture sealant kit *instead* of a spare wheel was a clearly misguided decision.

Some recent models are not supplied with a spare. However their Fix & Go puncture sealants cannot deal with serious tyre failures.

Although 'camping' grade tyres are made to suit motorhomes, their sidewalls eventually develop cracks. Unfortunately, getting replacements can involve long delays.

CHAPTER EIGHT

CHOOSING
PLACES TO STAY

Some motorcaravanners prefer to stay at camping sites that offer home comforts and modern amenities. A holiday might involve dining at restaurants, dancing at discos and using a washroom that's warm. In contrast, others seek places away from the crowds. A modern, well-equipped motorhome is fine in wild country if that's the experience you want. You make the choice, and here are some of the options.

137

A French municipal site at Allemont, near Alpes d'Huez.

L'Escale site on the outskirts of Le Grand-Bornand in the French Alps.

When you own a motorcaravan there is a wide variety of places you can stay. For instance, waking up alongside an empty beach on a Scottish island has a magic that's hard to describe. It's a very different experience from stopping at a lively site on the fringe of an Alpine village that's fully encircled by mountains; or sleeping on a remote roadside verge to cheer Tour de France cyclists who'll be tackling a Pyrenean summit. It would be impossible to catalogue the huge variation of places where motorcaravanners spend their nights!

You'll also find different facilities as you travel around Europe. For example, in Britain there are few places, other than campsites, where you can legitimately park to sleep. It's perversely annoying to see motorway signs exhorting motorists not to drive if they are tired when there aren't any places to stop for a snooze.

In many UK towns, height barriers prevent access to car parks; others have signs forbidding overnight sleeping in vehicles. The consumer magazine *Motorcaravan Motorhome Monthly* even runs an ongoing campaign called 'The Height Fight' that draws attention to towns that are unwelcoming to motorcaravanners, as reported by readers. The

Wild camping on the Col d'Aubisque, where Tour de France cyclists scale the French Pyrenees.

campaign's objective is 'to persuade authorities to provide dedicated daytime parking, and overnight halts, for motorcaravans'.

Attitudes about impromptu overnight sleeping differ profoundly from one European country to another; types of campsite are different as well. In France, for example, football pitches and adjacent changing rooms are often converted into municipal campsites in summer.

So are other spare grassy areas in villages and towns. Meanwhile, in Britain, members of the two major caravanning clubs have exclusive access to thousands of five-unit stopovers called Certificated Sites or Certificated Locations. These are popular too, and this excellent provision of rural facilities does not seem to have a counterpart in mainland Europe. So let's compare these different provisions.

Certificated Sites or CSs (The Camping & Caravanning Club) and Certificated Locations or CLs (The Caravan Club)

The Caravan Sites & Control of Development Act 1960 permits the establishment of these venues, which need neither a site licence nor planning permission.

These small sites are privately owned and are not permitted to accommodate any more than five units, ie caravans or motorhomes. Visitors are also limited on each visit to a maximum stay of 28 days. Typically located in rural areas, CLs and CSs are usually quiet, informal, and often on farms. Many provide club members no more than a tap, rubbish bins and an emptying point for a chemical closet. However, an increasing number are now offering mains hook-ups as well. Fees are remarkably modest and the two clubs have a total of more than 4,000 examples listed in their members' site directories.

This Alpine municipal site at Allemont is well laid out.

Regrettably, there are very few UK car parks that adopt this arrangement seen in the French Alps, where a motorcaravan is permitted to park for up to 48 hours.

This peaceful Caravan Club CL near Ludlow occupies an old orchard. Its five pitches are all served by a 16A mains hook-up point.

In France, Aires are strictly for motorcaravans (camping-cars) and can be used for overnight stops. This sign states that tokens that provide 230V electricity are obtainable in the village hall.

ⓘ Tip

Wild camping in the UK (*camping sauvage* in France)

In the UK, contrasting views are held about impromptu overnight sleeping in motorcaravans. It is sometimes claimed, for example, that all land in the UK is owned by somebody, and overnight parking without a landowner's consent is tantamount to trespass. On the other hand, there are many motorcaravanners who park by the roadside in wilderness locations for short spells and leave nothing behind when they leave. No harm is done, and in many instances, no one is any the wiser.

Different views are also held throughout mainland Europe, and tolerance of wild camping varies from country to country. However, a policy statement from The Caravan Club, affirms that it 'does not advise or condone so-called "wild camping". We would always recommend that motorcaravanners stay on a recognised site, for their own security, and out of respect for the local area and community.'

It is not unusual in French towns to come across emptying provision for motorhome waste water tanks – though not necessarily toilet discharge points.

Aire de Service/Stationnement pour Camping-Car

The provision of Aires des Camping-Cars in France receives frequent approval in magazines. These venues offer basic services and parking facilities together with a tap and an emptying point for waste water. Similar facilities are also established in Italy; one of these night halts is called an Area Attrezzata. In Germany there are Standplatz, complete with stay-and-display machines that issue 24-hour passes. In Spain, emptying points are signposted as Area de Servicios para Autocaravanas, and there's often overnight parking as well.

Regrettably, this provision is seldom seen in Britain, and motorcaravans seem to be regarded with less favour than they often are in mainland Europe. Presumably there's a general feeling abroad that motorcaravanners make significant contributions to local economies. Having said that, Aires in France generally don't permit an overnight stopover if you own a touring caravan. There also doesn't

seem to be much concern over vehicles packed tightly together. Safety issues such as these are discussed later in the chapter. Personal security is another concern; some people spending the night on motorway Aire de Service stopovers in Europe have been targeted by teams of professional thieves. Though rare, narcotic gas attacks have also been reported as a prelude to break-ins, which is why motorcaravans are often fitted with gas alarms. Away from the motorways, rural stopovers seem to be much more secure, and many motorhome owners use them when touring from place to place.

The eagerness to help motorcaravanners in France is clearly shown in this purpose-built motorcaravan service point on the edge of Annecy.

Commercial UK sites

There are many varieties of privately owned sites distributed throughout the UK. Some are small, others are large. In fact some of the large sites that offer facilities such as a clubhouse, restaurant, takeaway meal service, swimming pool, entertainment programme, crèche and cycle hire operation are often referred to as 'holiday parks'.

Organisational aspects also vary. On less formal sites, pitches might be merely indicated by numbered pegs around a field, whereas in high-

Individual pitches shielded with shrubs are found at Pencelli Castle, a high-quality site near Brecon, South Wales.

Above right: Known as La Plage Blanche, this riverside campsite in the French Jura lies south of Dole and is situated next to val'Nature adventure centre.

Above: Adventure activities for people of all ages are arranged by val'Nature, and in addition to offering formal classes in climbing and other pursuits, you can hire all-terrain bikes, kayaks, open canoes and a donkey to carry your gear on local walks.

quality parks, individual pitches can be formally enclosed by low hedges and enhanced by shrubs.

Moreover, an increasing number provide occupants of each pitch with their own mains hook-up, tap and drain for waste water. However, not many include a coupling facility for accepting toilet effluent; these are provided on many 'camping grounds' in North America, but the idea has yet to gain acceptance in Europe.

Commercial sites in mainland Europe

Commercially owned sites on the Continent similarly vary in size and style. However, many sites abroad have a remarkably short season; after an extremely busy July and August period, closures often start in early September.

During the height of the season, larger sites in the Netherlands, Belgium, France and Germany run elaborate activity programmes, especially for children. Playgrounds are often elaborately planned, and near the Alps and Pyrenees artificial climbing walls are sometimes included.

Because of its close proximity, France is especially popular with British motorcaravanners, although many retired owners spend their winters further afield in Spain and Portugal. French sites are marketed with great vigour and there are collective organisations like the Castel chain (inaugurated in 1959) and the Sites aux Paysage Group. As their names imply, the former includes sites established in the grounds of historic castles and chateaux, while the latter venues are beautiful countryside sites.

Club sites

These are owned or managed by The Caravanning and Camping Club and The Caravan Club. Most are purpose-built and have high-quality facilities. A few, however, are 'managed sites': these include racecourse sites that are used for caravanning between meetings, and sites run on behalf of local authorities. Some club sites are exclusively for

members whereas others welcome non-members on payment of a small extra charge. You can usually join the club on arrival as well.

Sites with restrictions

In the last few years a growing number of 'adults only' sites have been created by private owners. These are usually quiet, football-free places, and one site accepts no one less than 30 years of age. Another site accepts children at certain times, but requires them to reside in a special compound – which hardly sounds welcoming for future generations of motorcaravan users. Other sites with restrictions include places where dogs are not permitted, many of which are on farms where livestock is reared. Most sites do accept dogs, however, and some have special dog walk routes.

Owners of large motorhomes, especially American RVs, should also check in advance if a chosen site has restrictions applying to large vehicles. For example, if there are narrow, twisting site roads and a lack of hard-standings, very large motorhomes cannot gain access.

The delightful Camping and Caravanning Club site at St Neots, alongside the Great Ouse, offers in-season fishing, water activities, riverside walks and nearby ramps for skateboarders and BMX riders.

Owners of large motorhomes need to check if the site they plan to visit can accommodate this type of vehicle.

Through a joint venture, The Camping and Caravanning Club is running Forest Holiday sites for the Forestry Commission.

Forestry Commission sites

These wooded locations can be found all around the UK. Some have fairly extensive facilities whereas others are more limited. If you like woodland and wildlife experiences, these are delightful, sylvan settings. A recent joint venture has led to The Camping and Caravanning Club being entrusted with the management and running of the 20-plus Forest Holidays sites on behalf of their owners, the Forestry Commission.

Year-round sites

Though not usually open for a full 365 days per annum, some sites get extremely close to providing an all-year-round service. A number of these are club sites but there are some private owners in the UK who also operate for most of the year.

As a general rule, year-round sites are able to offer a large number of hard-standing areas, which are essential for owners of heavy motorhomes when grassy pitches are wet. A few site owners also organise Christmas and New Year packages that include a seasonal events programme. Heated marquees are erected, and these celebratory occasions are popular, so must be booked in advance.

A few private and Club sites are open for most of the year, including this Caravan Club site at Wythall near Birmingham.

CHOOSING, BOOKING AND ARRIVAL

Since there are many different types of site, guidebooks and site-searching facilities on the internet are helpful. You also need to be aware of the marketing groups whose members are made up of commercial and private site owners who pay for corporate marketing and inclusion in a site guide booklet. Just as there are groups in France like the Castels chain, the UK's Best of Britain chain comprises sites that fulfil the criteria required for acceptance. These are usually high-quality holiday parks rather than remote rural retreats.

Some guides only contain information on camping sites that have been successfully inspected by specialist assessors. The *Alan Rogers' Guides*, for example, are compiled with the help of independent assessors who travel all around Europe. Scrutiny of each listed site involves a rigorous inspection, and owners are visited, unannounced, on a regular basis.

It's not unusual to see inspectors conducting thorough checks of sites before details are published in high quality guidebooks.

Similar inspections are conducted by ACSI, based in the Netherlands, and it's not unusual to see their inspectors in the UK as well.

Awards of excellence
Several organisations, such as Calor Gas, run national competitions to find the best sites of the year in England, Scotland and Wales. There are various sub-categories too – for example, there's even a 'Loo of the Year' award! These competitions carry prestige, and winning sites are undoubtedly impressive. In a similar way, The Caravan Club conducts a contest to find the best Certificated Locations of the year.

Pencelli Castle site near Brecon has deservedly won many awards for its high standard of service and facilities.

In addition to these annual competitions there are 'tick' and 'star' schemes run by tourist boards and motoring organisations, which confer quality indicators on participating venues.

Booking

When it comes to booking, procedures can vary. Normally the process starts with a telephone call, and a deposit might be requested. However, more and more sites are accepting bookings on the internet and this trend will undoubtedly continue to grow.

Arrival protocol

When booking a site, enquire what time the site reception closes, especially if you're likely to arrive late in the evening. Legislation in the UK has affected the duration of employee's working periods and this has led to offices on some small sites closing earlier. Moreover, an increasing need for security measures has prompted many sites to be equipped with a barrier, and the reception staff provide a code number or loan a swipe card to lift the bar. It is therefore important to arrive before a reception office closes.

An increasing number of sites have a security barrier and visitors are given a card or code to lift the bar.

Before proceeding on to a site, it's important for visitors to complete the signing-in procedures at the reception.

On some sites, clients are also invited to walk around a site to choose their pitch. Whether a view over the sea is more important than a pitch close to a toilet block or the clubhouse is for you to decide. However, try to avoid pitches under trees that shed sap, particularly if you use an awning. Removing sticky deposits from fabric can require a lot of work.

Should you decide to use a mains hook-up, remember to ask how many amps are available. Chapter Twelve explains why that's important.

As regards late arrival procedures, some sites offer a small compound near the entrance where you can stay overnight until the reception opens next morning.

Recognising that some visitors arrive after the reception office has closed, a 'late arrivals' area is sometimes provided for overnight parking.

Facilities

Not surprisingly, many people locate the toilet block first. Washrooms and showers will be checked as well, together with fresh water taps, waste disposal points, toilet emptying points, ironing rooms, laundry rooms, and so on. Some sites also provide washing-up sinks and vegetable preparation areas.

Don't forget to confirm where the fire points are situated. Some motorcaravanners place their own

Most people want clean toilets. Few match the standard of Pencelli Castle's impeccable facilities.

With this system for receiving water from a waste tank, a motorhome has to be positioned with accuracy.

fire bucket on their pitch, although this practice is less common now that many motorcaravans are equipped with a fire extinguisher and fire blanket.

If there's a swimming facility, confirm what safety precautions are in place. You won't always find lifeguards on duty and several pools don't have a sign to indicate which is the deep end. Some countries are strangely lax in these matters.

Some motorcaravanners prefer to take dirty dishes to the site's sinks; children can play a part as well.

Emptying points for chemical toilets are often outdoors, although a few are situated in a covered cubicle.

It's all too easy to overlook a safety check regarding the location of a site's fire-fighting facilities.

Holiday sites at home and abroad often have swimming pools but lifeguards aren't always employed by the owners.

The rest depends on personal circumstances. Parents may want to inspect the children's playground; owners of dogs might want to find the dog walk. Others will check the site's restaurant menu before boiling a kettle and making a brew.

Below left: Some owners don't want to cook on holiday, so this Alpine restaurant's popular on L'Escale site at Le Grand Bornand.

Below: On-site play areas are often provided but it's the duty of parents to check on the welfare of their children.

In sharp contrast with the caravanning clubs' ruling about six metre spacing between units, the parking spacing on this French Aire de Camping-Cars was extremely unsatisfactory.

Contrary to many people's views, fires do occasionally break out, and it was fortunate that this nearly-new and unoccupied vehicle was parked away from a tightly-packed line of motorhomes.

Pitch spacing

A practice followed on club sites relates to the space required between adjacent units. This is mainly a precautionary measure in case of fire, although it also makes good sense where noise is concerned. Both clubs have similar rulings and The Caravan Club states: 'At the discretion of the Warden, caravan outfits may be positioned on the pitch in any way, provided that there is not less than six metres (20 feet) spacing between facing walls of adjacent caravans and that there shall be left a minimum clear space of three metres (10 feet) between adjoining outfits in any direction, in order to restrict the spread of fire. An "outfit" for this purpose

comprises all mobile and other equipment brought on to the site by visitors.' (*The Caravan Club Magazine*, March 2001.)

No one likes too many rules and regulations, but this proscription makes sense. Occasionally you'll find commercial sites, especially on public holiday weekends, where the close proximity of caravans and motorhomes is neither safe nor satisfactory. Moreover, the closely packed motorhomes seen often on many Aires de Camping in parts of France could pose a safety threat if one of the motorcaravans were to catch fire. Unlikely? Far from it, as the author recently witnessed when a gas supply pipe serving a motorhome fridge on a two-month-old model caught fire.

ARRIVAL PROCEDURES

When arriving at your pitch, carry out the following tasks:

• Decide where you want to position your motorcaravan, recognising that some sites give guidelines about orientation, awnings and ancillary equipment.
• Either reverse or drive your motorcaravan on to the pitch.
• On soft ground or during wet weather it's advisable to drive onto non-slip plastic mats to maintain traction. When a heavy motorcaravan remains unmoved for several days it can start to sink, which can cause problems when it comes to departure.

The levelling ramps and wheel-support plastic mats made by Fiamma are carried on board by many owners.

Both a non-slip plastic mat and a Grip Track were needed when leaving this muddy site.

- Some owners keep a small spirit level or part-fill a translucent plastic water container to check for slopes. Motorcaravanners also carry portable ramps to use when a pitch has a slope.
- Some motorhomes have rear corner steadies to minimise suspension movement, and these can be lowered once your vehicle is suitably parked.
- On the 12V fused distribution control panel, set the main switch to its ON position as described in Chapter Thirteen.
- To use a mains hook-up, follow the coupling procedures given in Chapter Twelve, and leave spare cable loosely unravelled underneath your van.
- Turn on the gas supply cylinder to run your refrigerator as discussed in Chapter Eleven. If coupled to the mains, you have a choice whether to run the fridge on gas or 230V.
- If your toilet hasn't been pre-prepared for use, add chemical and one litre of water to the waste tank, and top up the flushing water.
- If you use a directional TV aerial, you'll need to get this pointing in the right direction to achieve a good signal.
- Some owners fit a portable security device while staying at sites.

DEPARTURE PROCEDURES

Preparations before driving away:
Once you've stowed all your crockery, cutlery and other loose items, consider what else you need to do before leaving your site. Get into a routine and consider creating a check-list such as this:

Inside
Close roof lights
Close windows
Secure cupboards

Clear open shelves
Secure the fridge door
Select 12V operation on the fridge controls
Turn off the 12V switch on main panel
Make sure toilet waste is emptied.

Outside
Turn off the gas supply at the cylinder
Disconnect the mains supply (as described in
   Chapter Twelve)
Stow the mains hook-up cable
Retrieve any levelling devices.

If you'll be returning to the site later in the day, it's
often wise to leave a sign that indicates occupancy
of your pitch. Some owners erect a notice to this
effect; others have an independent awning for storing
a barbecue, bicycles or sun-loungers.

Leaving the site
Road safety advisers point out that road accidents
often occur in the first few moments of a journey.
Without doubt, if the exit gate of a site takes you
into a country lane that lacks road markings, extra
vigilance is needed – especially on the Continent.
Some British drivers leaving a foreign campsite have
a momentary lapse of concentration and drive away
on the left-hand side of the road.

*To secure a pitch when
using their motorcaravan
to drive off-site, many
owners display a small
notice confirming its
occupancy.*

153

*Another method of
showing that your pitch
is occupied is to erect a
free-standing awning such
as this Ventura product.*

CHAPTER **NINE**

ACCESSORIES

A motorcaravan has to fulfil the personal needs and interests of the owner. Some prefer to relax and a TV is very important to them: others enjoy active pursuits and derive pleasure from bike rides. Everyone's needs are different – which is why so many motorcaravan accessories are available, including satellite TV systems, equipment racks, and products yielding additional storage. Utility items such as awnings, support vehicles, levelling devices, solar panels and security equipment are also available.

155

Some owners tow a support vehicle like this Fun Tech Microcar which fits into a Ventura Space Storage 'shed'.

Motorcaravanning magazines provide plenty of in-depth advice about accessories. Apart from convincing claims made by the advertisers, more candid appraisals are often provided by reviews and editorial advice. Not surprisingly, the space dedicated to accessories is usually generous, as readers welcome reports on products they want to purchase, and comparison tests are helpful, too.

Inevitably, this chapter only focuses on a handful of items – many more could have been included. For example, useful products that are neither illustrated nor discussed in detail here include:

■ Reversing aids

Audible warning devices used when a vehicle is reversing can be helpful, although the author's experiments have shown that not all of them detect small bollards and high kerbs. Rear-mounted cameras are usually more effective, but when colour cameras superseded monochrome systems with microphones and built-in illumination, fully installed systems commanded much higher prices.

■ Security products

Remember when comparing security products that there are several different types. These include:

1 Physical deterrents such as wheel clamps and upgraded door locks
2 Electronically activated alarm systems
3 Tracking devices linked to detection centres.

Also be aware of work carried out by the Sold Secure Trust (www.soldsecure.com). This is an independent organisation that conducts laboratory attack tests on products and then publishes lists of successful items.

As regards motorcaravan security, one of the most notable system providers is Van Bitz, whose sophisticated Strikeback protection products are installed on both conventional motorcaravans and large American RVs.

This installer is one of the pioneers of a system that can send a warning to an owner's mobile phone whenever a protection device is activated. Many motorhome owners speak highly of Van Bitz products and the workshops are now supported by an attractive over-night site for customers to use.

■ Air conditioners

In small van conversions, a fan is an inexpensive accessory that helps when it's hot. However, some owners of larger motorhomes prefer to have air

Strikeback electronic alarm systems from Van Bitz are very effective but need to be installed professionally.

conditioners fitted. Two main types are manufactured: water evaporative cooling units (eg the Trav-L-Cool from CAK), and refrigerative air conditioners (eg those from Dometic). The former, which run on a 12V supply, are light and relatively inexpensive, but they don't work as well in humid conditions. The latter are efficient cooling appliances but are heavier, costly, require a 230V supply, and are sometimes quite noisy.

The water evaporative principle can be experienced if you inhale through a damp cloth that you've stretched over your mouth. To take the principle further, you need to create a more sophisticated arrangement using a supply of water, a pump, an absorbent filter and a 12V fan. This will give surprisingly good results as long as the device is switched on well before an interior gets desperately hot.

Refrigerative units work like domestic fridges, in which a compressor drives a refrigerant chemical around a complex system of pipes. This type of appliance needs a 230V AC supply and if you come across models that run on a 12VDC input, they incorporate a built-in inverter to boost this up to 230V AC. The trouble with inverter-driven products is that they place a heavy load on a battery. Given the variations between these appliances, talk to owners about their product's performance before making a purchase.

WARNING

Before purchasing any heavy accessory, follow the advice given in Chapter Six. Note the vehicle's MTPLM, check its empty weight on a weighbridge and then calculate its payload. Now check the weight of the accessory you're planning to buy, because the more items you install on the vehicle, the less scope will be left for carrying your personal gear.

■ Other products

Many other accessories are also described in later chapters, including water purifiers, suspension aids, gas leak detectors, inverters and portable battery chargers.

To find out more about these and other accessories, consult their suppliers using the addresses given in the Appendix on page 318.

POPULAR ACCESSORY PRODUCTS

Gaining space and carrying gear

Roller blinds and awnings

Many motorcaravans are fitted with a roll-out sunblind, some of which have 'zip-in' optional side panels. However, a fully enclosed unit generates extra work if you need to leave your pitch in a hurry. Furthermore, if circumstances dictate that a blind must be rolled when it's still wet, make sure you unroll it again as soon as possible to dry the fabric.

This roll-out Safari sunblind from Omnistor's range has smart side panels and curtains which run freely on tracks.

Above: The Khyam Motor-Dome Classic is a freestanding unit with a wide coupling valance and easy-fit interlocking alloy poles.

Right: This robust Swift Shelter from Pyramid, with concertina frame, guys and extra zip in the sides, is good in the garden as well as on a campsite.

Above: The roller blind on this Auto-Trail Cheyenne was quick to set up.

Several manufacturers supply roof boxes, some of which are suitable on van conversions. Check that access is easy.

As for freestanding awnings, it is almost impossible to design a universal shape that suits the profiles of so many dissimilar vehicles. Coupling and uncoupling isn't always straightforward either, and that is partly why gazebos and storage sheds have become popular too. Not only do these indicate that a pitch is occupied when you've driven off-site, but they can also be used in the garden at home.

Storage products

Many motorcaravanners would like more space to accommodate additional gear. Roof boxes are one option, but if you stow heavy items on top, your vehicle is much more likely to roll on bends, so roof boxes should be reserved for light but bulky items, such as lightweight folding picnic furniture.

Left: Back-boxes are easier to reach, and need secure locks. Check the back axle limit and only pack light items here.

Below: Every Beeny Box is made individually, although Auto-Sleepers and Auto-Trail are now licensed to fit them from new.

Incidentally, don't use an external box to stow costly equipment; items in boxes can be easily stolen.

Back-boxes are another alternative, but don't carry heavy items in them that might overload the rear axle limit. This problem has already been mentioned in Chapter Six and is raised again in the next section on bike racks.

Another option for owners of coachbuilt models is to have one or more low-level Beeny Boxes fitted. These high-quality, slide-out compartments have justifiably gained supportive reviews and every Beeny Box is painstakingly designed, fabricated and fitted in a workshop in Cambourne, Cornwall. Their sturdy stainless-steel support rails permit the carriage of heavy items and the contents seldom get wet in the rain. Not only do Beeny Boxes perform extremely well, they are also constructed so that they faithfully match the external finish of a coachbuilt motorcaravan.

Rear racks for bikes and scooters

Carrying heavy items at the extreme rear of a motorcaravan can lead to problems, particularly on vans that are built with a pronounced overhang rearwards of the back axle. Before having a rack installed it's important to check the advice given in Chapter Six relating to axle loading limits. So always have your rear axle load checked on a weighbridge before purchasing a rack for the back. Also find out what your bicycle, mobility scooter, motor scooter

Even in its weakest position, which is fully open, a Beeny Box will carry up to 45kg (99lb). These products look smart too.

This smart cycle rack from Thule is designed to clamp on a towball, but check the downforce limit on the towball first.

Above: This rack was correctly installed by bolting it through the panel, inserting spacer tubes and fitting spreader plates inside.

Above right: Rechargeable electric bicycles are becoming popular, but check that the rack is strong enough to bear their weight.

Right: Carrying two motorcycles on the rear of a coachbuilt model is very likely to exceed its rear axle weight limit.

or motorcycle weighs. Not only do the rack and its mounting points have to deal with the load, so does the rear suspension of the vehicle.

In addition, you need to be cautious about racks designed to be either mounted on a towball or bolted to the towbar assembly itself. Since towbars are not normally designed for any task beyond towing, it's hardly surprising to read magazine reports where an entire tow bracket assembly has been wrenched away from the host vehicle. Note, too, that the maximum permitted downforce on a towball is typically around 50–80kg and on new products the actual limit has to be shown on a label or plate. Regrettably this isn't always made clear by the manufacturers of some towbar-connected motorcycle racks. For obvious reasons you should never have a rack installed where the combined weight of its structure and the weight of its cargo exceeds the stated downforce limit. *Note: Not many motorcycles weigh less than 100kg.*

EXTERNAL ACCESSORY ITEMS

Towing using an A-frame

A safe way to transport a support car is to tow it using a purpose-made braked trailer. However, trailers take up space, both on campsites and at

home, so an A-frame is a popular alternative.

When towed with an A-frame, a car is defined as a trailer, so it is subject to the laws applicable to trailers. Since virtually all small cars exceed 750kg, the towed vehicle's brakes must be brought into use when it is towed. (Among the few cars weighing less than 750kg are French microcars such as the Aixam, the QPod and the Fun Tech.) In consequence, the majority of A-frames have to be fitted with the type of over-run coupling head that is used on touring caravans and heavy trailers. However, there are a

Above left: Equipping a support car with a rugged, bespoke, front-end towing assembly normally takes a day to complete.

Above: With the frame attached, its over-run brake cable is linked to an eyelet that activates the driver's brake pedal.

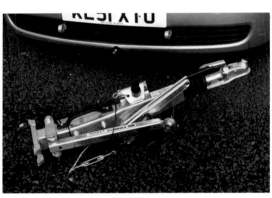

One of the endearing features of this braked A-frame manufactured by TOWtal is its compact size when folded.

An A-frame hinges up and down but doesn't articulate from side to side, so coupling needs accurate alignment.

If towing a vehicle using an A-frame is a 'grey' area, the use of a braked trailer is free from any doubt.

few alternative brake actuation devices available, such as an electronic device imported from the USA called the 'Brake Buddy'. Similarly, there are products such as the dual sensing vacuum-assisted braking systems supplied by Smart Tow.

When an A-frame is used, the castor effect of the car's front wheels means that it follows the course taken by the towing vehicle. Unfortunately this principle fails if you try to reverse a car that is attached using an A-frame. Equally, a car doesn't have the auto-release brake assemblies that are fitted to braked trailers and caravans. These special brakes disengage automatically as soon as the wheels recognise from their rotation that their trailer is being reversed.

This raises uncertainties about the legality of A-frame towing for anyone other than professional recovery specialists. However, it has been reported that no one in the UK has been prosecuted for towing with an A-frame.

Most people (including the author) who have had small support cars adapted by experienced specialists speak highly of the stability and overall towing behaviour when a braked A-frame is used. However, in some countries in mainland Europe, the local Police do not always tolerate the practice.

In the UK, some people declare that A-frame towing complies with current laws, some declare that it is illegal, and others regard it as a 'grey area'. Without question, A-frames used with small cars, *including* the Smart Fortwo coupé (which has a gross vehicle weight of around 990kg) *must* have a brake activation system fitted. It is therefore a matter of some concern that some owners of microcars like the Smart are breaking the law by using unbraked A-frames.

Whereas A-frame towing is a contentious area, the legality of towing a car on an appropriately constructed braked trailer is uncontested.

Above: After a day spent installing a Leveltronic system, its designer showed how a vehicle could be lifted completely clear of the ground.

Left: The Leveltronic system employs four jacks made in square section steel which are operated entirely by electric motors.

Levelling jacks

Many large American RVs are fitted with fixed hydraulic jacks that allow a parked vehicle to assume a level plane. Similar hydraulic systems, designed for both large and small European motorhomes, are now available from E & P Hydraulics whose UK division is based in Blackburn. (www.ep-hydraulics.co.uk). The standard product includes four jacks, each of which is able to lift 1.7 tonnes using air from a central electric 12V hydraulic pump. Larger units have a lifting ability up to 9 tonnes apiece and all versions have a manual lift/lower override facility just in case a battery supply fails.

The E & P system is remarkably easy to use. On arrival at your pitch, you depress a button on a small control panel that lowers all four jacks automatically. After that, there is an automatic activation of each telescopic unit until the vehicle is completely level. The entire operation seldom takes more than a couple of minutes, and includes built-in safety features for situations such as a premature attempt to drive away before the jacks are withdrawn. The

The E&P Jacking system has been shown at several exhibitions in the UK since its introduction here in 2011.

system was introduced in the UK during 2011 and has since been demonstrated at national and regional exhibitions.

As an alternative strategy, some owners have ordered the LevelTronic leveller and lifter from Italy, which was brought into the UK in 2006. This product has four jacks that operate using electric motors; installing the four motorised legs, the electronic 'brain' and the wiring harness usually takes a full day. In respect of performance, a high lift range up to 150mm (6in) means that a motorhome can be automatically levelled on slopes up to eight per cent. A remote control pad is used to control the levelling, and the jacks also have a manual operating mode.

A point to note is that when a LevelTronic system is fitted, a further portable jack isn't needed for dealing with a punctured tyre. Similarly the pressure can be taken off the tyres when a vehicle is laid-up for an extended period because the jacks are able to support a motorhome's weight. Furthermore, an elevated vehicle deters motorhome thieves.

Tyre safety

Anyone can get a puncture, and if you're driving at speed, a sudden loss of control can give you a rather nasty fright. If there is a complete loss of pressure, then a tyre's steel-reinforced beading will lose contact with the rim, whereupon parts of the tyre fall into the 'well' of a wheel. The exposed rims of the wheel make contact with the road, grip is consequently lost, and the vehicle starts to skid.

To avoid this situation, Tyron manufactures bands that fill the wells of wheels. Fitting isn't difficult and the benefits are great. If your vehicle has a blowout, the collapsing tyre is unable to fall into the well because the Tyron band occupies that space. In consequence, parts of the collapsing tyre will remain, like a buffer, between the rim itself and the road surface. The tyre will soon be useless, but that happens in blowouts anyway. The point is that you

Above: When the author agreed to drive this demonstration motorhome fitted with Tyron bands, good control was possible after a blowout even at fast speeds.

Left: Kwik-Fit mobile fitters have a simple device to compress a motorcaravan tyre when fitting a band in the well.

retain full control while bringing your vehicle to a halt. At special track demonstrations using a motorcaravan fitted with Tyron bands, a tyre is purposely detonated with a charge when the vehicle is at speed, and the driver is still able to negotiate a slalom course of cones with the tyre completely deflated.

Recently the company added two further features to its product. Firstly, wireless sensors affixed to each Tyron band inform a driver of tyre pressures on a dashboard-mounted panel. Secondly, the nationwide chain of Kwik-Fit independent mobile fitters can arrange for someone to come to your home to install a Tyron system.

Below left: Clipped on to the latest bands is a wireless transmitter which is able to measure the tyre's air pressure.

Below: A dashboard-mounted panel has a screen on which the pressure of each tyre can be displayed whenever required.

Above right: This compact flat-screen TV from Grade UK has a DVD player and a built-in rechargeable battery with a two- to three-hour life.

Below: A wide range of multi-section support arms are sold by Grade UK to enable a TV to face towards its viewers.

Below: The VESA couplings on the back of many sets will accept a quick-release plate to detach a TV for use indoors.

Right: The Status 530 directional aerials have a long mast that can be adjusted from inside while you monitor the picture.

ELECTRICAL ACCESSORIES

Portable flat-screen TVs and aerials

Aerial manufacturer Grade UK has been supplying products to motorcaravan manufacturers for many years. In fact, their familiar 'flying saucer' aerials have become a standard accessory on many UK models, including commercial long-distance lorries. These omni-directional aerials need no adjustment and can pick up signals in areas where the reception is good.

However, a better signal is obtained if you fit a 'directional aerial', which has to be pointed in the right direction to get a good-quality picture. Grade's Status 530 can even be raised from inside a vehicle and rotated while you monitor results on your TV screen. The company also supplies miniature signal amplifiers that increase or reduce the strength of a signal. Of course, the setting-up procedure has to be repeated every time you move to a new location.

In the last few years, Grade UK has also supplied flat-screen TVs for leisure vehicles, many of which incorporate a DVD player as well. There's even a range of support arms to position a TV screen wherever the viewer requires.

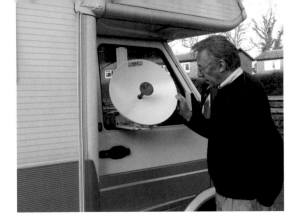

Many portable televisions also have universal VESA threaded fittings on the back that allow them to be either coupled permanently on a mounting arm or connected to a quick release clamp that lets you transfer the TV set for use in your home.

All portable 12V TVs currently on sale operate on digital signals and you normally have to retune a set every time you arrive at a new destination.

Satellite TV in motorcaravans

This has become a popular system for motorcaravanners who want a good picture, a wide range of channels, the benefits of free satellite stations and the chance to view British programmes when they're miles away in mainland Europe. Key items of equipment that are normally recommended include:

- Either an inexpensive portable dish or a roof-mounted product
- A cable-connecting socket on the motorcaravan wall or roof
- A satellite receiver box
- A satellite finder
- A modern TV set with appropriate connections.

The process of coupling-up a system, locating a satellite and fine-tuning the reception is often explained in booklets provided by the equipment suppliers. Specialists such as Maxview and RoadPro also provide helpful advice.

Above left: Portable dishes are available for mounting on tripods. Many can be secured to parts of a vehicle using clamps.

Below: Roof-mounted dishes controlled from inside can be operated manually or by motors. Domes are even self-seeking.

Below: Unless you buy automatic satellite-finding products, it's worth buying a satellite finder with LED and audible guidance.

Left: Satellite receivers usually run on 230V and some channels are free, but others require the purchase of a decoding card.

It's usually a case of the bigger the better – this 70W output panel is built in a frame and covered with glass.

Solar power

The idea of 'free' electricity is attractive, and photovoltaic (PV) panels that use light to create a 12V supply are popular with motorcaravanners. Their function is to keep a leisure battery topped up and they're at their most productive when directly facing the sun in clear conditions.

Clarity of light is important, and somewhat surprisingly, they work better in clear polar skies than in Mediterranean sunshine. That's because heat has little to do with PV panels – it can even reduce their effectiveness.

On a clear sunny day, an average-sized panel can give out 20V, which could ruin a leisure battery. That's why a charge controller, sometimes called a 'solar regulator', must be fitted in the system. These devices prevent a reverse flow of current when it is dark (which would flatten a battery) and reduce high voltages created on very bright days to an appropriate level. Some controllers also have digital

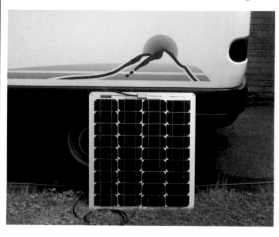

The 70W semi-flexible solar panel from GB-SOL weighs only 3.0kg and achieves current outputs up to 3.75 amps.

Apart from needing a hole to pass its output cable though the roof, this panel from GB-Sol was bonded to a mildly curving surface using Sikaflex-512 sealant.

readouts that reveal a panel's output at any one time; more expensive versions will also record how many amp-hours have been fed into a battery over several weeks.

The panel itself is the main determinant of power creation and these are often quite costly. In fact, it may take several years to recuperate the cost of a system, and the main reason for purchasing one is not so much to save money as to become less dependent on mains hook-ups for recharging your leisure battery.

Traditionally the panels are pre-mounted in an alloy frame and covered with heavy-duty glass. However, these are weighty, and an unsightly addition to some vehicles. In contrast, semi-flexible panels are covered in a special coating, and their 14mm thickness, coupled with their modest weight, appeals to owners of van conversions as well as coachbuilt motorcaravans. Most specialist suppliers publish helpful leaflets about solar systems.

A charge controller must be fitted in a solar power system. The more expensive ones provide digital readouts of battery state and input.

CHAPTER TEN

WATER AND SANITATION **SYSTEMS**

Obtaining drinking water and dealing with unwanted waste water are concerns of every motorcaravanner. Designers have adopted several approaches for meeting these needs, and a surprising number of variations can be found in different motorcaravans. It's much the same with motorcaravan toilets, which bear little resemblance to the ones in our homes.

171

Well-equipped sites have water service points for motorcaravans.

Only a few motorcaravanners use external waste and fresh water supply containers.

A few campervans have portable water containers that are housed indoors; larger models are normally fitted with tanks.

Most modern sites have a dedicated service point where a motorcaravanner can briefly park to release waste water and replenish the fresh water tank.

Water systems in motorcaravans are surprisingly different from systems installed in UK touring caravans. For instance, most caravanners use portable containers kept outside – one is for fresh water, the other is for waste. Only a few motorcaravanners adopt this practice.

The majority of motorcaravans are equipped with built-in tanks, most of which are permanent fixtures. It is only in small campervans that you might find inboard portable containers instead of fixed tanks.

So let's look more closely at these different arrangements.

FRESH WATER SYSTEMS

Tanks and portable containers

One advantage of having a fixed fresh water tank is that there is less likelihood of interference or contamination. After all, an external portable water container is exposed to wind-borne dust, inquisitive insects, slugs and leg-lifting dogs. On-board supply tanks eliminate these risks, but have disadvantages too. The main one becomes apparent when you need to empty a fixed waste tank or replenish your fresh water supply. Frequently, this will mean that you have to drive your motorcaravan to a purpose-built service area on your campsite.

Water service points

Motorcaravanners who often leave a site for day trips are not inconvenienced by an en route visit to a site's water service point. On the other hand, owners of large coachbuilt models may leave their pitch less frequently, especially if they have bikes, a

Some motorcaravanners will be seen using the portable fresh and waste water carriers used by the owners of towed caravans.

motor scooter or a support car. Others achieve semi-permanence by erecting a coupled awning complete with side panels. So don't be too surprised if you see some motorcaravanners unravelling a long hose to reach a fresh water standpipe.

Or others, heading for a service point with caravan-type portable containers.

Fresh water supply variations

Recognising that portable containers and fixed tanks both have their disadvantages, some van converters fit an alternative supply system that embraces the best of both arrangements.

Instead of having fixed tanks, conversions from La Strada and Middlesex Motorcaravans are often fitted with two portable fresh water containers that are housed inside their vehicles.

Below: Some motorcaravanners take a long hose pipe for replenishing their fresh water tank.

 Technical Tip

'Food quality' hose and fittings

When coupling-up to a water supply tap, you should fill your motorcaravan tank using a 'food quality' approved hose. Unlike a normal garden hose, these are intended for use with drinking water, yet there's no doubt that some short lengths of hose permanently attached to camping site taps are only garden products. That's less a cause for concern, of course, if your motorcaravan is fitted with a water-purifying device. It is also less critical if you drink bottled water and use the water from your onboard tank exclusively for showering, washing dishes or rinsing swimwear.

Right: Rather than having a fresh water tank, this campervan has been fitted with two portable containers.

These are coupled using a submersible pump and are easily disconnected for carrying to the nearest tap. This arrangement avoids the need to drive to a service point, which is especially useful if a container runs dry at an inconvenient moment. It also eliminates the need to carry a large coil of hosepipe for reaching distant water taps.

Above: An electric submersible pump needs a 12V supply, which is connected using a cigar lighter socket.

Above right: When one of the twin tanks is empty, the submersible pump is merely transferred to the full tank alongside.

Right: The empty container is now taken to a tap, and the supply pipe also has a disconnection joint.

By altering these controls, Whale's Smartflo pump can perform different supply tasks. (Photo courtesy of Bailey Caravans, Bristol)

Combined systems

A recent innovation is a combined system that comprises a fixed fresh water tank and a plumbed-in, externally mounted inlet for use with a portable container. This arrangement employs a permanently mounted diaphragm pump (described later), and the plumbing system includes bypass routes that are selected either by manual stopcocks or electrically activated valves. Operating these controls in different sequences provides the user with three choices of supply:

1 Enabling the pump to supply the taps or the shower by drawing water from the motorcaravan's fixed inboard tank.
2 Pumping water from an external portable container like an Aquaroll to supply the taps or shower.
3 Using the fixed pump to draw water from an external portable container in order to top up the fixed tank.

Having a choice of three operating modes is clearly a great asset for motorcaravanners, and this relatively new system was first installed in touring caravans that had fixed water tanks, like the Bailey Senator. At the time of writing, few motorcaravan manufacturers have recognised the benefits of a combined system, which is rather surprising.

Direct supplies

More and more UK sites are now offering visitors a pitch with its own tap that can be permanently connected-up using a special coupling hose.

To employ this arrangement when using a motorcaravan, it is necessary to fit a new input point on the side and to make a minor plumbing alteration to bypass its tank. Water can then be

This Camping and Caravanning Club site has some coupling points that permit connecting up a direct water supply.

Above: The Aqua Source Clear is an inline taste filter from Whale Pumps.

Below: At periodic intervals, fresh water supply components should be treated with a sterilising product such as Milton.

To draw a supply direct from a standpipe, the coupling hose must have a pressure reducer.

fed straight into the internal pipes from the mains – just like the system at home. However, the pipe couplings in a motorcaravan are seldom suitable for withstanding the higher pressure of water drawn from a rising main, so it is necessary to purchase a purpose-made coupling hose that incorporates a pressure reduction device. The Aquasource from Whale Pumps is one example. The Truma Waterline is another.

General issues

In the last few years, an increasing number of motorcaravanners have been purchasing bottled water for drinking purposes. Others consider this strategy expensive and unnecessary.

With regard to water quality, few, if any, brand-new motorcaravans are fitted with a water purifier, and some owners subsequently decide that it's worth adding one. However, it is emphasised in a later section that taste filters mustn't be confused with water purifiers. A taste filter might be useful for improving the palatability of mains water, but it is not a purifying device.

Other motorcaravanners are content to drink tap water but like to collect it as and when it's needed in a small plastic container. Their view is that water from the tank is principally for non-drinking purposes, unless it has been boiled. Suffice to say, we all have different views on water safety.

When considering the options, be aware that algae can form on the inside surfaces of a fresh water tank. Consequently, water purifying products like Milton should be pumped through systems and used for cleaning tanks and portable containers at the start of every season, or even more frequently.

Obviously, motorcaravan owners normally drain off their waste water as soon as possible. However, many are less inclined to drain off their fresh water tanks after every trip, especially when their motorcaravan is being regularly used for impromptu journeys. Arguably this might lead to an accumulation

of stale water, although the installation of a Nature Pure Ultrafine water purifier at least eliminates the likelihood of contamination.

Stability matters

Driving with full water tanks adds significant weight to a motorcaravan, which affects both its economy and its performance. In some cases full water tanks might be a factor in a vehicle exceeding its Maximum Technically Permissible Laden Mass (MTPLM). Moreover, driving an overweight vehicle is potentially dangerous and is obviously an offence. Roadside checks conducted by the police do lead to prosecutions, and in one recent inspection, drivers of over-laden motorcaravans were not permitted to resume their journeys. Emptying the water tanks was duly recommended, which then brought many of them within their respective MTPLM limits. Water is heavy and weighs about 10lb a gallon, or 1kg per litre.

Also be aware that some motorcaravan tanks lack baffles to reduce water movement, and water 'slurping' around a part-filled tank can pose greater instability problems than a tank that is filled to the brim.

Taking these issues into account, The Caravan Club advises its motorcaravanning members to drain both fresh and waste water tanks before driving. This is a wise recommendation, although some owners might consider it an over-cautious measure. In practice, many motorcaravanners want to have water available for use when travelling from place to place.

Ultimately the owner has to make an informed decision according to the circumstances, and the first task is to establish whether a motorcaravan has sufficient unused payload to travel with full water tanks. To find this out, load your motorcaravan with typical holiday gear, leave the tanks empty, and then take it to a weighbridge. Subtracting its measured weight from the stated MTPLM on its plate will reveal the spare payload. This represents what remains for the accommodation of the driver,

Nature Pure filters from General Ecology are used in the company's highly effective water purifying system.

Above: In this Dethleffs Esprit, the tank below a bench seat is emptied by pulling out a plug attached to the red cap.

Below: This Knaus Sun Ti has a removable overflow tube in its fresh tank that doubles-up as a drain-down plug.

On this Swift Kon-Tiki Vogue, the fresh water tank extended right across the vehicle and hard against the rear wall.

Tanks at the extreme rear

Heavy weights positioned at the extreme ends of a vehicle contribute to a phenomenon commonly referred to as 'the dumb-bell effect'. This is based on principles laid down in Newton's Laws of Motion. In practical terms, if you're negotiating a sharp bend on a wet or icy road surface, a heavy weight situated at the extreme back is disadvantageous, especially if the rear tyres lose their grip. Despite this basic rule of physics, a few manufacturers still mount freshwater tanks right across the back. That's when The Caravan Club's recommendation to drain a tank completely before driving becomes particularly relevant.

A waste water tank needs a large cleaning aperture, which is normally covered with a red screw-cap.

passengers, any accessories you might add, extra personal gear, and reveals if there's still enough leeway to include a full tank of fresh water.

Notwithstanding the laudable recommendation of The Caravan Club, and provided you know that your laden vehicle is well within its weight limit, you might decide not to drain your tanks, toilet flush water and water heater if you merely want to drive offsite to purchase a morning newspaper. Alternatively, you might wisely decide to reduce vehicle weight by draining off water prior to embarking on a long climb over a mountain pass or for some prolonged motorway driving. Common sense should always prevail.

When considering strategies, also bear in mind that in clear, calm weather on dry roads the stability of a vehicle is less threatened by a tank containing water than it would be when driving in snow or high winds.

Also be aware that some motorcaravan manufacturers mount water tanks in positions that might provoke instability. For instance, a part-filled tank mounted low down between the front and rear axles is far less likely to cause problems than a part-filled tank mounted right at the back, especially on a coachbuilt model with a large rear overhang.

WASTE WATER SYSTEMS

A waste water tank normally offers a slightly smaller capacity than its fresh water counterpart. During use, it will inevitably get dirty inside, so cleaning access should be provided. Typically, access is gained via a large opening fitted with a removable red cap. That is an important feature and it's regrettable that some manufacturers save money by fitting tanks without an access port.

Coupling hose

Another poor feature is the use of a convoluted

connecting hose with annular ridges on both the inside and outside surfaces. This is another penny-pinching feature; better quality hose has ridges on the outside but a smooth lining on the inside. Internal ridges in the former product tend to catch food particles that subsequently start rotting inside the pipe, whereas the latter has a more efficient self-cleansing effect.

Also disappointing are the routes that waste water hoses sometimes follow, and a few manufacturers disregard the fact that water doesn't usually flow uphill. Admittedly, it isn't always easy to achieve a constant fall (*ie* slope) in a pipe run, especially when chassis members present barriers, but with good planning and thoughtful design, it can be achieved. As the accompanying illustration shows, this is one of many reasons why potential purchasers are advised to look underneath the floor of a vehicle. You'll often find pipe runs that are poorly designed and inadequately mounted.

Installation of traps and interceptors

When comparing motorcaravans, enquire whether the manufacturer has fitted water traps under sink, basin and shower tray outlets. Also enquire whether there's a screw cap interceptor to catch food scraps *before* they flow into the tank.

To anyone new to motorcaravanning this advice must sound extraordinarily bizarre. One might presume that a professionally manufactured motorcaravan embraces all the good practices of construction in general, and plumbing in particular. Sadly this isn't always the case, and dreadful drain smells are a reality that has spoilt many owners' holidays.

This isn't to say that a salesperson always has the knowledge to provide the answers you want. Normally they have to seek the advice of a workshop specialist, but you would be wise to insist that they respond to your queries.

This convoluted hose has ridges on its inner surface; unfortunately these can trap scraps of food.

(i) **Technical Tip**   179

Rigid PVCu Pipe
Some manufacturers now fit domestic rigid PVCu pipe with a continuous fall (ie slope) to speed-up the discharge of water from a sink or wash basin. This can sometimes be fitted retrospectively, too, and installing an improved system is one of the practical projects included in the *Motorcaravan Manual* (3rd edition, 2012), also published by Haynes.

Below left: There were disappointing ups and downs in the runs of these convoluted waste pipes.

Below: Situated just before the waste tank, this food interceptor on a Swift Sundance is a useful item.

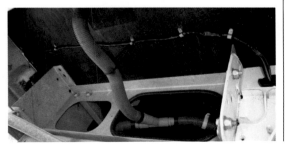

Above right: This Swift model's lack of rear mudflaps meant its drain-down tap was bespattered with road dirt.

Above: Weak clips prone to rusting and a dangling pipe are a poor arrangement on this Autocruise Starmist.

Right: The tap release lever on this TEC coachbuilt had no protection from rear wheel mud.

Right: This TEC system had a sturdy, wide bore pipe, robust clips and a good chance of stretching to a drain.

Below right: This plastic drain-down valve on an Orian looks fragile and is curiously close to the exhaust pipe.

Below: This sturdy lever and large bore pipe looks good; but the tank didn't drain when this Knaus Sun Ti was tested.

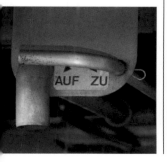

Tank position

A few years ago one of the UK's best-known manufacturers introduced a coachbuilt motorcaravan in which the waste tank was located just to the rear of the shower tray. Purchasers subsequently found that if the waste tank wasn't emptied before driving off, a determined application of the vehicle's brakes caused its contents to surge forward into the shower tray. Thankfully, however, most designers realise that a shower tray needs to be fitted rearwards of a waste tank!

Emptying mechanisms

There are more methods and mechanisms for draining-off a waste water tank than you could ever imagine, and the accompanying pictures illustrate just a few of them.

The contents of some tanks drain with impressive speed, some get blocked, others fail because the release tap seizes up after dirt is thrown up from the rear wheels, and a few have poorly secured emptying hoses. Consequently, a purchaser of a motorcaravan might consider asking a salesperson to demonstrate that the system works properly and is easy to operate.

Unpleasant odours

When a motorcaravan is brand new you won't get any odours coming into the living space via the sink, basin or shower tray. However, problems may occur once particles of rotting food get trapped in the waste pipe, or when water collected in the tank starts to stagnate.

Drain smells seldom happen in our homes because Building Regulations require odour traps to be mounted under sinks, basins and baths. Typically these traps hold water in a U-shaped pipe so that smells from the public sewer don't get into the house. Similarly, at the foot of a lavatory pan, water is retained in a moulding, without which rising odours would be both intolerable and a threat to health.

Water traps designed to provide a 'smell barrier' have been ignored by many motorcaravan manufacturers for far too long. It is only recently that miniature traps have been purpose-made to suit the plumbing systems fitted in motorcaravans. For example, Auto-Sleepers was one of the first manufacturers to fit a DSL Plastics water trap with removable interceptor bowl; this was used in the Company's 2006 Sandhurst coachbuilt. But if you look under the sinks of most motorcaravans you'll often find that there is no trap at all.

This water trap complete with removable bowl is now being fitted in some Auto-Sleepers' models.

Above right: Recent waste tanks have a drain-down low point – correctly used for the drain-off pipe on this Swift Sundance.

Above: On this Bessacarr, the intended outlet fell foul of the chassis so, disappointingly, an outlet was fitted higher up.

Above: Wastemaster Superclean from F.L. Hitchman is formulated to clean tanks and waste pipes.

Below: Accurate driving is often required in order to align a waste outlet with a site's drainage point.

On the other hand, food interceptors situated just before the waste tank are not unusual, and models from Swift have had these for several years. Curiously, no mention is made of them in many owners' manuals, so they seldom get cleaned out. That's a pity because the job only involves unscrewing a cap.

However, there is another contributor to the smell problem. On many waste tanks, the drain-down release pipe is mounted on the side of the receptacle rather than forming an outlet on its base. In consequence, when owners think they've drained the tank completely there can be a depth of around 25mm (1in) of water left in the bottom. Residual water like this, together with trapped food remnants, soon starts to stagnate and when the smell reaches the living space it is truly dreadful.

Recent tanks are now being manufactured with a low-level moulded take-off point to ensure that the entire contents are drained off. If you purchase a motorcaravan with an older tank that lacks this feature, check to see if it has a screw-capped cleaning point on the underside. If so, CAK sells a conversion outlet that can be mounted in this cap. Since the capped outlet normally represents the lowest point of all, it provides a better drain-down facility than an outlet pipe fitted on to the side of a tank.

Problems and curative measures aside, several water specialists also supply cleaning compounds such as Wastemaster Superclean for motorhome tanks and portable waste water containers. Their periodic use is certainly recommended, but tank cleaning products are usually concentrated, aggressive chemicals, so read the instructions with care.

Draining down a waste water tank on-site is usually easy, although you may have to lift the steel cover of an inspection chamber to reveal the drain. Some motorcaravanners carry industrial gloves for this task. Depending on your motorcaravan's water release system, careful driving may be required to get its outlet and the receiving drain in alignment.

Regrettably, a few sites do not have motorcaravan service points, and one was recently built on a five-star site in France by someone who had obviously never used a motorcaravan. To position your vehicle over the intended drain would have involved driving up a flight of five steps! If that sounds ridiculous, a similar mistake was made on a high-quality site in Cornwall. Although site owners always provide emptying points for portable waste containers, some haven't yet realised that motorcaravanners' needs are different.

These problems prompt some motorcaravanners to carry a bucket with them, although this is a laborious method of emptying a large tank. Of course, you should never drain a waste tank onto a public road (which is illegal) or onto a campsite pitch.

PRECAUTIONS IN WINTER

When stopping on a site during frosty weather, it is not unusual for fresh water to freeze in your tank. This can have implications for your water heater, so check its instructions. As regards preparing hot drinks, you'll have to collect water from a tap in a kettle or saucepan – just like in the old days before water pumps were fitted in caravans and motorhomes. It's hardly a great imposition.

A far worse inconvenience occurs if the contents of your waste tank freeze. This captive tutti-frutti iced lollipop will prevent anything draining from your sink, basin or shower tray, and the only way to empty a full and blocked sink is to bale out the water using a suitable receptacle.

To avoid this problem, experienced winter motorcaravanners copy the touring caravanner and purchase either a portable waste container or a large bucket.

Some owners take a bucket because several sites don't provide proper motorcaravan drain-down points.

183

Potable anti-freeze

Whereas the majority of owners drain down a water system prior to laying-up their vehicle, some adopt a different strategy. They pump potable antifreeze such as Camco Winterban into the system and leave it there until the vehicle is recommissioned. Winterban, which is imported from the USA, is often used in American RVs and is available from ABP Accessories of Great Dalby, Leicestershire. However, its use isn't officially approved by European appliance manufacturers (eg Truma) in case it has a detrimental effect on their products' components. Incidentally, the word 'potable' implies that it's fit to drink – though you wouldn't do that by choice.

In frosty weather, some motorcaravanners couple a portable container to the permanently open waste tank.

Above right: As emphasised on the label, tap levers must be centralised and open to prevent frost damage to the hot and cold pipes.

Above: When residual water in a downturn of pipe froze and expanded, rising pressure in the system split this component.

Below: All motorcaravans should have a fresh water drain-down tap at the lowest point, but some models don't have one at all.

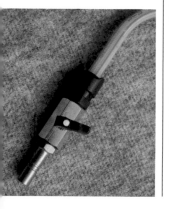

Then, before outside temperatures reach freezing point, the tank's drain-down tap is left permanently open so that it never gets filled, and the receptacle is placed under the outlet and linked using a short length of hose. Of course, this could freeze as well, so in severe conditions the screw cap is fitted to the receptacle before bringing it indoors at night. Alternatively, if you use a bucket, this must be emptied with prompt regularity.

Further precautionary measures are needed when your motorcaravan is out of use and parked for an extended storage spell. Long before the weather gets cold, you must drain down the entire water supply system. The water heater should be emptied too, in accordance with its manufacturer's instructions. The usual tasks are as follows:

- Open all the taps. In the case of mixer taps and shower controls that have lift-up levers, you must align these in a central position.

Opening taps acts as an air release point for both hot and cold supply pipes so that any pressure created by freezing water left in a pipe downturn will be released. *Note: Failure to do this during very cold conditions can lead to damaged pipe couplings and broken tap assemblies as shown in the accompanying illustration.*

- Find the drain-down release cock for your water system and open it fully.

Note: Some manufacturers don't fit a drain-down tap, which is a gross oversight. In this case you'll have to disconnect the lowest pipe coupling you can find, making sure you choose one where it is possible to catch discharging water in a receptacle.

- Follow the water heater instructions and release its contents as described by the manufacturer.

- Check your owners' manual for any other advice specific to your particular vehicle.

Note: There is another strategy for protecting a water system described in the Potable anti-freeze Technical Tip panel.

WATER COMPONENTS IN MOTORCARAVANS

This section provides a brief pictorial summary of the water supply components installed in modern motorcaravans. However, it doesn't include information on repair procedures or servicing because that kind of advice is included in the *Motorcaravan Manual* (3rd edition, 2012), also by Haynes.

Taps

Taps made out of plastic are light in weight and good quality examples perform well. Recently, however, it has become fashionable to fit domestic steel taps in many models. These reflect the comforts of home, although they add both weight and cost to a motorcaravan. Some units fold down into the basin as a space-saving strategy.

Most taps in motorcaravans merely open a valve to release water but occasionally you'll read about tap

Below: Stainless steel domestic taps have become popular in motorcaravans, although they're heavy and costly.

Below left: To maximise worktop space, the tap on this Knaus folds down into the sink.

Above: Microswitches are less common in motorcaravans, but wires under this Dethleffs tap reveal that one is fitted here.

Above right: Some taps, particularly those in caravans, embody a tiny switch to activate the water pump motor.

Above: Submersible pumps are seldom used in UK motorhomes but this blue and white pump is commonplace in German coachbuilts.

Below: This Mobilvetta Top Driver S71 is fitted with an accessible diaphragm pump, with a filter that's easy to reach.

assemblies that contain a small switch, referred to as a 'microswitch'.

This type is more commonly found in touring caravans. The function of the switch is to activate the electric water pump as soon as you operate the tap. To establish whether a motorcaravan's tap and its shower controls contain a microswitch, look under the assembly for two cables. You can see these in the accompanying photo, taken in a 2006 Dethleffs Esprit. These products work well provided damp doesn't get into a microswitch.

Pumps

Two types of pump are fitted in motorcaravans. You won't often find the submersible units that caravanners lower into the bottom of portable waste containers. These are fitted with a small paddle wheel, called an impeller, which pushes water along the supply pipes. Good ones last a long time, but will have to be replaced if the casing cracks. Submersible pumps are not normally repairable.

However, a submersible pump is occasionally held permanently in suspension in the fixed fresh water tanks installed in some German-built motorcaravans. The accompanying illustration shows an example of a Reich submersible tap in the bottom of a tank fitted to a recent Dethleffs motorcaravan.

In practice, the majority of European motorcaravan manufacturers, particularly in the UK, prefer to fit inboard diaphragm pumps rather than submersibles. These are well engineered, powerful, efficient, repairable, but also comparatively costly and sometimes noisy.

Pump switching devices

The practice of fitting a tiny microswitch inside a tap assembly to activate an electric pump has already been mentioned. However, most motorcaravans have a pressure sensitive switch instead, which is either mounted in the supply pipes or within the housing of a diaphragm pump.

As soon as you open a tap, the switch detects a loss of pressure in the pipes and automatically switches on the pump.

Unfortunately, a pressure sensitive switch will also react if there's a small air loss in a pipe connection. Reaction times can also vary according to the state of charge in a battery. Pressure switch sensitivity is sometimes adjustable but the fine tuning control is often hidden to prevent inexperienced users tampering with the set-up. There's also a tendency for these units to trigger a pump very briefly whereupon it gives one or two false 'beats'; the noise is sometimes distracting, especially at night. Accordingly, there is usually a pump override switch on a motorcaravan's main control panel so that you can disable it during the night.

Surge dampers
Sometimes, a diaphragm pump operates in a staccato, throbbing manner, and to stop this, a surge damper can be fitted in the supply to smooth out its delivery of water. The illustration shows an example.

Types of pipe
Not only are two types of pipe used for waste water systems (the disadvantage of the convoluted variety was outlined earlier), there are also two types of

Pressure sensitive switches are usually fitted; this Whale switch has a pressure adjusting control on the top.

Swift sometimes fits underfloor components to which a hatch affords access. The blue surge damper is on the left.

Above: Where hose negotiates a tight bend it often kinks; trying to remedy a deformed section isn't easy.

Above right: Hose is coupled with worm-driven clips, and the joints will be suspect if poor quality products are used.

Below: With JG Speedfit semi-rigid pipe, moulded bend-support channelling prevents kinks from occurring.

Above: When cut accurately, semi-rigid pipe is merely pushed deep into couplings to achieve an airtight joint.

Right: Grit filters mounted on the input side of diaphragm pumps need to be easily accessible for periodic cleaning.

fresh water pipe. Of these, flexible hose coupled-up using worm-driven ('Jubilee') clips is the more primitive system. Poor quality clips can fail and non-reinforced hose soon develops kinks when it passes around tight bends.

Semi-rigid pipe with push-fit couplings is a better product and has been used successfully in domestic installations for around 30 years. Versions are available from Whale Systems and there's the 'Speedfit' product from John Guest. Many couplings and components are available for domestic installations, some of which are used to good effect in motorcaravans too. For example, a 90° channelling prevents a length of pipe from kinking when it negotiates a tight bend. No less important is the ease with which sections of pipe and components can be coupled-up.

Filters/treatment: grit, taste and purifiers

You'll come across three types of filter and treatment products used in motorcaravans:

• Grit filters: These intercept waterborne particles and are an essential component to fit on the feed pipe supplying a diaphragm pump. If particles of grit are not intercepted, the tiny pistons and chambers

in a pump can be badly damaged.

Pump on the left, surge damper on the right, and a Nature Pure water purifier was later added in the middle.

- Taste filters: Although this type of product normally intercepts grit too, its main purpose is to improve the palatability of water. If a taste filter hasn't been installed as a standard component, it can often be fitted retrospectively. However, the filter cartridge needs to be changed periodically.
- Water purifiers: Several types are manufactured. The Nature Pure Ultrafine is particularly impressive, but it isn't cheap, and as long as a motorcaravan's pump is sufficiently powerful to force water through an Ultrafine filter, these American purifiers can usually be fitted retrospectively. The supplier's literature describes the huge array of disease bacteria, toxins, solvents and pesticides that the filter intercepts. The filters are so good that it is even possible to draw water from a canal, and with a Nature Pure Ultrafine installation this will then be converted into pure drinking water. When this product is installed in a motorcaravan the supply from its tank can undoubtedly be considered fit for drinking.

TOILETS AND SANITARY PRODUCTS

A *portable* version of the flushing toilets that have a detachable holding tank is often used in small campervans. The advantage of these free-standing products is that if you change your motorcaravan they can easily be transferred. Equally, there are some owners of small van conversions who occasionally erect an outside toilet tent and use that to house their portable 'loo'.

However, most motorcaravans nowadays are equipped with a fixed toilet, and there are two main types: bench-style products and models that feature a swivelling bowl. Both of these need flush water, chemicals, and both have a cassette that needs emptying when a gauge gives the warning.

Thetford cassette swivel-bowl toilets can be turned to suit the available space. Bench types have fixed bowls.

A filler hatch situated above the cassette compartment indicates that flush water is stored within the toilet casing itself.

More recently, vacuum toilets have been introduced, where the holding tank is mounted remotely and the contents of the bowl are removed using what sounds like a powerful suction process. These are similar in operation to the appliances installed in passenger aircraft and vacuum toilets are sometimes installed in RVs and A-class motorcaravans.

Emptying a holding tank is a straightforward operation, although you occasionally find European motorhomes that adopt the North American system in which effluent is instead stored in a fixed tank. The accompanying *Technical Tip panel gives further details*.

Flushing water

Fixed cassette toilets utilise two distinct flush water arrangements. In some motorcaravans the water is drawn directly from the fresh water tank, but the disadvantage of using this supply is that bowl-cleaning additives can't be mixed into the flush water. Others have their own built-in tank and are easy to spot because there's an extra filler inlet on the outside wall of the motorcaravan.

(i) Technical Tip

Waste from toilets

Whereas most European motorcaravans are fitted with a waste tank to collect unwanted water from a sink, washbasin or shower, the tank isn't made to accept effluent from a toilet. This is normally collected in a portable cassette and emptied separately. Just a few European motorcaravans – eg a few models from the Italian Laika brand – have a separate fixed tank to collect toilet waste.

This is very different from the provision in RVs built in the United States, where sink waste is collected in what is referred to as the 'Grey' tank while the waste from toilets is collected in the 'Black' tank. Furthermore, the camping grounds in North America are regularly equipped with 'dump stations' where both grey and black water can be emptied.

Anyone intending to purchase an imported RV would be advised to seek further guidance about these facilities from one of the UK's RV owners' clubs.

Few models sold in this country have a waste tank for toilet effluent. This Laika is one of the exceptions.

Chemicals

The cassette, or 'holding tank', is usually 'charged' with a chemical treatment, although some owners fit a ventilated 'SOG' modification kit that relies on natural bacteria to break down solids. Chemicals are not used in vacuum toilets because the receiving tank is vacuum-sealed.

Examples of chemical treatments include concentrated liquids, granular chemicals and sachets. Always check the dilution requirement of concentrated liquids and remember to put one litre of water into the cassette first of all. Recent Thetford toilets include a measuring facility for chemicals in the cassette cap.

When purchasing chemicals you'll find the blue type is usually based on formaldehyde. Though it breaks down solid matter efficiently, formaldehyde is considered detrimental to the environment, which has led to the introduction of alternative environmentally friendly 'green' treatments. However, some campsite owners discourage the use of green treatments, as they believe they contribute to drain blockages.

User advice

Explaining to adult readers how to use a cassette toilet might seem demeaning, but if it isn't explained here, how will you learn an all-important fact of life on the road? It certainly never gets mentioned in owners' manuals. So here goes...

Many motorcaravanners have 'house rules' which dictate that their toilet is normally only used for liquid waste. On most sites that's fine, but not when

Above: A Thetford cassette being withdrawn. Aqua Kem Green and pink Aqua Rinse are among the popular products.

191

Above: Recent Thetford caps are marked so they can be used to add the right amount of concentrated chemical.

(i) Useful Tip

- When adding a chemical, avoid spilling it inside your motorcaravan; the marks are virtually impossible to remove from carpets.
- It's best to introduce liquid chemical directly into a holding tank rather than via the toilet bowl. If undiluted chemical gets on the rubber seal that keeps the open/close blade watertight, it can cause damage.
- Flushing water additive does help to keep a toilet bowl shiny.
- Take note of the manufacturer's recommended cleaners. Thetford's Bathroom Cleaner (sometimes labelled as 'Plastic Cleaner') is both effective and easy to use.

There's a knack to emptying a toilet cassette without an airlock causing splashing.

you 'wild camp' or stop at farm sites (where you have to be self-sufficient). The rule also ignores the fact that there may be human 'emergencies'.

The time-honoured procedure when using a cassette toilet is to precede a 'performance' by flushing a small amount of water into the pan. Then you carefully place a few pieces of toilet paper to float on the surface like water lily leaves, making sure that they achieve surface contact around the sides of the pan as well. This origami exercise may sound bizarre but it brings its rewards.

Once a 'performance' is complete, you find that when the toilet-emptying blade is swung open, the solids drop unhindered into the holding tank and the paper encloses them completely with gift-wrapping panache. This means that no stains are left on the pan – or, more importantly, on the blade and its sealing rubber ring. Don't forget that you see this sealing ring every time the cassette is taken for emptying, so you don't want soil marks on it. Though experienced motorcaravanners know that this technique works they aren't always keen to pass on the secret!

Emptying advice

There's a knack to emptying a cassette, and it isn't wise to try this out for the first time with a brim-full container. Some points to bear in mind:

- When removing the screw cap, place it well away from the site's emptying bowl. Wardens are not happy when asked to retrieve a lost screw cap for butter-fingered guests. What's more, a lost screw cap invariably blocks a drain.
- As you point your cassette's outlet to the receiving pan, gently press the air release button. This can sometimes be difficult to reach, depending on how you hold the cassette. However, if you ignore this button, the contents tend to glug into the pan and you might get splashed.
- Add some fresh water to swill the last remnants

of paper out, but don't shake the water around too vigorously. This can damage the internal float mechanism that warns when a cassette is ready for emptying. Do it gently.

- It's often helpful if a new owner carries out their first ever emptying session using a cassette full of fresh water rather than effluent. This operation isn't quite as straightforward as you might imagine.
- Remember that you must realign the opening knob as shown in the accompanying illustration so that it is parallel with the long sides of the cassette. Failure to do this means that the cassette will not slide back into the motorcaravan.

Lay-up procedure

Obviously it is catastrophic to leave a toilet un-emptied all winter, even though cassettes are fitted with a pressure-relief valve. But you won't make this mistake if you always remember to leave the blade in its open position. Apart from acting as an emptying reminder, this prevents the blade sticking to the rubber valve – which often happens during an extended storage period.

It's an even better idea to lubricate the valve prior to laying-up. Do this as follows:

1. Clean the rubber seal using Thetford Bathroom Cleaner or a lukewarm diluted solution of washing-up liquid; never use a household detergent, which can damage the seal.
2. Dry thoroughly then spray with Thetford's Toilet Seal lubricant or use olive oil. Never use Vaseline or any other form of grease or lubricant.
3. Close the blade, return the cassette into your motorcaravan, then open the blade once again and leave it like that until you recommence using the vehicle.

Further advice, including a series of instructional video tips on toilet maintenance, can be viewed on the website: www.wickyworld.co.uk

Above left: You can use the yellow button to operate the blade, but return it to this position before re-inserting the cassette into its locker.

Above: To ensure the rubber seal stays supple and works well with the blade, Thetford sells a maintenance spray.

Above: The blade should be closed to reinstate a cassette; then open it again indoors and leave it open during long storage spells.

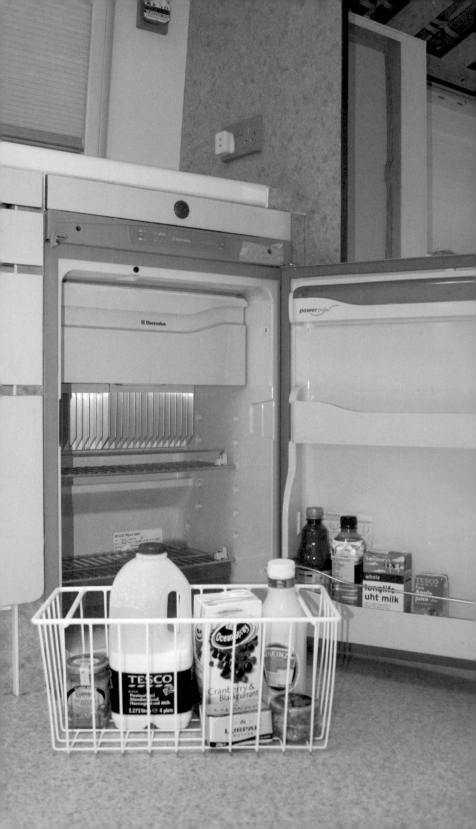

CHAPTER ELEVEN

REFRIGERATORS

Two types of refrigerator are fitted in motorcaravans and their operating principles are different. It is important to know which type has been installed because it affects the independence you can expect when using your vehicle. This chapter explains the respective merits of different products and gives advice on how to get the best from them. Without doubt, a fridge is an important asset, and only very small campervans use portable cool boxes instead.

195

A refrigerator is one of the most useful appliances in a motorcaravan.

A cooling unit on the rear of the casing withdraws heat from the food compartment via these metal fins.

Cooling appliances normally have a chemical refrigeration unit designed to reduce the temperature in their food storage compartment. Typically, this unit is mounted on the rear of the cabinet, and metal fins (which can be seen in the back of the food compartment) draw heat from the enclosure.

To achieve cooling, chemicals sealed within the unit have to be circulated around a series of pipes – and here lies the key difference between the two types of refrigerator fitted in motorcaravans. In those appliances referred to as 'compressor fridges', the chemicals are circulated by an electrically-driven compressor. In contrast, the chemicals in 'absorption fridges' are circulated by the application of heat.

COMPRESSOR REFRIGERATORS

In our homes we use compressor fridges, and it is not unusual to hear an appliance start-up whenever the thermostat registers that the temperature in its food compartment needs lowering. In a domestic kitchen, this noise is not intrusive, but when this type of appliance is fitted in the confined space of a motorcaravan, some people find the intermittent hum of the compressor pump rather annoying – especially at night.

Compressor fridges also rely on having a well-charged 12V leisure battery to operate the pump. That's hardly a problem if you drive around a lot because an alternator will help to keep a leisure battery charged. Similarly, if you frequently use sites with mains hook-ups, your motorcaravan charger will also keep the leisure battery in a good state of charge. Of course, its condition will also be governed by how many other 12V accessories are drawing current.

For reasons given later, a number of van conversions are equipped with compressor fridges, although this type of appliance is seldom fitted in large coach-built motorcaravans.

Product Identities:

Compressor refrigerators
For many years, the name WAECO has been associated with a wide range of motorcaravan products, especially compressor fridges. The many sizes of compressor fridges fitted in boats and motorcaravans is impressive but all WAECO accessories are now embraced in the Dometic Group's product range. However, the WAECO brand name is still retained by Dometic.

In the UK, the WAECO range of compressor refrigerators is well known and these appliances are one of many products supplied by the Dometic Group. Several medium and compact models are available for motorhomes, whereas several of the smaller units are often fitted in the cabs of long-distance lorries.

ABSORPTION REFRIGERATORS

This type of refrigerator is virtually silent in operation, and examples fitted in motorcaravans operate using one of three built-in heating systems: a gas burner, a 12V DV heating element, or a 230V AC heating element. This facility is called 'three-way operation', and having a choice of systems is valuable because it lets you keep your fridge running in a wide range of overnight venues. Its versatility is one reason why the majority of motorcaravans are fitted with absorption-type refrigerators.

Absorption fridges work efficiently as long as they are installed correctly, serviced regularly and used in accordance with the manufacturer's recommendations. When these requirements are met, specialists from Dometic state that their products will perform well in ambient temperatures

Several van converters prefer to fit compressor refrigerators in their products.

Product Identities:

Absorption refrigerators
For many years, the absorption refrigerators fitted in leisure vehicles were manufactured by Electrolux. However, in 2001, the leisure appliance division of Electrolux became an independent company and the name Dometic was adopted. This had been a brand name used in the USA for a number of years.

In 2003, many appliances were still bearing both Dometic and Electrolux badges, which was rather confusing. However, in 2004 the licence to use the Electrolux name expired. In this chapter, both names are used because thousands of motorcaravans are fitted with products previously manufactured by Electrolux. Only post-2004 models bear just a Dometic badge, and the Company's after-sales service covers both products.

This three-way Norcold absorption refrigerator is fitted in a Hymer Exsis.

up to 38°C (100°F). Dometic's products were formerly part of the Electrolux Leisure brand, while fridges manufactured by Norcold bear the Thetford badge and since 2002 are seen increasingly often in motorhomes sold in the UK.

Product ranges include portable cool boxes that operate using the absorption refrigeration principle. However, these must not be confused with portable units that have a 12V electric fan and employ what is known as the Peltier cooling process. Peltier products achieve mild cooling in picnic boxes, but do not produce low temperature refrigeration.

Large fridge-freezers fitted in coachbuilt motorcaravans also employ three-way absorption cooling systems and there are models in the ranges of both Dometic and Thetford.

PROS AND CONS

On the face of it, the case for purchasing a motorcaravan fitted with an absorption fridge might sound convincing. But there are some situations where compressor fridges offer advantages of their own. The pros and cons listed below will help to clarify the respective merits of these two types of refrigerator.

Compressor refrigerators

Advantages
- Normally less expensive than absorption models
- No routine servicing work is required
- Installation is easy and ventilation apertures are not required in a van's side wall
- If required, an appliance can be installed away from a side wall
- Available in unusual designs, eg with top access doors
- Cooling level controls are extremely simple to operate
- Compressor fridges continue working even when a vehicle is parked on sloping ground.

A compressor fridge can be mounted away from a side wall – as Bilbo's showed in the Cyclone van conversion.

Some compressor fridges are designed with access lids for installation in confined spaces.

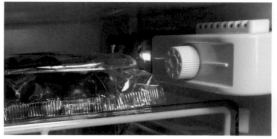

On this WAECO appliance, the self-explanatory cooling level control is situated just inside the storage compartment.

Disadvantages
- Wholly reliant on a 12V supply
- Cannot be run on gas
- Older models were surprisingly noisy; recent ones are much better
- Not convenient if you camp in the wild and have no means of recharging the leisure battery.

Absorption refrigerators

Advantages
- No need to depend on having a well-charged leisure battery
- When stopping in remote locations, you can run the fridge on gas
- You can remain parked for extended periods on pitches that aren't equipped with mains hook-ups
- Large fridge-freezer versions are available.

Disadvantages
- Efficiency can be compromised if the motorcaravan manufacturer hasn't installed the unit correctly
- Regular servicing is needed as defined by the appliance manufacturer
- Normally have to be installed against an external wall because of the flue outlet and cooling ventilators
- External ventilation is essential, and grilles might spoil external appearances, especially on the contoured sides of an MPV
- Costly; a three-way operation facility often makes small motorhome fridges more expensive than large household appliances
- Operation is dependent on a vehicle being parked fairly level, although recent models have improved 'tilt tolerance'. *Note: See Technical Tip 'Operating Angles' which appears later in the chapter.*

Being aware of these differences is important when purchasing a motorcaravan or having one built to order. Whereas most manufacturers of coachbuilts fit absorption models, some van converters prefer to install compressor appliances.

Most absorption fridges have two ventilators and a flue outlet that might look unattractive on some vehicles.

This Dometic refrigerator offers three-way operation and a setting system that selects the operating mode automatically.

Manufacturers' preferences

Van conversions from Bilbo's are normally fitted with compressor appliances, whereas models from Murvi usually have absorption fridges.

In some instances van converters give customers a choice, and Murvi will fit a compressor model as a special order.

To give other examples, Wheelhome exclusively fits compressor products, Auto-Sleepers exclusively installs absorption fridges, and small-scale manufacturers such as Middlesex Motorcaravans fits whatever type the customer wants.

If you have a strong preference one way or the other, keep this in mind when comparing different motorcaravans.

THREE-WAY OPERATION

There is no doubt that the versatility of a three-way absorption fridge is a very popular feature. However, if you haven't used a three-way appliance before it can be difficult to decide which operating mode you should be using. Fascia selector controls on earlier models were quite a challenge to understand, which didn't help newcomers to motorcaravanning. Fortunately, refrigerator panels are now much clearer and some of the more expensive appliances even incorporate what Dometic calls Automatic Energy Selection (AES) and Thetford calls Smart Energy Selection (SES). Appliances that incorporate these facilities are built with a 'computerised brain' that chooses the most appropriate heat source on your behalf.

AES and SES models employ a programme that always selects mains operation mode as the 'first choice' mode whenever you're hooked up to a 230V supply. If there isn't a mains supply, it chooses gas – provided the cylinder is switched for action and isn't empty. Alternatively, when you're driving, it selects 12V battery operation. This automatic selection

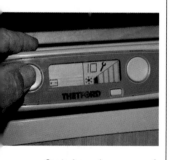

Control panels on some of the Thetford refrigerators employ LCD displayers with pictograms to illustrate different settings.

facility obviously adds to the cost of an appliance and most motorcaravans are fitted with manual selection controls. However, as pointed out already, recent fascia controls are far more straightforward to operate than they used to be.

Here are some points to remember:

Operation on gas

Applying heat from a small burner is a very effective way to circulate refrigerants in the cooling unit and you can alter the degree of cooling by adjusting a control on the front panel. Incidentally, absorption fridges are made to run on either butane or propane gas without any need for alteration.

The procedure for lighting a gas burner is not difficult on a modern refrigerator, although several different ignition systems have been fitted over the last 40 years. When leisure fridges first became popular at the start of the 1970s, you had to light the burner from outside using a match. That could be difficult, especially in windy weather, and things improved when spark ignition was subsequently developed using a Piezo crystal assembly. In truth, plenty of fridges on older motorhomes still employ spark ignition, and a red push-button igniter on their fascias is a familiar sight.

However, an electronic system was developed during the 1980s which is even better. Provided an appliance is switched on at its fascia, an electronic circuits generates an ignition spark automatically whenever the burner isn't alight.

Operation on 12V

You should never run your fridge on gas when the motorcaravan is being driven. It is also illegal and extremely dangerous to enter a filling station forecourt with an exposed gas flame. To avoid a potentially dangerous situation, fridge manufacturers fit a heating element that runs on 12V as an alternative heat source. This means you can keep your fridge working while driving without using the gas system.

However, a refrigerator takes a lot of current to heat the refrigerants (around 8 amps) and this would discharge a 12V battery very quickly. So it is entirely impracticable to run this appliance from a leisure battery when you're staying on a site. Consequently, a motorcaravan's wiring doesn't include a circuit that permanently connects this type of fridge to its batteries.

Nevertheless, as long as a motorcaravan has been correctly wired, a refrigerator can be switched to operate on 12V when the engine is running. Current for the 12V heating element is drawn from the

Ignition

Ignition systems only work if the spark gap is correctly set at the burner. Moreover, soot is created when a fridge runs on gas, which coats a burner assembly and hinders ignition. This is one of several reasons why a motorcaravan three-way fridge has to be serviced, and its electrode will then be checked and realigned if necessary.

Cooling on 12V operation

When you've set a Dometic three-way refrigerator to operate on a 12V supply, you can't control the cooling level as you would when the appliance is running on gas or a 230V supply. On 12V operation the refrigerator runs at a steady level and the fascia controls aren't able to alter the cooling performance. However, don't be misled into thinking that 12V operation is any less efficient than gas or 230V operating modes. This isn't the case.

Safety Tip

If you accidentally run a caravan fridge on more than one supply simultaneously, it might damage the system. This can happen on pre-1992 Electrolux appliances – especially when the user has been running the fridge on gas and then selects the 12V option in readiness for driving off-site. Even though the user turns the gas control knob to its lowest setting, this will NOT extinguish the flame on older appliances. The only way to extinguish the flame is to close the supply at the gas cylinder – which is a safety practice you're advised to adopt before driving.

The misunderstanding has caused some motorcaravanners to find, to their surprise, that the refrigerator has continued to run on a low gas flame – as well as 12V – while they've been driving. Entering a filling station with a fridge in this mode could have horrifying consequences. Consequently, the fascia gas control on Electrolux refrigerators made after 1992 does incorporate a shut-off valve.

vehicle by taking advantage of its alternator charging system. In other words the alternator keeps the vehicle and leisure batteries charged even though a power-hungry appliance is calling for current.

Operation on 230V

If you select the 230V option, a mains heating element comes into use for circulating the chemicals. On earlier types of refrigerator there was a specific control knob for altering the level of cooling when using a mains supply. This was similar to a second control knob intended for adjusting cooling when running on gas. However, recent models have a combined control instead.

Operating on a mains supply is not only useful on a campsite, it is also useful if the motorcaravan is parked on your drive and you're packing it ready for a holiday. It allows you to pre-cool the fridge before setting off, which is recommended practice.

Finally, when arriving at a site that has hook-ups on each pitch, you'll naturally prefer the 230V operating option, particularly if you've paid to use this mains supply.

HOW TO OPERATE A THREE-WAY FRIDGE

Manufacturers of absorption fridges advise that it is best to run a fridge for at least three to four hours before leaving home. However, don't leave it empty while you do this. Put several non-perishable products into the food compartment, such as bottles of water and other drinks, before coupling to a mains supply.

Pre-cooling on 230V mains

If you choose to save your gas and pre-cool the fridge using a mains supply, make sure you run the appliance using the motorcaravan's hook-up lead

Poor performance on mains

On crowded sites in summer, especially in popular parts of mainland Europe, the draw on a mains system is considerable. This becomes acute in hot weather when fridges and air conditioning units are running flat out. In some cases there's a significant loss of power, and tests on sites have shown that it can even drop below 195V. When this occurs your fridge's performance can be badly affected. If you can't get satisfactory cooling when running on mains, switch over to gas operation. This often improves fridge performance when a site is very busy.

so that the RCD and MCB safety protection devices in the 'van are employed. (These are described in Chapter Twelve.)

When using a standard hook-up cable you'll also need a plug adaptor to connect the coupling lead to a domestic 13A socket.

Moreover, to extend protection to cover your supply hook-up lead as well, remember to fit an RCD device in your home socket. These are often sold in DIY stores. RCDs are strongly recommended whenever running mains power tools and appliances outdoors.

Running on gas

If you haven't used your motorcaravan for some time, it can take several attempts to get a burner to light. Air in the gas supply pipe is the usual cause of problems and it may take repeated ignition attempts before the air is finally purged.

If the problem persists, poor ignition may result from a weak spark, dirty electrodes and an incorrect spark gap. This is a sure sign that a refrigerator is due for its annual service.

On some appliances, you're able to confirm when the burner is alight by looking through a small inspection port in the bottom left-hand side of the food compartment. Recent models don't have this inspection facility, although on appliances that have electronic ignition (as opposed to a push-button Piezo igniter) you'll hear the unit clicking while it tries to light the burner. In addition, there is sometimes a flashing red lamp on the fascia that shows if it still hasn't managed to ignite the gas.

Like most gas appliances, absorption refrigerators have a flame-failure device (FFD). This means that if the flame blows out in a wind, the gas supply to the burner will shut off automatically. Information on this device is given in the accompanying panel.

If pre-cooling a fridge at home using your hook-up lead, purchase an adaptor and an RCD to fit the 13-amp supply socket.

Flame-failure devices (FFDs)

An FFD uses a probe – called a thermocouple – which is angled into the gas flame; when it gets hot it creates a small electric current that automatically opens a gas valve in the supply pipe. However, when you start a fridge from cold, you have to hold down the main control for several seconds to manually open this valve while the probe is warming up. If the flame goes out when you release the control knob, the FFD needs attention. Cleaning and realigning the probe are jobs included in a refrigerator servicing operation; as is a check of its electrical connections. Never be tempted to jam a control knob open, because this overrides the protection afforded by an FFD.

The bronze coloured tube (centre right of photograph) brings current from the FFD probe to an electromagnetic gas valve behind the fascia.

(i) Technical Tip

Operating angles

For refrigerant chemicals to circulate correctly in an absorption fridge, it is important that your vehicle is parked level. Indeed, on motorcaravans built before 1986 this is critical, since refrigerators dating to this period seldom achieve cooling if they're 2°–3° from level. After that date, Electrolux introduced 'tilt-tolerant' refrigerators. For example, models like the RM122 and RM4206 operate correctly as long as the degree of tilt doesn't exceed 3°, while models like the RM4217, RM4237 and RM4271 operate at angles up to 6°. For further guidance, check the information given in your appliance's instruction manual.

As a point of interest, when you're on the road, the pitch and toss of driving is not a problem for fridge operation. As long as the refrigerator passes through a level plane now and again the cooling unit works effectively.

Running on 12V

Unless a motorcaravan is fitted with an AES refrigerator, it is the owner's responsibility to select 12V operation before taking to the road. As long as the installer has correctly wired the vehicle to the appliance, a 12V supply will keep the fridge in operation while the engine is running. Since there are no naked flames involved in this heating mode, there is no danger when you enter a filling station forecourt.

Efficiency

As long as a refrigerator has been installed in accordance with its manufacturer's instructions, a Dometic appliance is claimed to operate efficiently in air temperatures as high as 38°C (100°F). Unfortunately, some motorcaravan manufacturers don't install these appliances as well as they should, and cooling efficiency is impaired as a result. For the benefit of owners with a technical interest, this is discussed in more detail at the end of the chapter.

As regards operating difficulties that occur when a refrigerator is not level, further guidance on this subject is given in the accompanying Technical Tip panel: Operating angles.

If your fridge doesn't work on gas, check that the supply is switched on at the cylinder and also its gas control valve. The valve that supplies the fridge in this illustration is marked with a pictogram showing a snowflake.

SOLVING SIMPLE PROBLEMS

As a rule, an absorption refrigerator that has been serviced regularly and installed correctly will work efficiently. Check these points if you experience problems:

If your refrigerator doesn't work on gas

• Check that the gas cylinder isn't empty
• Confirm that the gas control valve serving your refrigerator is open

- If the burner doesn't ignite after repeated attempts, this may be because it needs an annual service.
- If the flame doesn't stay alight when you release the gas control knob, the flame-failure device needs attention.

If your refrigerator doesn't work on 12V
- Check that the fuse in your motorcaravan serving the refrigerator is intact
- Check that the 12V selector switch is in the correct position on the refrigerator fascia
- Ensure the motorcaravan's engine is running – the 12V option is unavailable when the engine is switched off.

If your refrigerator doesn't work on 230V
- Check that the 230V fascia switch is on
- If the fridge is coupled to the motorcaravan's mains circuits by a 13A plug, check that the fuse in the plug is intact
- Check that the miniature circuit breaker, which controls the fridge supply, hasn't 'tripped out' on the motorcaravan's 230V consumer unit (details in Chapter Twelve)
- If cooling is poor and the campsite is crowded, turn over to gas operation; busy sites often experience a mains voltage drop.

In the event of continuing problems consult your motorcaravan dealer.

GETTING THE BEST FROM A REFRIGERATOR

Refrigerators fitted in motorcaravans are obviously different from the appliances we use in our homes. For instance, when you've parked a vehicle in direct sunshine it can get extremely hot inside. In recognition of this, you certainly don't want to open the fridge door with the same casual frequency that you might at home.

Here is some advice that will help ensure you get the best from a motorcaravan fridge:

Normal use

To reduce the chance of condensation forming on a refrigerator's cooling fins, wrap anything wet – such as a lettuce – in plastic or cellophane. Also wrap strong-smelling items.

A common mistake is to place packs of drink cans hard up against the cooling fins. These fins draw heat out of the food compartment, so they mustn't be completely covered up.

Avoid packing food tightly in a fridge and try to position items so that air can circulate around them. This improves the efficiency of heat withdrawal from the compartment.

Apply safety catches before taking to the road. Failure to do this may result in the door flying open and the contents spilling over the floor. Yes, it can happen!

Cleaning

At the end of a holiday it is an important discipline to empty the contents of your refrigerator. If milk has been spilt and hasn't been mopped up, it doesn't take long before mould starts to form.

Keep the interior clean, but be warned that some household detergents damage plastic. Dometic recommends a teaspoonful of bicarbonate of soda added to a litre of warm water.

To clean the inside of Norcold fridges, Thetford (UK) now recommends the use of Thetford Bathroom Cleaner. This is marketed as a specially formulated cleaner for plastics.

To remove resistant marks on the plastic lining of a cabinet, Dometic recommends using a fine wire wool pad lubricated liberally with water to reduce its abrasiveness.

Airing a fridge during storage by leaving its door ajar is important, but some manufacturers fail to fit a securing system to override the magnetic door closer. This strut on a Thetford fridge works well.

Fitting a hinged wooden door might improve appearances, but on this Swift motorcaravan the manufacturer hadn't included a catch to hold it ajar during storage periods.

COLD-WEATHER MOTORCARAVANNING

Many owners take their main holidays in the summer, and poor cooling is sometimes reported. However, if you use a motorcaravan when the outside temperatures are low, you can instead experience *over-cooling*.

Models prone to over-cooling

This problem is only likely to occur on older Electrolux models fitted with a gas valve, such as the RM212, RM4206, RM4230 and RM4200. It doesn't normally happen on models fitted with a gas thermostat, such as the RM2260, RM4237, RM4271 and more recent appliances.

Cold weather covers

In response to the problem of over-cooling, Electrolux introduced accessories referred to as 'winter covers'. If your motorcaravan has Electrolux or Dometic ventilators, you can purchase suitable winter covers from your dealer. These reduce the flow of air across the rear of the appliance and should be fitted over the ventilators when outside temperatures fall below 10°C (50°F). Similar covers are also available from Thetford that clip on to its own range of plastic ventilator grilles.

Unfortunately some of the cheaper, non-standard vents used on motorcaravans have a different pattern, and you can't buy covers to fit.

Draughts

If a refrigerator has been installed in accordance with the manufacturer's instructions, the cooling unit at the rear of the appliance will be completely sealed-off from the motorcaravan's living quarters.

Consequently, if a strong wind blows towards the external ventilators it is unable to reach the occupants inside.

After removing a cutlery drawer above a fridge, you still shouldn't be able to see the wall ventilators from indoors.

In reality some motorcaravan manufacturers fail to seal off the rear section as required. Not only does this impair the cooling unit's performance in summer, but it also leads to draughtiness inside during windy weather. Some owners wrongly presume that winter covers are intended to overcome this. Although they might ease the problem, winter covers were not designed to act as draught excluders.

CHECKING AN INSTALLATION

If you are buying a motorcaravan – whether brand new or pre-owned – it is often possible to find out if the cooling unit has been sealed off correctly. For instance, if you look through the external ventilators you should not be able to see into the living space. On some models you can remove the grille by using a coin to undo the retaining catch, which makes it easy to check this detail.

Alternatively, if you remove drawers in the kitchen adjacent to a fridge and peer outwards towards the vents, you shouldn't be able to see any light from outside.

A further test to establish whether the cooling unit has been correctly sealed off is possible when an appliance is operating on gas. If there's a worktop or draining board directly over the appliance, put your hand on it. If it's warm, it is almost certain that the installer failed to fit an effectively sealed diffuser to direct heat out of the upper wall vent.

Creating a sealed ventilation pathway creates good

If a shelf or worktop over a fridge gets warm, the ventilation ducting may not have been effectively sealed.

cooling, and it is particularly important on large fridge-freezers because the flue also discharges into this ducted zone. On smaller refrigerators, exhaust gases are sent outside via a separate purpose-made flue.

If you carry out these checks and decide that the ventilation pathway has not been effectively sealed from the living space, the performance of the fridge in hot weather may not be as good as you'd expect. Equally there is a possibility that exhaust fumes from the gas burner might start to seep through into the living quarters.

REFRIGERATOR SERVICING

To ensure that their absorption refrigerators continue to perform well, both Dometic and Thetford recommend that their appliances are serviced every 12–18 months, depending on frequency of use. However, even with spasmodic operation, rust can form in the flue and fall on to the burner. Dead moths and spiders also upset the fine operation of gas appliances.

Be aware that if you book your motorcaravan for an annual habitation service, only cursory attention is given to individual appliances. For instance, a refrigerator's cooling will be checked and its gas flame inspected, but the appliance will not be given the full service recommended by its manufacturer.

Refrigerator servicing is usually an optional 'extra' that incurs an additional charge. Although this operation only takes an hour or so to complete, if it becomes necessary to remove and transfer an appliance to a bench, this may take a further hour or more. On many fridges, service jobs are virtually impossible to complete if an appliance is left in situ, so it is regrettable that the fridge in one well-known

Italian motorcaravan takes a full day to remove and reinstall! Fortunately the majority of refrigerators are far easier to disconnect, remove and reinstate.

Service jobs include:
- Fitting a new gas jet on Electrolux and Dometic models (but not Thetford fridges)
- Cleaning the burner, flue, FFD probe and ignition assembly
- Checking spark gaps and realigning the components if necessary
- Checking operation of the flame-failure system.

These tasks must be carried out by a qualified engineer. More detailed information on servicing, operation and installation are given in the *Motorcaravan Manual* (3rd edition, 2012), also published by Haynes.

Finally, be aware that a full fridge service is not included as part of a normal habitation service – as discussed in Chapter Sixteen. This is a separate operation and it is no secret that some owners don't ever bother to have their refrigerator serviced as recommended. Then they become annoyed when the appliance lets them down ... and as you might guess, this typically occurs during the hottest spell of the year.

Servicing a fridge is not a DIY job. One of the tasks on Dometic and Electrolux models is to fit a new gas jet, because an old one should never be cleaned.

A service engineer will clean the gas burner, flame failure probe and check the ignition system.

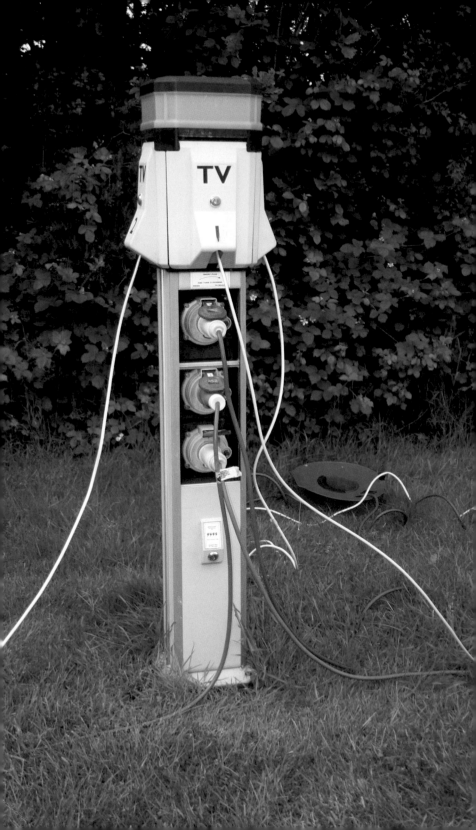

CHAPTER **TWELVE**

MAINS
ELECTRICITY

When The Caravan Club decided to
fit 12 experimental mains sockets
on one of its sites in 1977, it could
scarcely have predicted the outcome.
Today, mains 'hook-ups' are available
on all major sites throughout Europe.
Having a supply of 230V electricity is
a great asset to a motorcaravanner, but
observing safety standards is crucially
important.

213

*These hook-up pillars are
often seen in Britain. This
one also houses TV sockets
linked to a large site aerial.*

In a technical guide published by The Camping and Caravanning Club, it is stated: 'Electricity is a very good friend but an even worse enemy.' This view is endorsed here – safety advice is important to follow.

Just because we have mains electricity in our homes it doesn't mean we'll know how to use it in a motorcaravan. Installations in houses and leisure vehicles are surprisingly different. For instance, there are hook-up supply pillars to understand, limits to the amount of current you can use, and wiring procedures that aren't used in a house.

When early trials on campsites found that many caravanners and motorhome users liked having a 230V mains supply, matters of health and safety concerning temporary supplies were given careful thought. For example, a site's supply points – often called 'hook-up pillars' – have to comply with strict regulations. So, too, does the link cable that brings power to your van. Also, a motorcaravan's rather special wiring system differs from a domestic installation. The mains installation in a house doesn't get bounced about like the ones in vehicles driven on roads!

Even when suitable equipment has been installed, it is necessary to learn how to use it correctly. This chapter therefore gives attention to four specific areas:

- The supply source
- Components fitted in a 230V installation
- Putting a system into operation safely
- Two popular accessories.

Technical Tip

Loss of power

Throughout this book, 'mains electricity' refers to a 230V supply. However, on very busy caravan sites, particularly abroad, a high demand for mains electricity sometimes results in hook-up pillars yielding only 195V or less. That ought not to happen, of course, and it is why refrigerators sometimes run poorly on their mains setting, as described in the previous chapter.

THE SUPPLY SOURCE

Hook-up pillars

A site supply is drawn from a hook-up point, and the voltage in EU member countries has now been standardised. However, supply pillars do not follow a universal pattern and differ both in structure and the sockets they offer.

The accompanying photographs illustrate these dissimilarities, and the one shown at the beginning of the chapter includes sockets for TV aerial cables, too. At the base of this pillar there's also a locked door, and if the user overloads the supply, a trip-switch is activated and the site manager has to be notified. A member of staff will subsequently unlock the enclosure door and reinstate the supply. Other types of hook-up point are shown alongside.

Above: A few hook-up pillars have 'pay-as-you-go' credit card swipe systems, but they're expensive to install and you won't see them very often.

Left: On this site in Wales, overload resetting switches are easily accessible, although it might not be intended for members of the public to operate these controls.

Left: Newly-built sites in France are fitted with the industrial sockets that we use in the UK. This older site still has traditional French sockets, for which British visitors need an adaptor.

Left: This French site offers different levels of supply (in Amps) and the user-fee varies accordingly. The site warden inserts one of the switch blocks shown here to activate a visitor's chosen supply.

Technical Tip

Quality of hook-up cable

The girth of the required three-core flexible cable is conspicuously substantial. For the technically minded, each of the three individual cables within the cover sheath (usually orange) should have a cross-sectional area of 2.5mm² and comply with British Standard/European Norm (BS EN) 60309-2. On the ends of the cable, industrial connections compliant with this BS EN standard include one that has brass pins for coupling to the site pillar, while the other has deeply recessed brass tubes for coupling to your motorcaravan.

Although these connectors are weather-resistant, they are not intended for submersion in the kind of puddles illustrated later on page 223. Summer downpours occasionally take us by surprise, which is why extra lengths of cable should never be linked together.

Note: Thinner cable must NOT be used for hook-up purposes. If you see connecting lead being sold at an unusually low price, it could be sub-standard. It has been alleged that some orange-sheathed products sold in the past have enclosed non-compliant 2.0mm² cable inside.

Mains hook-up cable is sold in 25m lengths with a plug and socket pre-fitted on either end. It has to comply with British Standards/ European Norms.

COMPONENTS FITTED IN A 230V INSTALLATION

Hook-up cable

Visitors using a site, people driving vehicles, and children at play may all come close to your hook-up cable, which is why it has to comply with British Standard/European Norm regulations. When sites first started offering mains supplies, wholly unsuitable cables were often used, especially on popular sites abroad. Twisted wire joined with insulation tape wasn't unusual, yet was clearly hazardous. Fortunately, these dreadful practices are seldom seen nowadays and safety standards are strictly implemented.

Hook-up cable is sold in most motorcaravan accessory shops, complete with a pre-fitted blue plug and socket that adopt an industrial pattern. The 'Technical Tip' panel above adds further points of detail.

Note that the supply pillars on a site should always be situated so that any pitch offering a mains supply is close enough to a hook-up point to be reached by a 25m length of approved cable. For safety reasons, lengths of cable should never be joined together.

Input sockets

There are several variations in the type of socket installed by motorcaravan manufacturers. At one time face-fitting sockets were mounted on the underside of floor panels but that is no longer considered acceptable because grit and water spray pose a threat to electrical connections.

As shown alongside, some sockets are mounted on a side wall, whereas others are located inside a locker. Also be aware that some sockets have a clip that secures the hook-up plug and a détente lever has to be depressed in order to withdraw it.

Above left: This type of motorcaravan inlet has a détente lever that holds the connector firmly in place.

Above: The coupling here forms part of a purpose-made battery box and the socket is well protected.

Below: The socket on this TEC motorhome is fitted in a rear 'garage' and cable entry is via a floor aperture.

(i) Technical Tip

Amps, Volts and Watts

Expressed simply, the word 'voltage' refers to electrical 'pressure', and in Britain a mains supply traditionally provided 240 Volts (V) alternating current (AC). Lower voltages were often used elsewhere in mainland Europe. However, as a result of European standardisation, supplies are now 230V AC albeit with a permitted variation between +10% and -6%.

'Volts' relate to electrical pressure, but this is not a measure of quantity. The amount of power consumed by different electrical appliances is measured in Amperes (Amps or A), and the word 'current' is used in this context. That is important, because the electrical power available from site hook-up pillars is also expressed in Amps and the provision varies from site-to-site. This has a profound implication for the number of mains appliances you can use simultaneously – as explained later.

The term 'Watts' (W) is the rate of electrical consumption and is a combination of both Amps and Volts (Watts = Amps x Volts). It is generally understood that a mains light bulb rated at 60W is brighter than an equivalent 40W bulb, although it is also more costly to run. Electrical appliances are usually rated in Watts as well, and to find out how many Amps they consume, you divide their Wattage by the Volts. So a domestic 2,000W fan heater consumes nearly 9 Amps (2,000W divided by 230V = 8.78A), which is more than the current that can be drawn from some hook-up pillars. *Note: In some parts of rural France, you will occasionally find sites that offer no more than 5 Amps from their hook-up pillars.*

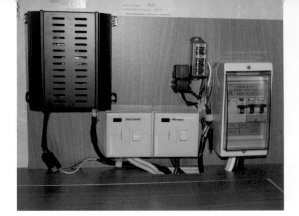

Above: Installing a consumer unit in the bottom of a wardrobe is a curious arrangement but it's not uncommon.

Right: Sargent Electronic Control units are often installed in British motorcaravans and include controls for the 230V system.

Consumer unit

Perhaps the most important component in a motorcaravan's mains system is the 'consumer unit'. It is both a safety item and a master control unit.

As the accompanying illustrations show, consumer units are either 'stand-alone' products that get fitted in obscure places like the back of a wardrobe, or they are housed in a casing that also contains 12V control switches, fuses and a battery charger.

As soon as power arrives at the 230V input socket of a motorcaravan, a short cable (that must not exceed 2m) conveys it to the consumer unit. This unit has two important controls, each of which has a different function. *Note: See page 224 for guidance on how to use these correctly.*

1 A residual current device (RCD) is fitted with an isolating switch. In 40 milliseconds or less, this automatically breaks the flow of current in all live

In this integrated Power Management unit, the 12V fuses are in the right-hand section; the mains consumer unit is on the left.

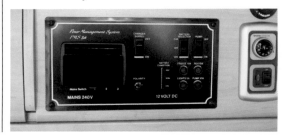

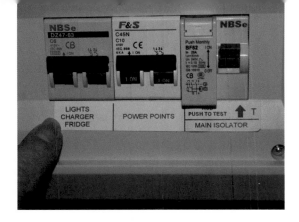

conductors, if, for example, someone accidentally touches a live connection. Essentially, an RCD is a life-saving device, and there's a test button so that an owner can confirm that its trip-switch is working correctly.

2 Miniature Circuit Breakers (MCBs) are a modern version of old-fashioned re-wirable fuses. Usually there are at least two of these. An MCB rated at 5 Amps typically protects a motorcaravan's battery charger, its lighting circuits, a TV socket, and the refrigerator. An MCB rated at 10 (or sometimes 16) Amps protects sockets likely to be used by higher wattage appliances, eg an electric kettle. Their function is to protect a motorcaravan's wiring circuits from damage as a result of overloading.

A consumer unit also has an earth connection, and BS/ENs require that extraneous conducting components such as the chassis, the gas piping, and items such as steel sinks are bonded using 4mm^2 cable and permanently labelled with a warning tag.

Supply sockets

On British-built motorcaravans, sockets fitted internally are 13A, three-pin products, and on imported models these have usually been fitted in place of the original sockets that were intended for users abroad. Sometimes 'switched' sockets are specified, but as a penny-pinching measure the switching facility is sometimes omitted. Of course, when a socket is used to run a low wattage

Above: Miniature circuit breakers (MCBs) protect different types of mains appliances, and these should be marked on the casing.

Below: An earth cable from the consumer unit is bonded to the gas pipes, with a label stating 'SAFETY ELECTRICAL CONNECTION – DO NOT REMOVE'.

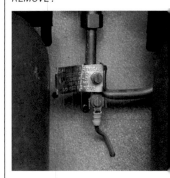

Two 13A three-pin sockets are usefully positioned on this worktop but it's a pity they lack switches.

appliance such as a table lamp, a 3A fuse should be fitted in its plug – just as it should when running table lamps at home.

Typically, the number of sockets installed in motorcaravans is insufficient for many people's needs, especially when we now want to keep batteries charged for our mobile phones, laptop computers and other electronic gizmos. In fact, many owners get further sockets added retrospectively, and if you entrust this to an electrician it is important to check that he or she is aware that a different type of cable is used for motorcaravan wiring.

The reason for this is quite simple. In buildings, sockets are normally connected-up using cable manufactured with a solid copper core. However, this shouldn't be used in motorcaravans because solid copper wire tends to shake loose in a socket's screw-fit connectors. Instead, $1.5mm^2$ flexible mains cable is used because the array of copper strands in the live, neutral and earth wires gives better flexibility and achieves a more secure attachment in screw-fit connectors.

PUTTING A SYSTEM INTO OPERATION SAFELY

Before coupling to a hook-up pillar you should ask at the site reception office how many Amps are available (supply variations were explained earlier). For example, some site hook-up pillars offer no more than 5A, whereas others offer 16A. To find out what this means in practical terms you will have to carry out some simple calculations.

To calculate how many electrical items you can run from a site hook-up, find the wattage of all your appliances.

Calculating which appliances will operate within your limit

To establish what appliances you can and can't run on your pitch, the first task is to check the wattage of each item. Here are some typical ratings.

• Mains light bulb: 40 or 60W
• Small colour LCD-screen TV: 50W
• Built-in battery chargers vary, but 250W is not unusual
• Truma Frostair 1700 Air Conditioner: 650W
• Truma Ultrastore water-heater running on mains: 850W
• Dometic medium capacity RGE 2000 refrigerator: 135W
• Dometic large RGE 400 fridge-freezer: 325W
• Typical domestic pop-up toaster: 1,000W
• Typical fast-boil domestic kettle: 2,500W (often referred to as 2.5kW).

Then you need to decide which appliances will be running at the same time and add up their respective wattages. When carrying out this calculation, do not forget that a fixed battery charger is sometimes operating in the background and some chargers are not fitted with an on/off switch. So include this item in your calculations.

Once the combined wattage of your working appliances is calculated, divide the result by 230 to establish how many Amps you'll draw when they're running. On some small rural sites offering only 5A you will probably have to reduce the number of items that are operating simultaneously, whereas on club sites offering 16A there's much more power available.

Having to undertake these calculations might sound onerous, so for a quick check you can work on the basis that a site offering 5 Amps will allow you to run

A hook-up might offer 16 Amps, but on a full site on a dark winter evening you're asked to draw as little current as possible.

a selection of appliances provided their combined power requirement doesn't exceed 1,000 Watts. In practice that's not particularly generous and it is fortunate that an appliance like a 'three-way' refrigerator will also run on gas. Similarly, you can avoid using an electric kettle by boiling water on the hob. Your supply of electricity can then be reserved for keeping the 12V leisure battery in a good state of charge, for running lights, charging a mobile phone and operating a colour TV – depending on your priorities.

To eliminate the need for carrying out calculations, devices have been designed such as the 'Fuse Control', which displays current consumption and operates its own trip system when the demand is too high. Regrettably, this product is no longer on sale, although some control panels in modern motorcaravans are now able to display how much current 230V appliances are consuming at any one time.

Note: On cold, dark, winter nights a site's supply will be placed under heavy pressure, especially when all the pitches equipped with hook-ups are occupied. Although an individual pitch might be able to receive a 16A maximum supply, a site's mains installation isn't designed so that every pitch occupant can draw 16A at the same time. Consequently, posters are often displayed advising visitors to be sparing in their use of electricity. Disregarding this request may result in a site being plunged into darkness.

Coupling-up procedures

This step-by-step list enables you to couple-up to a mains supply safely and to perform each task in the correct order.

☐ Inspect the hook-up pillar nearest to your pitch. If you find a multitude of dodgy-looking cables around it, or have doubts about its safety, you might decide not to couple up. Fortunately, there are few examples of inappropriate products on most modern sites.

☐ Check that all appliances in your motorcaravan are switched off and move the RCD switch on the consumer unit to its off position.

☐ Unravel your hook-up cable, and don't be tempted to leave the surplus in tightly wound coils. If left tightly coiled, especially on a drum, cable can overheat when high-consumption appliances are in use. In severe cases its insulation might even start to melt. The correct procedure is to place the unravelled hook-up lead in loose coils underneath your motorcaravan and away from any places where puddles might form during a downpour.

☐ Always insert the cable's 'female' connector (that's the one with the recessed brass tubes) into the motorcaravan's inlet first.

☐ Next insert the cable's 'male' coupling into the socket on the hook-up pillar. (This is the one that has three brass pins within its moulded casing.)

☐ On some systems the connection has now been completed at this stage. However, on others, the

Above left: It might look more tidy, but don't put surplus hook-up cable into tight coils.

Above: Don't leave surplus cable tightly wound on a drum – tight coils sometimes generate heat.

Below: When there's spare cable, leave it in loose, open coils under your motorcaravan.

Left: This is dreadful! When laying out cable bear in mind that downpours often leave puddles.

Above: Some hook-up sockets don't provide a supply of current until the plug is twisted clockwise.

Above right: To release a plug from this type of socket, you have to depress the red button first.

This isolation switch forms part of the residual current device which cuts off the power.

Below: Two miniature circuit breakers protect individual circuits and are a modern type of fuse.

Below right: To check an RCD trips-out correctly, pressing a button recreates the effect of someone touching a live wire.

power doesn't start to flow until you rotate the hook-up pillar's coupling clockwise and hear a click. On couplings where this is necessary you'll also see a red button. This is part of a retaining system that locks the plug in place and prevents it from being accidentally pulled out.

Note: There's usually a label that explains this twisting requirement, though in many instances you'll find that the instructions have been obliterated by constant exposure to sunlight.

☐ Check that the cable is laid out in a tidy fashion between the supply point and your caravan – projecting loops might cause passers-by to trip.

☐ Now go to the consumer unit (described earlier) and move the RCD main control switch to its ON position. Check, too, that the MCB switches are also in the ON position.

☐ To confirm your RCD is working correctly, press the small 'check button' to confirm that the emergency trip-switch comes into operation instantaneously. Providing it does, reset the RCD switch to its ON position once again, secure in the knowledge that your all-important safety device is operating correctly.

☐ Use a test device in one of the 13A sockets to confirm that the supply is correctly wired. If this

confirms that the system is sound, you can now run your appliances.

Uncoupling procedures

When leaving your pitch, disconnecting a mains hook-up is principally a reversal of the above sequence. In particular, it involves:

1 Switching off your appliances and the RCD switch on the consumer unit
2 Withdrawing the plug from the site pillar to terminate the supply (on some sites you have to release it by depressing a red button)
3 Withdrawing the plug from the caravan input socket (on some models this involves depressing a release lever).

On damp mornings you'll then want to dry off the hook-up lead before stowing it away.

Reverse polarity

The issue of reverse polarity is something that confronts anyone travelling abroad. Moreover, it is something that many motorcaravanners haven't experienced before, so here is a simple explanation.

In Britain, the switches that control 230V 13A wall sockets, lights and other electrical appliances are connected up to the live cable, which provides an appliance or socket with power. This means that when a switch is moved to its OFF position, electricity isn't able to reach an appliance. Thanks to that feature, as long as an operating switch is turned to its OFF position, we can safely change a light bulb at home without having to switch off the entire incoming supply that serves the house.

Unfortunately, the safety of the British system is completely lost if the live and neutral cables serving an appliance have been connected up the other way round. For example, a switch that interrupts the flow of electricity on the way out of an appliance certainly prevents that appliance from working,

Above left: Socket testers are available from electrical dealers and show when a system is wired correctly.

Above: The display on this socket reveals that its earth connection has become detached.

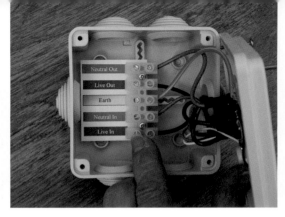

Above: If you find that the polarity of a site supply is reversed, this device fitted inside your 'van rectifies the problem.

Above right: Inside this device, the connecting block is clearly labelled and an electrician could quickly wire it up.

Technical Tip

Double-pole switching

Motorcaravans manufactured since 1994 have a double-pole switched RCD and double-pole MCBs, so the level of protection is improved. It is a pity however, that 13 Amp double-pole switched sockets are not fitted in motorcaravans as well, even though these can be purchased in Britain. Their installation would add the final protection for motorcaravanners stopping on sites where the supply has been wired-up in reverse.

but this reversed connection does mean that an appliance or light socket remains live, even though it isn't operating. This presents a potentially dangerous situation when a light bulb is being replaced.

However, this problem doesn't arise in wiring systems installed in mainland Europe because the usual practice abroad is to fit switches which operate simultaneously on both the live and neutral cables. These are referred to as 'double-pole' switches and ensure that an appliance still doesn't become live even if the live and neutral feeds have been wired-up in reverse. Arguably this is much safer than the British practice of fitting single pole switches.

Recognising that double-pole switching systems are regularly used abroad, it is interesting to note that you will quite often find that a 230V supply at hook-up pillars has been connected-up the other way round. This is referred to as 'reverse polarity', and while it might affect polarity-sensitive appliances, it doesn't pose a safety threat when double-pole switches are universally used. But as stated above, British wiring traditionally uses single-pole switches.

The implications of this is that British tourists travelling abroad need to check mains polarity as soon as they couple-up at a site. If a site pillar has been wired-up the other way round, you sometimes get a reverse polarity light illuminating on your consumer unit to warn of the situation. For example, if you look back to the earlier illustration of a Sargent Control unit on page 218 you'll see a red light marked 'Reverse Polarity' on the top right of the display panel. Alternatively, you can establish polarity status using one of the testers shown on page 225. So what should you do if a site's supply pillar has its live and neutral cables coupled-up in reverse?

- Many motorcaravanners acknowledge the potential danger and decide not to use the site's 230V mains supply.
- Some recognise the fact that polarity-sensitive appliances may receive damage and that their

appliances will remain live, even when switched off, but decide to use the supply in spite of the inherent risks involved.

- A few motorcaravanners have a pole-reversal component like the RYD product fitted retrospectively in their vehicles. (See accompanying illustration.)
- Alternatively, many owners get an electrician to construct their own reversal adaptor using a short length of hook-up cable complete with a plug that is purposely wired the other way round and boldly marked. You can't purchase these, but when one is fitted into a site pillar that was originally wired-up in reverse, your supply is rectified right at the source. You then couple your hook-up cable via this homemade adaptor and duly take power to your van.

Adaptors

Nowadays the blue industrial-style sockets used on site hook-up pillars in Britain are being fitted on new installations in many European countries. In fact, on some sites abroad you occasionally find hook-up pillars offering traditional national sockets alongside the new ones. But this is unusual, and British motorcaravanners touring abroad usually take adaptors to suit the countries they're planning to visit.

In addition, you may want to couple your motorcaravan to a supply at home when it's parked in the drive. For example, it was recommended in the previous chapter that a refrigerator should be pre-cooled before you leave home. To save gas, many owners prefer to do this using mains electricity, so they purchase an adaptor that fits a household 13A socket. In addition they purchase a small portable RCD unit to fit the supply socket so that the orange hook-up cable running from the house to the motorcaravan is protected. An adaptor and a portable RCD are shown alongside.

Above: This adaptor allows your hook-up cable with its blue industrial plug to be coupled to a 13A three-pin socket at home.

Below: To protect a hook-up cable running from house to motorhome, put a portable RCD into the domestic socket.

Adaptors for use on traditional French hook-up sockets. The one with red/white tape is reverse-wired to correct polarity reversal at the hook-up connection.

Right: There is a 13A 230V mains socket on a Honda EU 10i, but there is also this 12V DC socket for battery charging.

Below: The Honda EU 20i is a sought-after high-quality product, so make sure it's protected against theft.

POPULAR ACCESSORIES

Petrol generators

Modern portable leisure generators are smartly designed, compact in size and much quieter than their industrial counterparts. On the other hand, they are surprisingly heavy, as are models designed to be installed permanently in motorcaravans. This means they take up a significant amount of the payload allowance.

Also be aware that the output from a leisure generator is usually far less than what you get from an average hook-up point. To achieve a high output you'd need to purchase an industrial generator and these are both noisier and heavier.

The output from portable leisure machines is typically from 650W (around 2.8A) to 2,000W (around 8.5A). Also be aware that generators often have two settings – 60Hz and 50Hz. To achieve a claimed 650W output you have to select the 60Hz setting, which provides a less stable supply that may not be suitable for operating sensitive appliances.

And there's a warning. As the mains appliances in a motorcaravan are switched on and off, you'll often hear the generator engine altering its note, and on many models this is accompanied by a brief irregularity in the output. A similar change of note can occur when a generator is first started-up and is running on its choke. Only more recent models, such as the Honda EU10i and EU20i generators, feature electronic systems that eliminate power irregularities.

Brief surges upset some types of electrical appliance, especially if you couple a generator to a motorcaravan's mains inlet to run its battery charger. Most built-in battery chargers now feature 'switch mode' circuits, and supply irregularities can easily damage their electronic components. On account of this problem, some generators have a 12V outlet for

battery recharging that will completely bypass the built-in charger in your motorcaravan. You merely have to purchase a suitable coupling lead to fit the generator's 12V outlet and take this directly to the terminals on your battery.

Good-quality generators are costly, and there are often reports of them being stolen, so make sure you are able to secure the product you plan to purchase. There has also been a recent influx of very cheap products imported from the Far East. If you intend to buy one of these, check that it is supported by a reliable after-sales, repair and spare parts service.

Inverters

When an inverter is connected to a 12V battery it will convert its 12V DC input into a 230V AC output. This can be useful, and even low-rated 100W inverters will enable you to run a mains light bulb from a 12V battery.

However, the more you run through an inverter, the sooner your leisure battery will reach a state of total discharge. To give an example of this, if you were to run a 250W inverter it typically draws more than 20 Amps from a leisure battery (250W divided by 12V = 20.8A). In other words, a 60Ah motorcaravan battery running only the inverter would be 'flat' in less than three hours. Moreover, some inverters have low-voltage sensors that shut them down before a battery gets too low.

Of course, a larger 90Ah battery would work longer between recharges; the situation is also less acute when using an appliance that operates intermittently, such as an electric shaver. Similarly, if a compact 230V colour TV is used to watch a half-hour episode of a favourite serial, a pure sine wave inverter might be the answer when using a site that isn't equipped with hook-ups. On the other hand, long evenings of TV watching would soon leave you with a completely discharged battery. That is why mains hook-ups are so popular.

Above left: Portable inverters like this 350W ProPowerQ quasi sine-wave model are available from RoadPro and detailed descriptions are given in the company catalogue.

Above: This inexpensive Mobitronic inverter is rated at 100W and has no trouble running a 230V 60W light bulb.

Technical Tip

Inverter limitations

For sensitive equipment like TV sets, a pure sine wave inverter is recommended, and these cost around three times the price of a modified sine wave inverter. They are complex products and one of the best explanatory guides is a leaflet supplied by Road Pro. Visit www.roadpro. co.uk or call 01327 312233.

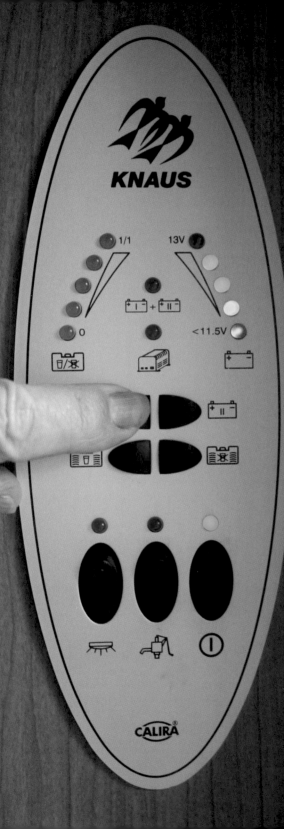

CHAPTER THIRTEEN

THE 12-VOLT
SYSTEM

To ensure that a vehicle's battery is left with enough charge to start the engine, 12V appliances in the living area are run from an additional power source described as a 'leisure battery'. However, some motorcaravans are fitted with a surprising number of 12V accessories, and this means that a leisure battery needs charging quite often.

231

The 12V control panel on this Knaus Sport is clearly marked.

On this TEC motorhome, an ON/OFF master-switch is conspicuously located on the left of the panel.

Many Murvi motorcaravans built between 2003 and 2008 had Kigass electronic panels that had helpful pictogram switches.

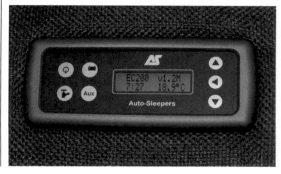

Marked switches and a meter are easy to understand on the Sargent panel fitted in this Swift Sundance.

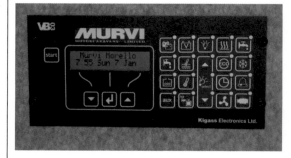

This Sargent panel on an Auto-Sleepers Sandhurst is full of information, but you need to learn how to use the display.

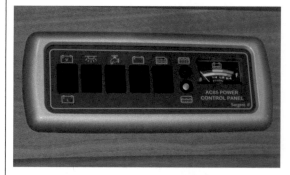

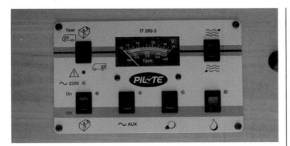

Operating a 12V supply system is usually quite simple. Provided your leisure battery is in a good state of charge, you merely go to a control panel and flick a few switches. Having said that, control panels are often surprisingly different and the accompanying photographs show several examples.

CONTROL PANEL INFORMATION

Fortunately, motorcaravan manufacturers have moved away from the idea of fitting complex panels with a galaxy of light emitting diodes (LEDs) reminiscent of the flight decks on aircraft. Although some owners like exuberant displays, they don't always suit a motorhome lounge.

When comparing panels, look for the following switches and indicator displays:

• **A battery selection switch:** These often employ a rocker-type switch that can be set in one of three positions. In the middle, the 12V supply is switched off, while the two side positions allow you to draw current from either the base vehicle battery or the leisure battery. However, it is best to regard the base vehicle's battery as an emergency supply source for brief use only.
• **Accessory controls:** Usually, a control panel has on/off isolation switches for the water pump, interior lighting, and auxiliary 12V accessories, including a socket that serves a TV.
• **Water and battery charge information:** A panel also employs a device to show you:
  (a) the water levels in fresh and waste water tanks,
  (b) the charge levels in the starter and leisure batteries.
Information is often displayed using a series of indicator lights, as shown in the illustration at the start of this chapter. Alternatively, there may be an analogue meter (with a needle indicator) or a digital display as discussed in the 'Technical Tip' panel.

Above left: There's an analogue meter on this Pilote Reference to show both water levels and battery charge condition.

233

Above: In this Auto-Trail coachbuilt, the 12V control panel provides a digital display that gives voltage readings.

Level condition indication

Water levels in fresh and waste tanks are often shown by a series of LEDs, and these fulfil that objective. However, the indication of a battery's charge condition is less helpfully shown using lights. For instance, the appearance of a red light might warn that a battery is getting low, but how low? The later section on batteries explains that a reading of 12.7V indicates that a leisure battery is fully charged, whereas 12.4V shows that it is 50% discharged. This level of precision is more accurately shown by a needle on a graduated meter scale or by a digital readout.

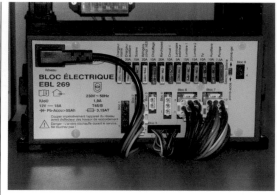

Above: On this 2006 Mobilvetta Top Driver S71, fuses on the driver's seat base are marked with pictograms.

Above right: Fuses in this Pilote are found under the double-bed, and their designations are marked in French.

Above: It's good to see a battery master-switch on a cab-seat base in the 2006 Mobilvetta Kimu.

Below: Fuses on the positive cable coming from the battery in this Auto-Sleepers Sandhurst are enclosed in a tight case.

FUSES AND SHUT-OFF SWITCHES

Sometimes control panels are fitted with fuses to control 12V circuits in the living area. However, in many motorcaravans, fuses for the living area are not housed in the main control panel but are mounted in a separate fuse box. These fuse boxes are sometimes fitted in unexpected places, such as under a bed, or even on the plinth that supports a seat in the cab.

Blade type fuses are preferred nowadays, on account of their accuracy, and their Amp rating is clearly marked on the plastic moulding. Since these are readily available from auto accessory shops, it is wise to purchase some spares to keep in your motorhome.

A few motorcaravans are also fitted with a master 12V shut-off switch that is normally situated near the leisure battery. This is a good safety feature, and if a motorcaravan doesn't have one of these, it is not too involved to have one fitted retrospectively.

There should also be a 12V master fuse fitted on the live cable coming from your leisure battery's positive (+) pillar. Since a battery sometimes emits an explosive gas when it's being charged, and since fuses often spark when they fail, the master fuse should be mounted in a purpose-made airtight case. Alternatively, if the battery is installed in an enclosed box, a standard fuse holder can be used as long as it is safely situated *outside* that box.

LEISURE BATTERIES

The primary function of a leisure battery is to supply power to 12V appliances in your living area. However, its secondary function is to act as a buffer that will absorb and smooth out any power surges that might come from a motorcaravan's built-in battery charger.

Finsbury Library

245 St John Street
EC1V 4NB
Phone: 020 7527 7960
Email: finsbury.library@islington.gov.uk
Fax: 020 7527 7998
www.islington.gov.uk/libraries

Borrowed Items 21/01/2017 14:20
XXXXXXXXXX5023

Item Title	Due Date
30120025295460	11/02/2017
* motorcaravanning handbook : buying, owning, enjoying	
30120025022336	11/02/2017
* France on two wheels : six long bike rides for the bon vivant cyclist	
30120025603580	31/01/2017
Drawing on the right side of the brain	

* Indicates items borrowed today

To explain this further, when you've connected your motorcaravan to a mains supply, its built-in charger will provide 12V DC electricity. This supply not only charges the battery but it also helps to run 12V appliances. However, the output isn't always smooth, and even a small surge can damage a sensitive 12V accessory. Irregularities can be eliminated by directing a charger's output via the leisure battery on its way to the accessories it is serving.

Vehicle and leisure batteries compared

These products are not only constructed differently; a conventional battery (called a 'wet lead-acid' battery) is either made for engine starting or for running motorhome accessories. Moreover, these different versions of wet lead-acid battery do not perform each other's job very well. Inside the casing, a genuine leisure battery is constructed differently from a starter battery, and that is why it usually costs more. So remember: a standard type of leisure battery is not good for starting engines. Conversely, a starter battery is not good for repeatedly running 12V accessories and will soon fail if used in this way. The distinctive tasks they need to perform are as follows:

- **Vehicle batteries** have to produce a lot of power to start an engine. It's a tough challenge, but as soon as the engine fires up, its alternator immediately replenishes the battery so that it doesn't discharge any further. This instant response is important, because if you frequently draw power from a starter battery until it's nearly flat, then apply a recharge, it won't last for long. Quite simply, it hasn't been constructed to work like that.
- **A leisure battery** is made to perform a completely different job. Its task is to supply an array of 12V accessories until its condition is pretty low. Then you recharge the battery and it returns to its full state. In effect, its entire life is spent providing electricity for long spells before it then receives a long recharge. This pattern of use is referred to as 'deep cycling'.
- **Traction batteries** have a similar discharge/recharge pattern of use. However, they are larger and usually run for longer periods between charges because they have to drive vehicles like forklift trucks, mobility chairs and golf buggies. Some motorcaravanners have fitted traction batteries in their vans, but considerable space is needed to accommodate these larger and heavier products.

Inside a vehicle battery are six compartments containing a thin lead mesh 'plate' that holds a paste. This is immersed in acid.

If the electrolyte drops low in a cell, add de-ionised water.

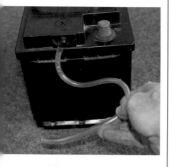

When charged with a high voltage, a 'wet' lead-acid battery gives off a gas that needs to be directed outside via a plastic relief tube.

Battery constructions compared

A leisure battery is installed as standard equipment when you purchase a motorcaravan, and this is most commonly a 'wet' lead-acid type. Inside each of the six separate cells is a fluid (called the electrolyte) consisting of a dilute solution of sulphuric acid. Removable caps on the top enable the electrolyte to be checked and topped-up if necessary.

In a leisure battery, as opposed to a starter battery, layers of glass fibre mat are also included to press against a paste that is held within the lead plates. That is important because it helps a battery cope with the repeated charge/discharge cycles. There is also a ventilator tube, so that if any gas is created during a heavy charge it can be safely dispersed outside.

Considerably more expensive are Absorbent Glass Mat (AGM) batteries, which have individual cells packed tightly with a fibre that absorbs all the acid. The casing is also sealed completely and air is drawn out of it during manufacture. Unlike standard leisure batteries, AGM products can perform both engine starting and leisure supply functions with equal success. However, they are seldom fitted in motorcaravans on account of their considerable price.

Similar in concept is the gel battery, in which the electrolyte is an acidic paste rather than a liquid.

The sealed AGM batteries in the Optima range have a distinctive shape and the cells contain tightly compressed fibre that presses against the lead plates.

Like the AGM product, a gel battery is sealed and nothing leaks if you turn the casing upside-down. Moreover, this type of battery has to be charged at a lower voltage than a 'wet' battery (14.2V max.). This means that it won't produce gas so doesn't need a ventilation tube.

Gel batteries are ideal on jet skis and quad bikes, which occasionally roll over. For safety reasons they're now being fitted on many German motorcaravans as well. Convenience aside, most battery specialists point out that from an electrical viewpoint, a gel battery performs no better than a standard 'wet' lead-acid product.

Note: For technical enthusiasts, the construction and characteristics of batteries is explained in greater detail in Chapter Five of the Motorcaravan Manual *(3rd edition, 2012), also by Haynes.*

Quality accreditation

Purchasing a good-quality leisure battery is often difficult and some products sold for leisure use are essentially car batteries that have been remarketed for caravan and motorhome owners. The labelling is not always helpful, and one product, designated as the 110 model, turned out in the 'small print' to have a 90Ah capacity. There have also been non-regulated products imported from the Far East, with a surprisingly short performance life.

Naturally, it is difficult to evaluate the quality of a true leisure battery since the quality and thickness of its lead plates and the use (or not) of glass fibre in the cells is completely hidden from sight. As a broad distinction, a product that is light in weight is unlikely to perform well because its lead plates won't be very substantial.

It certainly helps that the standards set down in EN50342 provide assurance of quality in construction, materials, and accurately claimed Ah credentials. At present, a number of leisure batteries do not achieve EN50342 accreditation. However, long-established EN50342 compliant brands include the models shown below.

Battery capacity

The external dimensions of batteries differ and this is often related to their capacity, which is rated in Amp hours (Ah). The greater an Ah rating – marked on the side – the longer a leisure battery will provide power before it needs recharging.

Owners who spend most of their time on sites that offer mains hook-up points usually find that a battery with a 65Ah capacity is adequate. At the other extreme there are owners who want as much self-sufficiency as possible and prefer to stop at remote locations or on farm sites, where mains power is seldom supplied. Equally, if you are winter touring, when daylight hours are short and fan-driven heat is essential, a battery offering a higher Ah capacity is much more likely to meet your needs.

In practice, many owners of modern motorhomes find that their 65Ah leisure battery becomes discharged after only a couple of days. If that is the case, a 120Ah battery would be much better, although the greater the Ah capacity, the longer it takes to recharge it from a discharged state. Those travelling a long way to remote locations sometimes use two batteries of this size.

The speed of discharge is also influenced by the number and type of appliances fitted in a motorcaravan. It was explained in Chapter Eleven, for example, that a compressor refrigerator places a heavier demand on a 12V supply than a three-way absorption fridge that can run on gas. Similarly, diesel-driven heaters usually consume more 12V power than gas heaters. Halogen lights are also quite greedy. None of this matters, of course, if you stop only at sites equipped with mains hook-ups.

Inspections have revealed that the all-important fibre-glass mat used in this Banner EN50342 Leisure Battery is missing from many non-accredited products.

Battery location

A praiseworthy feature of the caravanning industry is that touring caravans are built with purpose-made lockers for housing leisure batteries, complete with an external access door. In contrast, motorcaravan manufacturers seldom fit purpose-made lockers and their leisure batteries are installed in all sorts of strange places. The Bailey range introduced in 2012 is one of the exceptions; it is even possible to specify a larger locker than the standard one in order to carry two batteries.

In small van conversions there are fewer locations available, and this necessitates fitting batteries in tight spaces where routine inspections of cells is sometimes difficult.

However, there's hardly a problem finding a good location for a leisure battery in a coachbuilt motorcaravan, yet some pretty odd places get chosen.

For instance, the battery on a 2002 Buccaneer Cruiser 760 is exposed to the elements at the extreme rear of the chassis where it is mounted on an elaborate hinged support structure. This poses considerable problems if a tow bracket is later required. Equally, accessing the leisure battery on a 2003 Bessacarr E745 necessitates removing the driver's seat – designated as a job to be done 'by your Dealer'. But that is not unusual, and the unsatisfactory situation of having to remove a seat to check a battery's cells is found on several other makes and models.

Fortunately, manufacturers are now adopting better practices. In some models, for example, specially made boxes are being mounted in the floor of coachbuilt models complete with a useful access hatch.

Less pleasing is the fact that these neat, under-floor boxes don't usually include any space to add a second battery. Only a few motorcaravan manufacturers, eg Knaus, have had the foresight to provide room for a spare, as is evident in the 2005 Knaus Sun Ti.

Of course, owners who are desperate for more battery power make improvements themselves. In the DIY book *Build Your Own Motorcaravan*, also published by Haynes, the following advice is given:

Good locations for a leisure battery:
- Where cells can be easily checked and topped-up
- In a compartment sealed-off from the living space
- Where there's warmth, to achieve optimum Ah capacity

It's hard to find a space to install leisure batteries in small 'van conversions but this one is pleasingly accessible.

Below: The battery in this Auto-Sleepers Sandhurst is mounted in a box under the floor but there's no space to add a second one.

Below left: The locker in this 2005 Knaus Sun Ti is pleasing because there's space to fit a second battery if required.

Above: Beeny Boxes are bespoke sliding units fitted to motorhomes at the Cornish HQ. They're strong enough to carry batteries.

Above right: If you want to purchase a second battery, purpose-made boxes like this are available from Towsure.

- As near to an alternator as possible to minimise voltage drop through the length of its coupling cable
- Where battery weight suits the overall weight distribution in a vehicle
- In a position where it is easy to fit a ventilation tube.

WARNING: Never fit a battery in a gas cylinder locker (cylinder valves can leak; battery terminals can spark; explosions can happen).

Incidentally, if you do need to carry a spare battery on special expeditions (either wired-up or ready to swap over), accessory specialists such as Towsure sell portable battery boxes. Beeny Boxes (mentioned in Chapter Nine) can also be installed in the sideskirts of most coachbuilt models, and these are strong enough to carry a battery or two.

Ventilation
The panel below explains why a lead-acid 'wet' battery sometimes emits an explosive gas when it is

---

 Technical Tip

Emission of explosive gas

When a battery is charged at a high rate it creates an explosive gas (a mixture of hydrogen and oxygen) that often lingers around the cells, even after charging has ceased. If you connect-up a portable charger to your battery, make certain that no-one nearby is smoking when the charger is disconnected from the terminals. Also, switch the charger off at its 230V supply socket before unclipping the connections on the battery pillars.

If a battery does explode, the casing often disintegrates and acid can get splashed in your face. Explosions also occur if a flame is nearby, such as a pilot light on a gas appliance.

The gas normally only forms when a charging voltage exceeds 14.4V, but it sometimes gets emitted at lower voltages if one of the battery cells is faulty. For this reason, always ensure there are no naked flames or sources of sparks near a battery when it is undergoing a charge or its cells are being checked.

Also note that this gas is lighter than air – so if a battery is fitted in a sealed compartment, there must be a high-level outlet to allow escaping gas to discharge and disperse outdoors. Alternatively, if a leak-proof tube and connecting elbow can be coupled to a battery, this may be routed down through the floor, since gas will be forced downwards under pressure.

being charged. That is why a ventilation facility in the form of a plastic relief tube is important, though it is not needed on AGM or gel 'sealed' batteries for reasons outlined above. Of course, like any other battery, both gel and wet lead-acid batteries have to be firmly secured using clamps or straps. Damage would undoubtedly result if they were to break free during a journey.

The actual Ah performance of a battery depends on its rate of discharge and the label on this EN50342 product reflects this by quoting three Ah capacities.

241

Life between charges

Battery manufacturers emphasise that you should never run a leisure battery until it is absolutely flat. In addition, a battery is claimed to last for many more years if you start recharging it as soon as its charge level drops to 50% ie 12.4V or less. Whether the majority of owners heed this advice or not is anyone's guess.

The output period is also determined by a battery's Amp hour (Ah) rating and this is usually quoted by manufacturers for batteries operating in an ambient temperature of 25°C (77°F). The accompanying panel indicates how lower temperatures significantly reduce the Ah performance shown on a battery's label.

Lastly, if you use a battery to run a lot of appliances simultaneously, this obviously hastens the time when a recharge is needed. But it is worse than that, because a high demand in a short space of time also reduces an Ah rating more than a simple calculation might suggest. The effect of a rapid discharge rate undoubtedly leads to surprises, and this is why batteries built to EN50342 standards have two or three Ah ratings marked on the label. Where a single Ah rating is given on a leisure battery, this refers to a normal 20-hour rate of discharge. On the label shown in the accompanying photograph, this EN50342 battery achieves 180Ah at the 20-hour rate, whereas if it is supplying considerably more appliances it would drop to a reduced 135Ah capacity.

Checking battery condition

When you've been charging a battery – including charging via the alternator while you've been driving –

(i) Technical Tip

Temperature effect on a battery's output

A stated Ah capacity presumes an ambient temperature of 25°C (77°F); one well respected battery manufacturer states that for every drop of 1°C there's a 1% reduction in capacity. So at 0°C, ie freezing point, the nominal Ah capacity is reduced by 25%. This means that a battery nominally rated at 60Ah effectively becomes a 45Ah battery at 0°C. Bearing this in mind, a battery mounted externally performs less well in cold conditions than an identical one that is fitted indoors in a warm locker.

Though called a '12V battery', a reading of 12.7V is required to signify that a leisure battery is fully charged.

a misleadingly high voltage figure will be shown when charging first ceases. To get an accurate indication of charge condition, a battery should be left to settle for at least four hours before a voltage reading is taken. An even truer picture is obtained if you wait 12–24 hours. This is because the condition of any battery appears impressively good when charging is first terminated. Some hours later, however, the voltage reading for an older battery has usually fallen, whereas a newer battery is able to hold its charge much longer.

Keep this in mind when using your motorcaravan's control panel, and if you want more information than is provided by a panel warning light system, purchase a good multi-meter, which is inexpensive – even digital models are now available for less than £20.

The voltage reading you've obtained should be interpreted as follows:

Voltmeter reading	Approx charge state
12.7V or over	100%
12.5V	75%
12.4V	50%
12.2V	25%
12V or under	Discharged

Notes
1. Some electrical specialists assert that these percentage indications should be regarded only as an approximate guide.
2. Remember to take the reading four hours or more after charging has been terminated.
3. Make sure 12V appliances are switched off when the reading is taken. For complete accuracy this should include a clock, although in practice this item doesn't make a great deal of difference.

Looking after a leisure battery
When new, a leisure battery is unlikely to need a lot of attention although it should never be regarded as a 'fit and forget' accessory. For example, the electrolyte in a wet lead-acid battery should be

The individual cells on a lead-acid battery should be checked periodically and topped up using deionised water.

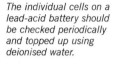

checked periodically by removing the cell caps. The dilute sulphuric acid should just cover the lead plates. If its level has dropped, top it up using deionised water, which is sold at auto accessory stores. *Do not smoke and do not use a naked flame to see inside the cells.*

Other points to remember:

- If a leisure battery is left in a totally discharged state for a day or more it will often be irreparably damaged. Many leisure batteries are ruined this way.
- If your motorcaravan is not in use and you want to transfer a battery to a bench for charging, always disconnect the negative terminal first; and when reinstalling a battery, connect the negative terminal last.
- To prevent a battery's terminals getting covered with a white powdery substance, lightly smear them with petroleum jelly ('Vaseline').

CHARGING A LEISURE BATTERY

Alternator charging

When driving a motorcaravan, the charge coming from the base vehicle's alternator will be fed into its starter battery. However, some of the charge can also be fed into the leisure battery. To achieve this, motorcaravan manufacturers fit an electrically operated switch called a 'relay', which is activated as soon as the engine is running. This arrangement links the two batteries and they remain in this coupled state until the engine is switched off. At that point their independence is re-established – which is especially important when starting an engine because you don't want to get the leisure battery involved.

An alternator can undoubtedly play a useful part in charging a leisure battery but you may have to drive for several hours if it has become heavily discharged. Equally, if a leisure battery is fitted at the rear of a vehicle – as it sometimes is – the cable linking it to the alternator is so long that there is likely to be a drop in voltage before it reaches the battery. To minimise voltage loss, a thicker cable reduces the 'fall-off', although it obviously makes sense to install a leisure battery as close to the alternator as is reasonably possible.

Several other factors play a part too. For instance, some motorcaravan manufacturers don't purchase base vehicles that are fitted with an 'optional extra'

(i) Technical Tip

System shutdown

When a motorcaravan is being driven, an automatic switch called a relay enables a leisure battery to receive a charge from the vehicle's alternator. However, a second relay automatically cuts off the 12V supply to all other services in the living area apart from a three-way refrigerator. If its 12V operating mode has been selected, an absorption refrigerator continues to operate, whereas all other 12V items, like interior lights, are disabled.

This system shutdown feature was introduced in the late 1990s when more and more electronic systems were being fitted in motor vehicles. Essentially it is a precautionary measure concerned with 'electromagnetic compatibility' – described in more detail in Chapter Five of the *Motorcaravan Manual* (3rd edition, 2012). Suffice it to say, recent engine management systems, braking systems and stability programmes are electronically controlled, and the disabling of 12V supplies in a motorcaravan's living quarters is intended to minimise the likelihood of electrical activity upsetting these control systems.

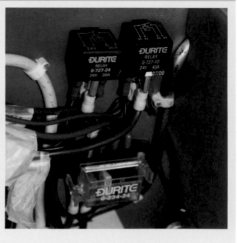

The black cubes in the upper part of this illustration are 'relays', which is the name for electrically-operated switches.

high output alternator. In addition, if you park your motorhome for an extended period on a pitch that isn't served by a 230V hook-up and you then use a support car, scooter or bicycle for all local trips, no charge is drawn from the alternator either. To recharge a battery in these circumstances it is useful to own a portable generator like the products mentioned in the previous chapter.

Fixed battery charger

Chargers fitted permanently in motorcaravans as standard items start to operate when the vehicle is coupled to a mains supply. Some have an on/off switch but many start operating automatically as soon as a 230V supply is connected.

Not only does the output from one of these devices charge the leisure battery: it provides a 12V supply to run domestic appliances as well. These two functions operate simultaneously, and that is why built-in chargers are designed not to yield more than 13.8V. The restriction also means a battery won't start 'gassing', and it falls well within the 14.2V limit for charging gel batteries. Of course, it will

Left: When a battery's removed from a motorhome you can charge it with an initial boost of 15V, which is good for its plates.

Left: The CTEK Multi XS 7000 charger can be switched to give higher voltage charge regimes as well as a 13.6V supply.

make your 12V lights glow more brightly, but as long as the charge voltage remains within 13.8V, it is unlikely to cause them to fail.

Portable stepped chargers
Notwithstanding the earlier point about a built-in charger's output being limited to 13.8V, wet lead-acid batteries respond better when recharged with an initial input around 15.0V or more. After this initial 'boost charge', the battery then benefits from a gradually reducing charge level. This regime causes an emission of gas and a battery's cells then need topping-up more often with de-ionised water. However, 'gassing' is known to extend the working life of a battery.

In response to this, portable chargers are now available which offer 'stepped charging' regimes. These sophisticated products have electronic circuits that monitor a battery's progress while it is being revived, and which then make continual reactive changes to the output level. For example, a charging regime might start with a boost voltage which then tapers off as the battery responds.

The batteries in classic cars, motorcycles and motorcaravans that remain unused for long periods are often kept in good condition with the help of a permanently connected, electronically controlled trickle charger.

Some technically-minded owners even disconnect their leisure battery from the 12V circuits in their motorhome and transfer it to a bench. Using portable chargers from manufacturers like CTEK, they can then provide the charge regime that suits their battery best. More information on technical issues like this are dealt with in the *Motorcaravan Manual* (3rd edition, 2012).

Trickle chargers

These are designed to keep a battery that is already in a good charge condition fully maintained by providing an occasional input of power. Trickle chargers are used by many owners of vehicles that are parked for extended spells, such as classic cars, motorcycles in winter – and motorcaravans. Most can be left permanently connected to both the mains supply and the battery because their electronic circuits monitor voltage and activate charging only when it's needed.

Solar and wind generators

Neither of these products is cheap and purchasers don't necessarily fit them with the hope of saving money. When conditions are right, however, both are able to provide a battery with a trickle charge, thereby helping to extend its output before it needs a renovating recharge.

Wind-generators are often fitted on boats and work best in exposed places where prevailing winds are strong. They are less frequently used by motorcaravanners.

Solar panels only need light but they undoubtedly work best in bright sun, clear skies and during a summer's long hours of daylight.

To give an example of performance, a 70W Solar Kit that typically costs around £480 (plus fitting charges) can yield around 3 Amps in a sunny position on a clear day. The output might be higher at midday but would be considerably less when it is raining and dull. In one hour of continuous, favourable light, your battery might, at best, receive

a sustained 3 Amps, but that represents only a small fraction of the capacity of a 65Ah battery.

So the results are not dramatic, but during an eight-week test conducted in the Midlands between mid-July and mid-September 2007, a roof-mounted 70W panel produced a logged total of 540 Amps. Inevitably, the yield would be considerably less in the shorter daylights hours of winter, but solar panels do make a useful contribution.

Sharing excess power

Since the starter and leisure batteries in a motorcaravan are normally kept separate, built-in chargers are usually only wired to recharge the leisure battery. Only a few motorcaravans include a switching facility to recharge a starter battery instead. However, there's another strategy that many owners adopt.

Inexpensive 'power-sharing' products, such as the Battery Master Balancer from Van Bitz or the EuroE848 charger, are easy to fit and they monitor voltage in both batteries. When the voltage in a leisure battery becomes significantly higher than the voltage in the engine battery, a controlled transfer of current automatically takes place. This also occurs when you are using a mains hook-up or if a solar panel is permanently feeding the leisure battery.

If there isn't any charging taking place, the vehicle battery on a parked motorcaravan still has to run items like its clock and an electronic alarm. A power-sharing product then ensures that the discharge won't be drawn from the starter battery alone. Arguably, it is a pity that these products are rarely fitted as standard.

Consumption issues

It was stated earlier that some owners are surprised at how quickly their leisure battery needs recharging. It was also suggested that some leisure batteries are not as good as they ought to be, and some are built exactly the same as starter batteries. In contrast, products complying with EU 50342 specifications do perform well but are not the cheapest by far.

The GB-SOL Flexible 35W solar panel is easily bonded to the roof of a campervan and weighs only 2kg.

The Euro E848 device monitors voltage in both batteries and creates a transfer of current if the starter battery drops a lot lower than the leisure one.

Traditional car-type tungsten filament bulbs are not economic to run.

Though more economical, fluorescent lights aren't to everyone's taste.

Halogen fittings give pleasant light but get hot and consume a lot of power.

One halogen bulb consumes roughly eight times the power of an LED cluster like this.

Without doubt, a good source of power is important. However, there is also the matter of consumption demands and most modern motorcaravans are fitted with a variety of accessories, some of which are surprisingly power-hungry.

Perhaps the most significant change in recent times has concerned the light fittings used in motorcaravans. When car-type bulbs were first used, it was well known that tungsten filament lighting placed significant demands on a 12V supply. In contrast, when fluorescent lights were introduced, these were immediately recognised as being far more economical to run. However, the type of light produced wasn't to everyone's taste, and halogen light fittings then became fashionable instead.

There is no doubt that a ceiling liberally equipped with halogen units produces a bright interior, but it comes at a cost. Not only do halogen bulbs require a surprising amount of current, they also get remarkably hot and some have even caused damage. Many recent motorcaravans have been equipped with halogen fittings, but practices are once again changing.

A decade or so ago, light emitting diodes (LEDs) were introduced for 12V leisure applications, but these were costly and mainly fitted in boats. Then prices dropped dramatically – but some motorcaravanners didn't like the cold, clinical light produced by most LED fittings. Then different tints appeared, including the introduction of 'warm white' units and that met most people's taste.

Three things have since contributed to the popularity of LED fittings:

1 Economy: Eight LED ceiling-lights require roughly the same amount of current as one halogen bulb with a comparable output.
2 LED lights do not get hot, which is a useful safety feature.
3 A good quality LED fitting is better able to cope with power irregularities compared with a halogen unit.

These points have now led to the increasing use of LED light assemblies in motorcaravans and some owners have replaced their original halogen fittings with LED products instead. Specialist suppliers like CAK stock a huge variety of lamps including LED products that are made to fit into holders that hitherto housed halogen and tungsten bulbs. In fact at the time of writing, LED products in motorcaravans are notably well established, whereas similar products are slow to appear in our homes.

CHAPTER **FOURTEEN**

UNDERSTANDING **GAS**

The most popular fuel used in motorcaravans for cooking and heating is liquefied petroleum gas – or LPG, as it is usually called. However, LPG is also highly flammable, and it is crucially important that all users treat it with care, respect and understanding.

In winter conditions, propane performs better than butane.

Technical Tip

Installed gas tanks

Although some motorcaravans are fitted with a supply tank to provide gas for domestic needs, these products mustn't be confused with tanks installed to run LPG-adapted engines. In the automotive context, gas has to be injected in its liquefied state into an engine compartment and changed to vapour prior to injection into the engine. That cannot be achieved using a domestic supply tank and more information about these installations is given later in this chapter.

252

Some motorcaravanners have a refillable gas tank fitted to run their domestic appliances.

Liquefied petroleum gas is readily available in purpose-made cylinders, although some motorcaravanners prefer to have a fixed tank installed to supply their domestic needs. It is also used as an alternative fuel for vehicle propulsion, and in both contexts matters of safety must be fully understood and always observed.

Useful Tip

Terminology

Terms that are ambiguous or inaccurate should be avoided when dealing with LPG. For example:

1. Some people incorrectly refer to LPG as 'liquid' petroleum gas, and that is a contradiction of terms: gas engineers correctly refer to it as 'liquefied petroleum gas'.
2. You will often hear motorcaravanners state that they need a replacement gas 'bottle', which might confuse a new owner – beer is sold in bottles: LPG is sold in 'cylinders'.
Ambiguities can lead to misunderstandings and for the sake of clarity, terms preferred by gas specialists will be used throughout this chapter.

CHARACTERISTICS OF LPG

A rudimentary understanding of LPG's characteristics helps to reinforce why precautionary measures must never be treated lightly. Note the following points:

- In its natural state, LPG is not poisonous
- LPG does not have a smell, which means that leaks might not be noticed
- To warn of leaks, distributors add what is called a 'stenching agent'
- LPG is denser than air, and if a leak occurs the gas sinks to the lowest point
- The gas escape outlets in a motorcaravan are called 'drop-out holes' and must never be covered up
- Motorcaravanners use two types of LPG – butane and propane
- When an appropriate regulator is fitted, the gas appliances installed in British motorcaravans will run on either butane or propane
- Since LPG is highly flammable, it must be stored in accordance with the LP Gas Association's Code of Practice.

(i) Safety Tip

Leak detectors

As a safety precaution many owners have a leak detector fitted and several types are available. Devices which react to smell run on a 12V supply and emit a loud noise if a leak is detected. Carbon monoxide detectors work in a similar way, and these are often fitted in order to warn if there's a dangerous emission from a faulty gas appliance.

It is useful having safety devices installed but this shouldn't be regarded as a substitute for periodic servicing checks conducted by a qualified gas engineer.

Note: All National Caravan Council (NCC) Certificated motorcaravans built from 1 September 2011 are obliged to be equipped with a carbon monoxide alarm as a standard item of equipment.

The 12V alarm from Van Bitz reacts to many kinds of escaping gas.

This carbon monoxide alarm, manufactured by Honeywell, is sold in the UK by Calor Gas Ltd.

STORAGE

At point of sale

Retailers and site operators supplying gas have to comply with strict rules when storing and handling LPG cylinders. For example, on rare occasions cylinder valves have become faulty and a leakage occurs. Noting the earlier point that this gas is denser than air and sinks to the lowest point, storage facilities must allow leaking gas to disperse safely. That is why mesh cages are often used and these are situated outdoors, well away from any potential source of ignition.

Strict regulations apply to the storage facilities used by the suppliers of gas cylinders.

Although situated inside this van conversion, the gas locker has low escape holes and a fully sealed door.

A gas locker must have adequate escape outlets and these should not get covered up.

In your motorcaravan

Manufacturers have to comply with strict specifications, and gas cylinder lockers must have low-level drop-out holes. In fact some of the recent Auto-Sleepers coachbuilt models have a base fabricated in steel mesh that affords a particularly good means of gas escape.

A storage locker should also offer a minimum of 30 minutes' fire resistance. However, in view of a motorcaravan's structure, some manufacturers regard compliance with this expectation as unreasonably hard to achieve.

External access is required too, although small van conversions sometimes have an interior door that is totally sealed from the living area.

Either way, a gas cylinder locker must never be used to accommodate a battery, contain fuses, include a light or be used as a route for electrical cabling unless it is entirely sealed in a conduit. Anything that could create a spark is considered dangerous,

---

(i) Technical Tip

DON'T DO THIS! Even when collecting a replacement cylinder, never lay it on its side – valves can sometimes leak.

Always keep cylinders in their upright position

It is not unknown for valves on cylinders to develop a small leak. For instance, if grit or grass gets caught in the spring-loaded steel ball that forms the seal on a Campingaz cylinder, the obstruction may lead to gas seepage. Sometimes you might hear a faint 'hiss'.

This problem is usually solved by taking a Campingaz cylinder outdoors, checking that there are no flames nearby and no-one smoking, before depressing the ball very briefly with a small screwdriver. A sharp blast of escaping gas occurs instantaneously and usually dislodges the obstruction, whereupon the steel ball then reseats itself correctly.

The valves on other types of cylinders sometime develop leaks too, and that is why it is extremely dangerous to lay a cylinder on its side. A tiny drop of liquefied butane trickling from a cylinder that isn't upright will multiply in volume around 230 times as it converts into gas. The increase in volume of propane is approximately 274 times greater. The potential hazard of this is abundantly clear.

although a few models now have recessed, sealed and covered niches containing light emitting diodes (LEDs) for illumination.

Also required is a means of securing cylinders effectively in an upright position, bearing in mind that bumpy roads pose a challenge to any fixing system.

At home

Some owners remove their cylinders during a long lay-up period, but it is usually unsafe to store them in a house. In fact, the worst place is in a cellar, since this is normally devoid of low-level ventilation outlets. In the event of a cylinder valve developing a leak, the denser-than-air gas then has nowhere to escape, so accumulates around the lowest parts of the floor.

A garage is often unsafe too, especially if it's used for parking a car, charging a battery or storing a petrol can. It's far safer to store a gas cylinder outdoors in a weather-protected, well-ventilated and secure location.

TYPES OF LPG

Two distinct types of LPG are used by motorcaravanners in Britain. One is called butane, the other is propane, and their respective characteristics need to be recognised.

Butane

Key points about butane:
- It is widely sold throughout Europe and there are many suppliers, most of whom use different sizes of cylinder and dissimilar connecting systems.
- It has a higher calorific value than propane and since it burns at a slightly slower rate it is a more efficient heat producer.
- It presents problems in extremely cold conditions because it doesn't change from its liquefied state into a gas. This occurs when temperatures fall to -2°C (around 29°F) at atmospheric pressure. Accordingly, butane is not the preferred gas for winter use or for visits to cold regions.

Butane has a higher calorific value than propane, burns at a slightly slower rate, and is a more efficient heat producer.

(i) Technical Tip

Temperature issues

When temperatures fall, the rate at which liquefied butane changes to gas decreases progressively. So, even when the temperature in a gas cylinder locker is a little above freezing point, a significant reduction in the output of gas might become apparent if you're cooking a meal and trying to run a space heater and water heater at the same time. On noting a lower-than-normal flame on the hob, many motorcaravanners wrongly presume that the cylinder is nearly empty and prepare to fit a replacement.

Propane is the preferred winter fuel because it vaporises in temperatures as low as minus 45°C.

• It is heavier than propane. Taking the smallest cylinder sold by Calor Gas as an example, the butane version holds 4.5kg (10lb) of liquefied gas, whereas an identically-sized cylinder of propane holds 3.9kg (8.6lb).

In Britain, butane is usually sold in BLUE cylinders but you cannot rely on that colour designation.

Propane
Key points about propane:
• This is the preferred winter fuel because it changes from a liquefied state into a gas in temperatures as low as -45°C.
• Outside the UK it is harder to find propane in portable cylinders for leisure activities, although 11kg and 13kg cylinders are available in France, Italy and Spain.
• Some processing companies add a small amount of propane to their butane cylinders in order to improve cold weather performance.
• Propane is lighter than butane in its liquefied state. If you check two cylinders of identical size, you'll see from markings on the side that the recorded weight of propane is less than the recorded weight of butane.
• It has a vapour pressure approximately four times that of butane. This has implications when regulators are coupled-up and further details appear in the accompanying Technical Tip panel and later in the chapter, on pages 266–270.

In Britain, propane cylinders supplied by Calor Gas are red but other suppliers employ different colour designations.

Which gas should you use?
Taking note of the differences between butane and propane, motorcaravanners who only use their vehicles during warmer times of the year often prefer butane. In contrast, year-round owners who tour

Technical Tip

Pressure regulation

Since 1st September, 2003, dual gas butane/propane 30mbar regulators have been fitted in UK motorcaravans. Before these new regulators were developed, gas-specific 28mbar butane or 37mbar propane regulators had to be used in accordance with your preferred choice of cylinder. Accordingly when changing from one gas to the other, owners of motorcaravans built prior to 1 September 2003 have to change the regulator, too. More detailed information on regulators is given later in this chapter, on page 268.

mostly in Britain generally use propane. However, propane in portable cylinders is less easy to purchase in some parts of mainland Europe.

In this country, Calor is probably the largest supplier of gas cylinders to UK caravan and motorhome owners and you get a wide choice of cylinder sizes and both types of gas. Depending on the national availability of different cylinders, many Calor Gas dealers often allow you to trade-in an empty butane cylinder for a full propane one, and vice versa. It doesn't work like this, however, in many parts of mainland Europe.

In addition, you can't purchase Calor Gas cylinders or Calor-approved refills abroad. The most common product sold in Europe is Campingaz, which is butane. However, it is generally believed that Campingaz cylinders contain a small quantity of propane mixed with the butane, thereby making the product reasonably satisfactory if you visit a cold place like the Alps in winter.

If you don't want to purchase a purpose-made regulator or coupling hose to fit the unique Campingaz connection, you can buy an adaptor instead. These fit directly on to a Campingaz cylinder and have a turn-tap on the top. Their outlet connector adopts a screw thread pattern that accepts the screw-nut coupling used on regulators and factory-made hoses that couple-up with Calor's 4.5kg butane cylinders.

This coupling-up versatility is fine, but there's still the disadvantage that the largest Campingaz cylinder (called a Type 907) only holds 2.72kg (6lb) of butane. This is a very modest amount compared with Calor cylinders' capacities, as the table on page 259 shows. Many British tourists consequently take a full Calor cylinder abroad (even though it can't be replaced on the Continent when empty) and a Campingaz 907 cylinder too. Unfortunately, that doesn't solve all the problems. Whereas Campingaz is quite widely available, it is unobtainable in some European countries.

Above left: A Campingaz 907 cylinder has a coupling that's unique. The regulator here is made to fit all Campingaz cylinders.

257

Above: Adaptors for Campingaz cylinders offer a threaded outlet to match the regulators and factory-manufactured coupling hoses used on Calor Gas 4.5kg butane cylinders.

ⓘ **Useful Tip**

Campingaz cylinders are seldom available in Finland, Norway and Sweden. If you visit these countries for longer than the normal output life of your Calor cylinders, you may have to switch to the countries' own products. This would entail purchasing the appropriate regulators and couplings – though Gaslow can supply these before you leave the UK.

To find the list of countries where Campingaz, is available, contact Coleman UK Inc (see Campingaz in Appendix, page 319).

Obtaining your preferred type of gas cylinder

If you decide to use Campingaz, you start by purchasing a cylinder full of gas. When it is empty, you exchange it for another and merely pay the price for the LPG. The charges are reasonable and in Spain the costs are remarkably low – it appears that the product is government-subsidised. In the case of Campingaz, you own the cylinder.

The situation is different if you want to use Calor Gas in your motorcaravan. To obtain a cylinder of gas you have to enter into a cylinder-hire arrangement, which involves completing a form and leaving a deposit. Thus when you exchange an empty cylinder for a full one, you only pay for the LPG. Strictly speaking you never have ownership of the cylinder, even if you use a motorcaravan for years and years. In fact, if you cease motorcaravanning, you can get this deposit back by taking your Calor cylinders to an approved specialist – as long as you can produce the original hire contract papers!

Above: BP Gas Light cylinders are large in diameter, light, and you can see the gas level through their semi-transparent sides.

Below: The hope of finding universal couplings is a long way off but the BP Gas Light clip-on adaptors are easy to connect.

The supply difficulties that face motorcaravanners visiting different countries prompted revisions to the European Norms applicable to gas systems, which many manufacturers implemented in 2003. The acute urgency to achieve greater standardisation thus led to the introduction of new gas regulators and cylinder coupling methods. The revised components are now being fitted on recent motorcaravans and are described later on pages 269–270.

Finally, the dissimilar sizes of cylinders and the many types of motorcaravan being sold make it difficult to give definitive guidance on cylinders that would fit your own motorcaravan's gas locker. So before purchasing a cylinder, check this with the supplier; some lockers are too small to accommodate several products included in the tables on pages 258–261.

Cylinders often used by motorcaravanners

The weights quoted here relate to the gas content and don't include the weight of an empty cylinder (known as its 'tare weight').

The dimensions of cylinders vary a great deal: so do the sizes of gas lockers. Check with your dealer regarding the suitability of cylinders for your gas locker before making a purchase.

BP Gas Light

5kg (11.02lb) propane
10kg (22.04lb) propane

☐ BP Gas Light cylinders are duo-coloured green and white.

Note – Introduced in 2006 by BP in partnership with Truma UK, these light, composite cylinders are around half the weight of similar steel cylinders. Their semi-transparent material lets you check the gas level inside and the 27mm clip-on valve is easy to connect. Cylinders are supplied under a hire arrangement, although a 50% reimbursement fee is only available on returned cylinders that are less than six years old. The success of this new venture will depend on whether a large chain of Gas Light suppliers becomes established.

Calor

3.9kg (8.6lb) propane 4.5kg (10lb) butane	Same external size of cylinder
5kg (11.02lb) propane	Patio Gas with level indicator
6kg (13.2lb) propane	Calor Lite version
6kg (13.2lb) propane 7kg (15.4lb) butane	Same external size of standard steel cylinder
13kg (28.7lb) propane	Patio Gas with level indicator
13kg (28.7lb) propane 15kg (33lb) butane	Same external size of cylinder

☐ The Calor 19kg (41.9lb) propane cylinder is too large for motorcaravan lockers.
☐ Calor Lite propane cylinders are made of lightweight recyclable steel and the plastic collars offer comfortable lifting points. These are among Calor's newer products and their full weight of gas and cylinder amounts to 10.52kg. This is 3.36kg (7.4lb) lighter than the standard steel product that

Left: Propane 'Patio Gas', marketed by Calor in distinctive cylinders, is intended for use at home as well as in motorcaravans.

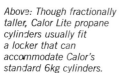

Above: Though fractionally taller, Calor Lite propane cylinders usually fit a locker that can accommodate Calor's standard 6kg cylinders.

Above right: The weight of an empty Calor Gas cylinder is marked on its metal collar in pounds and ounces.

holds an equivalent amount of gas. The Calor Lite is also fitted with a Gas Trac level indicator as shown on page 262.

☐ Calor Gas butane cylinders are blue; Calor Gas propane cylinders are red; Calor Patio Gas propane cylinders are green with red handles.

Notes

The weight of an empty Calor cylinder is marked on a silvered aluminium disc attached to the top near the connector. Perversely, it expresses the tare weight in pounds and ounces.

Some of the smallest micro van conversions cannot accommodate any of Calor's products. Similarly, you'll find that only the larger coachbuilt motorcaravans have room in their gas lockers to accommodate a pair of 13kg propane or 15kg butane Calor cylinders. Calor Patio Gas cylinders are also large in diameter and are often sold at Garden Centres. In spite of their useful level-gauge indicator, they haven't yet achieved popularity among motorcaravan users.

Campingaz

0.45kg (1lb) butane
1.81kg (4lb) butane
2.72kg (6lb) butane

Campingaz cylinders are blue.

The largest and smallest Campingaz cylinders: only the 907 on the left holds sufficient gas (2.72kg) for motorhome use.

Note – Only the Type 907 Campingaz 2.72kg butane cylinder is a practical proposition for the motorcaravanner. The two smaller cylinders are really intended for camping use only. However, owners of micro campervans that only have room for one Type 907 cylinder often take a 0.45kg cylinder to use as an emergency back-up to run the hob.

Gaslow refillable cylinders

6kg (13.2lb) propane 11kg (24.22lb) propane	Normally fillable at autogas stations

Note – Designed for permanent installation in a gas locker, these cylinders have to be connected to an autogas filling point mounted on the side of a motorcaravan. This coupling-up is achieved by installing Gaslow's flexible stainless steel pipe.

The cylinders have European Pi approved filler valves that automatically shut off when the container is 80% full. Coupling-up a cylinder to the motorcaravan supply pipework is via the same type of screw connection used on 4.5kg Calor butane cylinders. The cost of gas supplied at autogas stations is significantly cheaper, and once Gaslow's components are purchased, both the cylinders and the stainless steel connecting pipe carry a 15-year warranty.

Above: A cylinder in a Gaslow system is coupled to an autogas filler permanently mounted on the motorcaravan.

Above left: The link between a Gaslow refillable cylinder and the autogas filler is made using a fixed, flexible, stainless steel pipe.

Above: Gaslow offers refillable cylinders in two sizes; these are fixed in a locker and have to be decommissioned and exchanged after 15 years.

(i) Safety Tip

Safety precautions when fitting and removing gas cylinders

When changing a cylinder, make sure there is nothing nearby that could ignite escaping gas. Check that no-one is smoking and ensure that the area is nowhere near electric fan heaters, gas heaters, pilot lights on a gas appliance, a fridge running on gas, an outside barbecue, a gas-operated portable awning lamp and so on. Equally, check there is no battery nearby because sparks can sometimes occur at a terminal.

Turn off the cylinder you want to change. If you have an approved twin-cylinder coupling device with a manual or automatic changeover valve, it is permissible to let the active supplying cylinder remain connected and switched on. But always turn off the cylinder you want to change – it may still contain a small amount of gas, even if it is insufficient to run a motorcaravan's appliances properly.

Like Calor patio gas cylinders, the Calor Lite also has a float-operated gas level gauge.

The gauges from Gaslow can identify when there's a leak in a system as well as indicating the amount of gas in a cylinder when it's in use.

It is possible to monitor gas consumption if you weigh an unused cylinder on accurate scales.

HOW FULL IS YOUR CYLINDER?

Keeping a check on the amount of gas left in a cylinder can be difficult. However, the recently introduced BP Gas Light product, with its semi-transparent casing, makes it delightfully easy. Similarly, the introduction of the Gas Trac float-activated level indicator on Calor Lite and Calor Patio Gas cylinders is helpful too. This starts to operate with best accuracy when the level falls below halfway.

Inexpensive gauges from Gaslow that measure cylinder pressure are also useful, but they only give an indication of a cylinder's contents when it's coupled to an appliance that is in use.

The more costly Sonatic system from Truma uses ultrasonics to check a cylinder's 'state of fill', and its findings are relayed to a liquid crystal display (LCD) mounted inside the motorcaravan. At present the Sonatic is available for operation with Calor 7kg butane or 6kg propane cylinders and its accuracy is notably good. However, some gas engineers point out that its measuring mechanism requires an electrical supply and usually you are not permitted to have cable running in a gas locker without full conduit protection.

Although numerous other devices are also on sale, you can actually work out a cylinder's content using an accurate set of bathroom scales and a calculator. This describes how:

1 As soon as you've collected a full cylinder from a supplier, put it on the scales and take a note of its total weight.
2 You'll know the weight of gas contained in the cylinder from its supplier's information – Calor always displays this in bold white lettering on the side.
3 If you want to establish the weight of the empty cylinder, subtract the weight of the gas from the total.
4 After a period of use, rechecking the total weight of the cylinder will reveal the amount of gas remaining.

Technical Tip

Procedure when fitting and removing gas cylinders

1. Campingaz cylinders
Since there's a screw thread on top of a Campingaz cylinder, it means that when the regulator or adaptor finally loosens, a small quantity of gas usually hisses out while the valve ball reseats itself. So, meticulously follow all the safety recommendations described in the previous Safety Tip. Also, act promptly to complete the disconnection. The same thing occurs very briefly when connecting a new cylinder.

In view of this brief moment of leakage, some users prefer to hold a partly tightened regulator or hose coupling and then rotate the cylinder, rather than the other way round, which merely contorts the connecting hose.

263

2. Screw-thread Calor cylinders
1.When connecting and disconnecting a cylinder, always first make sure that the cylinder's handwheel is off – ie turned fully clockwise (this has a conventional right-hand thread).
2.When a new Calor butane cylinder is supplied, it sometimes has a small black cap over the threaded outlet. Remove this by turning it clockwise when looking at its dome (the coupling has a left-hand thread). Keep it for when you return the empty cylinder.
3.When a new propane cylinder is supplied, it similarly has a small plug in the coupling. Remove this with a large slotted screwdriver, turning it clockwise when looking at the slot (the coupling has a left-hand thread).
4.Check the connection surfaces (whether it is a butane or propane cylinder) to confirm they are clean and unobstructed. Then offer-up the threaded coupling. Hand-tighten it first, turning it anti-clockwise, and complete the job using an open-ended spanner. Since they do not employ a washer, propane couplings have to be tight.
5.Turn on the gas cylinder's hand-wheel, checking immediately for a hiss or smell that would indicate a poor connection. For a more thorough test, apply a proprietary leak-detecting fluid or a prepared mix of soapy water to the coupling areas. Then look closely for bubbles, which signify an escape of gas.
6. When returning an empty cylinder to a supplier, the plastic cap (butane) or plastic plug (propane) should be refitted.

3. Fitting a 541clip-on regulator to a 7kg Calor butane cylinder
No tools are needed to connect or disconnect this type of coupling. Furthermore, there isn't an on/off turn-wheel on the cylinder itself; instead, the on/off control is an integral part of a regulator or adaptor. As a safety feature the regulator's detachment mechanism won't operate until you've turned the tap to off.

Preparing a new cylinder: Rotate the orange cap so that its arrow points towards the opening in the cylinder shroud. Remove the cap by pulling on the plastic strap and lifting as you do so.

Attaching a clip-on regulator: The retaining collar is lifted up with the thumb while the regulator is pushed down onto the cylinder connection.

Switching on the gas: Once the regulator has seated properly and the retaining collar has been lowered you can rotate the operating tap to the vertical ON position.

Disconnecting a clip-on regulator: The design of a clip-on regulator intentionally ensures that the release collar can only be pushed upwards when the turn-tap is in its off position.

When a cylinder is exhausted the orange cap is pushed back onto the coupling.

Fuel stations in Australia often have staff able to refill portable cylinders from a supply vessel like this one.

Note: Strictly speaking, on a newly-filled Calor cylinder you don't need scales to establish the cylinder's weight because it's marked on the collar plate in pounds and ounces. Firstly, convert this to ounces (there are 16 ounces in one pound). Secondly, take a calculator and convert the ounces into kilograms by multiplying your result by 0.0283495.

For example, the collar plate on the Calor 6kg propane cylinder illustrated on page 260 shows a tare (cylinder weight) of 17lb 6oz, ie 278oz. When converted to kg (278 x 0.0283495) this comes out as 7.88kg. Since the freshly filled cylinder contains 6kg of propane, the total weight of the cylinder plus its gas content should be around 13.88kg.

Refillable cylinders

The introduction of portable refillable gas cylinders raised a number of safety concerns. For example, refilling a cylinder isn't like filling a can with petrol. Liquefied gas is often delivered from an autogas pump at some force, and any spillage on your hands leaves painful injuries. There are other safety issues, too.

For example, it is most important that a gas vessel is never filled more than 85% because its contents can expand if temperatures rise. That is why a gas tank or cylinder must have a European Pi approved filler valve that automatically shuts off gas acceptance as soon as the container reaches its limit. Unfortunately, some of the early refillable portable cylinders did not incorporate any form of automatic cut-off device.

Gas specialists became extremely concerned because this places the onus on the customer to ascertain when to cease the filling process, which isn't easy. In consequence, many suppliers decided to forbid the refilling of portable cylinders on their forecourts.

Some coachbuilts are fitted with Gaslow's refillable 11kg cylinders; this one also has an automatic changeover

The arrangement is slightly different in Australia, where refilling portable cylinders is a normal practice at fuel stations. However, it is the staff who refill a customer's gas cylinder and the LPG is drawn from a small tank intentionally made for the purpose. The arrangement is wholly different from an autogas forecourt in Europe.

In response to the many concerns, a statement published by the LP Gas Association or LPGA (IS24, June 2007) made the position clear. This document clarifies that permanently fixed gas 'vessels' related to heating and cooking 'may be permitted to be refilled at autogas refuelling sites provided they:

- remain in situ for refilling; and
- are fitted with a device to physically prevent filling beyond 80%; and
- are connected to a fixed filling connector which is not part of the vessel.'

In other words, appropriately installed tanks are deemed acceptable. So, too, are the specially made cylinders, sold by Gaslow, provided they are permanently installed and coupled with Gaslow's stainless steel fill-up pipe, which links to a filler point mounted on the vehicle. The components in this system carry a 15-year warranty, at which point the cylinder (which is marked with a date) has to be uninstalled and exchanged.

Of course, not everyone wants to spend a three-figure sum to have a tank or a fixed-cylinder system installed, but safe and easy-to-use systems are available. Moreover, a Gaslow system can often be uninstalled, transferred, and fixed in another motorcaravan without requiring major alterations to either vehicle.

Underfloor refillable tanks

With an increasing number of autogas stations opening for vehicles that run on LPG, many motorcaravanners have wanted to use these facilities to refill their domestic supply. In spite of the cost of having a refillable tank installed, and the matter of its additional weight, it offers benefits such as these:

- For heavy gas users, such as motorcaravanners touring in Europe, having a domestic tank installed can eliminate worries about finding suitable portable cylinders
- Winter users who rely heavily on gas for their heating needs sometimes have a tank installed
- Some owners find it tiresome carrying heavy

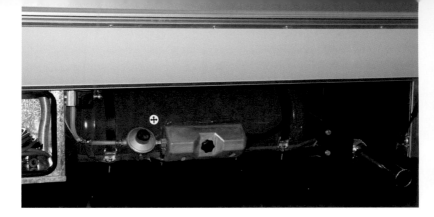

The design, installation, maintenance and guidance relating to under-floor LPG tanks is now being clarified in a new Code of Practice.

portable cylinders to a supplier when replacements are needed
• Once a tank has been installed, the cost of gas purchased at autogas stations is considerably less expensive.

However, for many years there have been few guidelines relating to safe installation procedures. Accordingly, a Code of Practice (CoP) is now in the final stages of preparation regarding all fixed or underslung LPG tanks fitted on motorcaravans. The content of this CoP embraces issues such as design, installation, maintenance, user instructions and decommissioning. Following consultations with industry, it is anticipated that the final CoP will be available during 2012. Many gas experts have strongly asserted that guidelines like this are long overdue.

Regulators

A regulator is an essential component in a motorcaravan's gas supply system. Its function is to ensure that gas is supplied to appliances at a consistent and appropriate pressure regardless of whether the supply cylinder or tank is full or approaching exhaustion. The pressure of gas in a cylinder is also affected by changing temperatures, which is another reason why regulators are important.
   A regulator has a diaphragm inside that stabilises the flow of gas and delivers it at the pressure required by the installed gas appliances. It must be

For a diaphragm to work properly, the tiny breather hole on a regulator's casing mustn't get blocked.

wholly weather-protected, and for the diaphragm to work, a tiny breather hole in the casing must not get blocked.

Rain entering this hole during winter can soon freeze, and the diaphragm's operation then promptly fails. Check one of the outcomes of a faulty regulator in the Technical Tip panel alongside.

Apart from this need for vigilance, there is nothing in a motorcaravan regulator to service or adjust. Accordingly its casing is sealed, and a regulator usually gives unfailing service for several years. Opinion on routine replacement is divided. Some specialists recommend every five years; others quote ten. However, both agree that an earlier replacement should be made if there are any external indications that the item might be damaged.

Changes to systems

For many years it has been necessary for anyone buying a motorcaravan to also purchase a regulator that matches the type of gas cylinder they want to use. This is the case when regulators are 'cylinder-mounted' because their coupling has to match the type of coupling on the cylinder. Similarly, a different regulator is required for a cylinder containing butane, as opposed to a cylinder containing propane.

Unfortunately for those motorcaravanners who tour widely throughout Europe, the huge variety of cylinder connections means that an array of regulators might be needed. There have also been problems for companies importing and exporting motorcaravans. In Germany, for example, gas appliances installed in caravans and motorhomes used to be manufactured to run at the higher pressure of 50mbar. In Britain, however, appliances used to be fitted to run on both 28mbar (butane) and 37mbar (propane) without needing adjustment.

Quite simply there was a desperate need for standardisation among European Union member states. New European Norms were therefore published in 2001 (BS EN 12864) and 2002 (BS EN 1949) and these made radical changes affecting both regulators and cylinder coupling arrangements. The new standards were implemented by UK manufacturers on 1 September 2003; a few German motorcaravan manufacturers were fitting the revised components a month or two earlier.

Recognising the fact that some readers own or intend to purchase a motorcaravan built before autumn 2003, the earlier systems need to be explained. So, too, do the gas systems installed in post-2003 models.

Technical Tip

Over-gassing

If you ever get a frightening tall flame on a stove burner, this is an example of 'over-gassing', which is usually caused by a faulty regulator. The condition sometimes occurs when the tiny breather hole on a regulator gets blocked.

The Calor Gas 4.5kg butane cylinder has a threaded coupling, and a spanner is needed when making a connection.

Systems in motorcaravans built before 1 September 2003

Mounting a regulator directly on top of a supply cylinder has been customary practice for many years, and such cylinder-mounted regulators have to match the type of gas and the style of coupling. To avoid errors, a propane cylinder always has a different coupling from a butane one.

On some butane cylinders there's a push-fit arrangement; on others there's a threaded coupling that you need to tighten using a spanner.

Remember, too, that Calor Gas screw-type couplings have a reverse thread. So forget the usual convention for threaded fixings; in this instance you have to rotate the nut anti-clockwise to tighten your regulator and vice versa if you want to remove it.

One of the implications of fitting a regulator directly to a cylinder is the fact that gas pressure is immediately reduced and it can then be fed to a motorcaravan's fixed copper pipes with a short length of approved low-pressure hose. The low

 **Technical Tip**

Regulator spanner

Coupling a regulator to a Campingaz cylinder doesn't need a spanner, and a regulator to suit Calor's clip-on system doesn't require special tools either. However, all the Calor Gas propane cylinders, together with Calor's 4.5kg butane cylinders, require a spanner to tighten the regulators' couplings. Accordingly, open-ended spanners are sold at motorcaravan accessory shops and these are intentionally rather flimsy to prevent anyone from over-tightening the attachment nut.

But be warned: if someone else coupled your regulator using a plumber's wrench and over-zealous strong arm tactics, a Calor spanner isn't likely to be tough enough to loosen it when you cylinder needs changing. That isn't something you want to discover when it's dark, cold, and pouring with rain.

Calor cylinder sealing washers

Neither propane cylinder 'pole' couplings nor Calor clip-on couplings have sealing washers. However, if you use a screw-on butane regulator to suit Calor's 4.5kg butane cylinder, it has a flexible washer that must be changed regularly. A packet of three washers costs pennies rather than pounds.

Some motorcaravanners think they can reuse the washer fitted in the screw-on cap that is sometimes supplied with a refilled 4.5kg cylinder. *Don't do that!* It is not made of the correct compound and will soon be the source of a leak.

pressure designation will be marked on the hose, together with the date when it left the factory. It can also be coupled satisfactorily to the main supply pipe and the regulator using good-quality hose clips.

During an annual habitation service, this short length of flexible coupling hose will be replaced. A replacement needs to be fitted and tested even sooner – by someone competent – if premature wear or distortion is noted, particularly near the clipping points.

This coupling system, which has been used successfully for many years, has much to commend it, apart from the fact that regulators have to be cylinder-specific. Even then, regulators for cylinder mounting aren't unduly expensive and are often sold for well under £10.

Systems in motorcaravans built after 1 September 2003

The publication of new European Norms/British Standards prompted changes in gas regulators and the type of hose used to couple-up to cylinders. Here are some of the main innovations:

- A new design of 'universal' regulator was developed that would operate using either butane or propane.
- A new standardised working pressure of 30mbar was introduced. Gas appliances being installed after 1 September 2003 are set to work at this pressure and are labelled accordingly.
- The 30mbar regulators are almost always fixed on the wall or ceiling of gas cylinder lockers, thereby forming part of a motorcaravan's factory-installed supply system. This practice means that regulators now receive manufacturers' soundness checks, together with the rest of the installation, before leaving the factory.

 **Technical Tip**

Regulator and appliance compatibility

Since gas appliances fitted in a motorcaravan have to be matched to its installed gas supply system, gas specialists have strongly asserted that anyone owning a pre-2003 motorcaravan must not attempt to install the wall-mounted universal butane/propane regulators and supply arrangements that are used in post-2003 models.

More detailed technical information on this subject can be found in Chapter Six of the *Motorcaravan Manual* (3rd edition, 2012), Haynes Publishing.

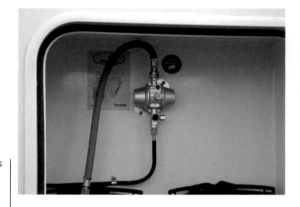

Since 2003 motorcaravans have usually been built with a wall-mounted 30mbar regulator. Customers have to purchase a coupling hose for their chosen cylinder.

- The only component that a new owner has to purchase is a factory-made high-pressure coupling hose with crimp-fit connectors. These connectors are important, and the types of hose clips hitherto used on low pressure hoses must not be fitted.
- High-pressure hoses with a variety of different couplings are available for purchase. Whereas the connector for coupling to a wall-mounted regulator is standard, the connector on the other end has to suit an owner's choice of gas cylinder.
- Although there are coupling hoses to suit most types of cylinder connections used throughout Europe, a few systems require the owner to purchase an adaptor.
- Notwithstanding the benefits offered by wall-mounted regulators, a few German manufacturers (eg Dethleffs) still supply cylinder-mounted regulators instead. Although the latest types are 30mbar regulators handling both butane and propane, they still have to suit an owner's preferred type of cylinder.

To minimise the chance of contaminated condensation running into a system, a 30mbar regulator should be mounted high up.

Although regulators are now mostly wall-mounted, in this 2006 Dethleffs a 30mbar cylinder-mounting type is supplied.

Problems with the new system

The change to wall-mounted, universal butane/propane 30mbar regulators, together with a high-pressure coupling hose, offers improved convenience when travelling in Europe. However, since the new system was introduced there have been several incidents where motorcaravanners have experienced gas blockages and the failure of appliances.

There have also been reports of 'oily liquid' appearing in gas supply pipes as shown in the accompanying photograph.

Intense investigation and laboratory analysis of the curious liquid has revealed that it contains a plasticising agent. It transpired that this was the product used in the manufacture of flexible rubberised hoses. It was duly concluded that this liquid was condensation mixed with plasticiser and was almost certainly responsible for the failure of diaphragms in regulators. If the liquid subsequently got into the supply system it might then lead to blockages as well as interfering with the operation of gas appliances.

Problems of gas blockages and evidence of an 'oily liquid' getting into systems was first reported around 2004.

Gaslow's semi-rigid stainless steel pipe, with or without a red handwheel, is often fitted instead of a rubberised hose.

A document published in January 2007 by The National Caravan Council (NCC) and available on the NCC's website explained that in some circumstances, condensation seems to form in high pressure coupling hoses. With the passage of LPG, the condensate subsequently absorbs the plasticising agent used in the manufacture of flexible hoses. Furthermore, when a fixed regulator is mounted lower than the supply cylinder outlet, the resulting 'oily substance' is then able to trickle down the hose and enter a regulator's mechanism. This affects its performance and blockages could follow.

In response to NCC recommendations, dealers are now remounting regulators at higher points in gas lockers so that any condensation can then run back into the supply cylinder rather than into the regulator. In addition, Gaslow has introduced a semi-flexible stainless steel pipe fitted with reinforcing ribs and covered with a steel braid. This is completely free of plasticising compounds and acts as a logical alternative to traditional rubber-composition coupling hose. Then in 2011, Truma introduced a revised butane/propane 30mbar regulator and gas filter designed to make further improvements.

Time will tell whether these recommended measures will end the blockage problems and the NCC concedes that the phenomenon was totally unexpected. The published document also affirms that there is no inherent fault in either LPG or the individual components. It is interesting to note, too, that blockages don't seem to occur in systems that employ cylinder-mounted regulators. In conclusion, if anyone owns a motorcaravan that was manufactured post 1 September 2003, make sure that the gas system receives an annual check, which is included, of course, as part of a habitation

A variety of cylinder changeover devices is available, bcth for pre- and post-2003 gas supply systems.

service. (See Chapter Sixteen for information on Servicing Operations.) What's more, if there is a hint of poor performing gas appliances, get a dealer to consider carrying out the modifications described above. On a positive note, it has been suggested that malfunctions have only been reported on around 5% of all post-September 2003 caravans and motorhomes.

Changeover systems

It is a poor design feature if a motorcaravan's gas locker only has space to accommodate *one* gas cylinder. Motorcaravanners need a subsidiary back-up supply, and when two cylinders are installed, some owners have a manual or automatic changeover device fitted as well. This permits hasty switching when a supply cylinder runs out and eliminates the immediate need for disconnection. Several products are manufactured and there are changeovers to suit many combinations, including:

- Systems conforming to earlier British Standards with cylinder-mounted regulators
- Post-2003 supply systems with a 30mbar wall-mounted regulator
- Post-2003 supply systems with a wall-mounted regulator matched with a pair of Gaslow's refillable cylinders
- Post-2003 supply systems with a wall-mounted regulator and supplied by one Gaslow refillable cylinder paired with one normal propane cylinder.

As stated earlier, LPG is certainly a convenient product to use but it helps to know something about gas supply components in order to get the best from a system.

CHAPTER FIFTEEN

COOKING AND HEATING

Although the majority of motorcaravans are fitted with gas-operated cooking and heating appliances, 230V hot plates and 12V fans are often fitted too. In addition, there's increasing interest in appliances that run on petrol or diesel fuel drawn from the base vehicle's tank.

275

The stylish kitchen in this Auto-Trail Cheyenne is equipped with a large domestic stove.

Most British motorcaravanners like a hob fitted with a grill but few imported models offer this facility.

The increasing popularity of motorcaravanning throughout Europe has resulted in a lively export and import market. British-built models are purchased abroad, just as some owners in this country drive motorcaravans manufactured in Belgium, France, Germany, Italy, Slovenia and Spain. However, this burgeoning interchange of products has drawn attention to national differences, together with the varying requirements of owners.

In Britain, for example, the majority of motorcaravanners want good cooking facilities, kitchen worktop space and a grill for their toast. Equally they expect to have electronic ignition to light the burners on their hob and consider that matches and hand-held devices are hardly appropriate in costly habitation vehicles. These expectations pose a problem for UK residents planning to purchase an imported model.

For example, German motorcaravans are often characterised by impressive washrooms bespangled with lights, whereas kitchens are small and modestly equipped. As pointed out in Chapter Four, many owners in that country don't expect elaborate kitchens because they frequently take meals in restaurants and bars. Alternatively, barbecues are popular when the weather is fine. In consequence, many Continental motorcaravans have hobs offering only two or three burners. Moreover, if their kitchens

Below right: The kitchen in this Dethleffs Esprit is pleasingly spacious but it doesn't include a four-burner hob with a grill.

Below: This tiny oven fitted in a Knaus Sport coachbuilt doesn't meet the expectations of many British owners.

include an oven it is usually small, worktop space is limited and grills are seldom installed.

Putting aside national preferences, a universal element is the design of the gas supply system that serves the appliances. In this regard, check the accompanying panel describing supply control valves. After that, let's take a discerning cook's tour of UK kitchens.

Closing the glass lid on the sink makes a small improvement to the modest worktop space in this imported motorcaravan.

(i) Technical Tip

Supply control valves

Since motorcaravans are usually equipped with several gas-operated appliances, a supply system is constructed as follows: typically, a main trunk pipe from the cylinder and regulator subdivides into branches, thus providing individual supplies to the appliances. To isolate certain items, many motorhomes have a bank of gas valves, as is shown below. These valves are either labelled or identified by pictograms and there should be further guidance in the owner's manual.

If you purchase a pre-owned motorcaravan and find the labels are missing, you can often follow the route of each branch pipe with the help of a torch and a mirror. When their respective functions have been noted, operation of appliances can be checked one-by-one before finally adding labels of your own.

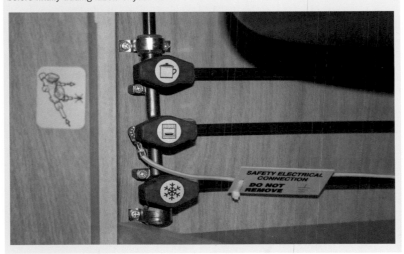

Many hobs fitted in imported models have to be lit using either a match or a hand-held igniter like this Zippo product.

HOBS AND GRILLS

In recently built European motorcaravans, it is obligatory for the burners on hobs to be fitted with a flame-failure device (FFD). Accordingly, each burner will have a small probe that derives heat from the flame. When it heats up it creates a small electric current, which is sufficiently powerful to hold open an electro-magnetic gas valve. The panel that described FFDs on page 203 pointed out that if a draught extinguishes a burner, its probe cools down, a coil spring in the gas valve then shuts off the supply, and gas can't escape from the burner. This is a good safety feature, although when you first light a burner, it takes several seconds for the probe to get hot. That is why you have to keep the control knob depressed for a short while. Your action thus overrides the spring-operated shut-off valve and gives the burner's FFD probe time to heat up.

A close inspection of the burners may reveal a thinner component, too, and this is the spark igniter. You'll seldom find these fitted on Cramer hobs, which were originally manufactured in Germany. If your motorhome has one of these products you'll

For several years Auto-Trail coachbuilt models have included a hob with an electric hotplate.

either have to purchase matches or a purpose-made igniter. Dometic, the latest owner of the company, points out that Cramer hobs can be ordered with built-in spark igniters but few Continental manufacturers request them.

On a different note, some hobs are now being manufactured with a 230V hotplate amidst the gas burners, which is fine if you regularly use sites with mains hook-ups.

Different yet again is the practice of fitting a ceramic hob with burners that run on diesel fuel drawn from the vehicle's tank. These appliances have been fitted in narrow boats and Webasto introduced a revised version that is suitable for motorcaravans. This product isn't often specified but Wheelhome decided to offer one of these hobs as an option in its 2012 Skamper, Skarpa and Vikenze campervans. If matched with diesel space and water heating appliances, this eliminates the need for gas cylinders.

Finally, please read the accompanying panel on the subject of space heating and hobs.

The diesel-powered ceramic top hob from Webasto is often fitted in canal boats; it is also an option in 2012 campervans built by Wheelhome.

 Safety Tip

Heating and hobs

Never use a hob to act as a space-heating appliance. Admittedly, when a kettle is boiled or a saucepan is in use, the living space gets warmer. However, in some kitchens, heat rising from a burner that hasn't been covered by a pan may be sufficient to damage a locker or shelf fitted above.

As a second safety warning, note that if the gas/air mix on a hob is slightly out of adjustment, there is a possibility that small quantities of carbon monoxide are present in the products of combustion. For instance, if you find that the underside of cooking implements gets badly covered with soot, this is a warning that the flame pattern is incorrect. Get the hob checked by a qualified gas engineer as soon as you can.

This is why leaving an incorrectly adjusted hob running as a heater for a prolonged period can be extremely dangerous. An article in a South Wales newspaper reported how two tourists did this in a campervan to keep warm at night; both were found dead in the morning.

Many British coachbuilts such as this Avondale Seascape are fitted with a large cooker complete with hob, grill and oven.

OVENS

Whether you need an oven in a motorcaravan at all is a personal matter – some people, who regularly use their full-size domestic cooker when at home, are less inclined to use one in a motorcaravan. Other owners see things differently, therefore many British manufacturers install large cookers in coachbuilt motorhomes – which do claim a significant part of a vehicle's payload. Smaller products are normally confined to small coachbuilt models, whereas some van conversions don't have an oven at all.

Microwave ovens have also become increasingly commonplace, and these have both supporters and detractors. Some owners contend that a microwave oven that is fitted at head height is dangerously situated when you are reaching, for example, for a hot mug of coffee. Others point out that you need a generous 230V supply to run a microwave, adding that the current draw is particularly high during the start-up period in a cooking cycle.

Above: Some owners are content with compact cooking appliances in their motorhome.

Below: Microwave ovens are being fitted more frequently but normally they'll need to run on a 230V hook-up.

 Technical Tip

Electrical consumption of microwave ovens

The cooking power of a microwave oven is often expressed in Watts – a medium-sized product might be rated at 600W: compact models are 450W. This relates to their *output*.

However, motorcaravanners owning a microwave oven need to establish its *input* requirements, especially if they want to purchase a portable generator. To calculate the requirement, a rough rule of thumb is to double the output and then subtract 10%. In other words, the absolute minimum wattage required from a generator to run a 600W microwave oven is 1,080W (1,200W – 120 = 1,080W).

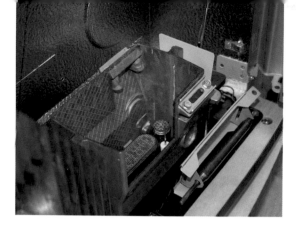

SPACE HEATERS

The term 'gas fire' has long been superseded, and for good reason. Moreover, the word 'heater' is also imprecise because many motorcaravans are fitted with two – one is a water heater: the other heats the living space.

Gas fires
About 30 years ago caravans and motorhomes were often fitted with a 'gas fire'. These appliances had an exposed burner, and this was potentially dangerous. For example, a gas burner needs oxygen, and that was simply taken from the living area. Equally, there was no flue to discharge the products of combustion to the outside world. That meant the fumes were released into the living space.

Such fires were often lit with a match, which risked carbon monoxide emissions – described above with relation to hobs. Another disadvantage is the fact that when LPG is burning, it produces a large quantity of water vapour that subsequently settles on cold surfaces as condensation. This isn't welcome in a leisure vehicle and these features eventually prompted the introduction of 'room-sealed' heaters instead of open burner 'gas fires'.

Room-sealed space heaters
A 'room-sealed' heater has these features:

- Its gas burner is mounted inside a room-sealed enclosure
- A duct, or specially constructed inlet, draws oxygen into the enclosure from *outside* the living space
- The products of combustion are returned directly outside via a flue system

This cutaway display unit shows how the burners in modern heaters are mounted in a room-sealed enclosure.

Technical Tip

Exposed flame gas fires

If you buy an older motorcaravan fitted with a gas fire that has exposed flames and no permanently installed flue, get it removed and scrapped at once. It might even cause a fatality, and if it hasn't been checked by a qualified gas engineer do not use it.

The flue outlet for the space heater installed in this Swift Sundance was roof-mounted.

This heat exchanger in a Truma heater includes an inspection port to show when the burner's alight.

Below: Compact space heaters from Propex, like this Heat Source 2800, have been fitted in many van conversions.

Below: The underfloor version of Whale's space heater is used by Elddis in order not to take up wall space.

Below right: Whale's room-sealed heaters employ stainless steel air intake and exhaust outlet pipes, which are directed down through the floor.

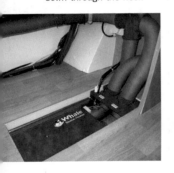

• When the sealed enclosure gets hot, it warms the air around it
• The enclosure, called a 'heat exchanger', is designed to release its heat efficiently into the living space
• There is either a warning light or a sealed inspection port to show that the main burner is alight
• A room-sealed heater can usually be left in operation all night – however, confirm that this is the case either by checking the owner's manual or seeking advice from a dealer.

Understandably, you can't light a burner using a match when it is mounted inside a chamber that has been sealed off from the living area. Instead, an efficient and reliable ignition system is utilised, and as long as you have your heater serviced regularly, neither Piezo nor electronic ignition systems are likely to give trouble.

Types of space heater

Van conversions have often been equipped with either compact gas heaters manufactured by Propex or the E Series products from Truma.

More recently, two new space heaters from Whale have also attracted interest, and Elddis has been installing under-floor versions of these products as a space-saving strategy. Whereas the main heating function is achieved by a gas burner, some models include a 230V electrical element, too.

These self-contained appliances distribute ducted warm air and one of their advantages is that they don't take up wall space and can even be mounted in small lockers. As regards performance, the Trumatic E 4000 fan-driven version achieves a useful 3.7kW and although quite costly, E-series products are exceptionally reliable. All these compact products are ideal in smaller motorcaravans but are not normally used for heating spacious interiors in large coachbuilt models.

With more interior space available, many coachbuilt motorhomes are fitted with wall-mounted room-sealed gas heaters, and the output of some models is augmented by a subsidiary mains-powered electrical element. The Trumatic S series is a popular example and models in the range offer thermal output levels from 1.85 to 5.5kW.

Apart from the fact that they take up wall space, these heaters are efficient performers. However, a separate water heater is also required, and examples are described later.

A third category of gas heaters, often known as 'combination' or 'combi' products, integrate both space and water heating tasks within one appliance. The Truma C range, introduced several years ago, is one of the best-known examples, whereas Atwood's combination heater, imported from the USA, was unexpectedly withdrawn from production.

Depending on the model, Truma Combination heaters achieve thermal outputs between 2kW and 6kW. They include a mains facility for alternative water heating, but do be aware; not all Combi models include a 230V facility for space heating. In other words, if your gas supply runs out unexpectedly, some models don't offer a mains electricity-operating mode to fall back on.

Combination heaters can be installed in large motorhomes by several different manufacturers and the Truma products are impressively built.

Above left: Truma wall-mounted space heaters like this are efficient room-sealed appliances.

Above: Not all models in the Truma C Range of combination heaters include a 230V space-heating facility.

The latest Truma Combination heaters are impressive products and routine service work must only be undertaken by appropriately trained personnel.

Many winter users pack a domestic fan heater as a back-up item, but its consumption may be too great for some sites.

Domestic fan and radiator heaters

Recognising that gas supplies can run out at inopportune moments, some owners take a small 230V portable domestic fan heater on winter trips as a backup.

These should be operated via a vehicle's RCD and MCB-protected mains system, described in Chapter Twelve. Whether the use of a 230V portable household product in a confined space is a wise strategy is a matter of debate.

There are other considerations too. Many mains hook-up supplies at campsites do not provide sufficient current to run a domestic heater in the way you would at home. The amperage available at sites varies enormously and a 230V fan heater might overload a site supply if used on more than its lowest setting (see Chapter Twelve). That said, many owners exercise the appropriate caution and use a small fan heater if their gas system fails, but it would be ill advised to leave one running when a van is unoccupied.

However, mini 230V oil-filled radiators are sometimes used for keeping internal temperatures above freezing in motorcaravans parked at their owners' homes. Many of these appliances incorporate an over-heat safety shut-off, a timer, and frost activation switching. In advertisements, these products are sometimes described as a reliable heating source, although it would be an owner's responsibility to establish whether a particular oil-filled radiator is deemed suitable for use in the close confines of a motorcaravan – particularly if it is unoccupied.

Electrical assistance

The effectiveness of gas heaters is often enhanced by distributing warmed air through a system of ducts with the help of an inbuilt 12V fan. This makes it possible to heat a separate shower room and to control temperatures in specific zones.

Most space heaters are fitted with a network of ducts so that warm air can be distributed throughout the living space.

In spite of this, you sometimes find that one end of a motorcaravan is cooler than the other. If that is the case, some heaters have a balance control fitted on the main outlet at the point where the main trunk of the ducting splits into two separate branches. Some Carver and Truma wall-mounted heaters have this control adjacent to the fan itself. This may be hard to reach and some owners are unaware that it exists. A good owner's manual should provide further information.

As regards the inclusion of fixed 230V space-heating elements in gas appliances, opportunities to bring these into use will also depend on the Amp output of a site's hook-up pillar. Moreover, in some (but not all) space heaters, an electrical element can be operated at the same time that its gas burner is in operation. In the case of recent Trumatic S3002(P) wall heaters fitted with an additional Ultraheat electric element, a user is able to select from these five operating modes:

500W from the electric element	Subject to site Amp output
1000W (1kW) from the electric element	
2kW from the electric element	
3kW (controllable) from the gas system	
Up to 5kW from the combined systems	

This versatility is particularly welcome for cold weather travellers.

Wet heating systems

A few motorcaravans are fitted with a central heating system that uses radiators. The efficient 3000 Compact Alde system, for example, is highly regarded and is often installed in top specification models.

Several gas heaters can be fitted with a supplementary 230V element such as this Truma Ultraheat unit.

To achieve an equitable distribution of ducted air throughout the living area, some heaters have an adjusting control.

Useful Tip

Spare parts

Two names traditionally associated with space and water heaters are 'Carver' and 'Truma'. In the mid-1980s the German company Truma supplied many components to Carver, which was based in Warwickshire. When this co-operative venture terminated, the companies carried on independently. However, in the late 1990s Carver ceased production of caravan and motorhome accessories.

The supply of spare parts for many of Carver's products was then taken over by Truma, although this service is not intended to continue for long. However, Arc Systems is noted for its repair of many obsolete Carver heating models. In addition, a copy of Carver's much-liked Cascade Water heater is manufactured and sold as the Henry GE. This replica product is distributed by Johnnie Longden Wholesalers, Poole, Dorset and some of its spares are claimed to be suitable for use in original Carver Cascade water heaters.

The situation is less satisfactory with regard to Atwood combination heaters, which were fitted by several UK manufacturers including Murvi. Although the parent US company established an Atwood base in Europe, this closed down unexpectedly. Purchasers of pre-owned motorhomes fitted with these heaters find it very hard to obtain spare parts.

As regards the recent heating products introduced by Whale, spares are easily obtainable; there is also an adaptor plate that allows a Whale water heater to make use of the flue aperture left in a side wall after an obsolete appliance has been removed and scrapped.

WATER HEATERS

Many small van conversions do not have the space to fit a water heater. This isn't a serious shortcoming and campervan owners seldom complain when they have to boil a kettle to produce hot water for washing-up. However, owners of coachbuilt models usually have higher expectations.

A few older motorcaravans still have 'instantaneous water heaters', such as the appliances from Paloma and Rinnai. These operate with exposed burners and since many have an internal flue outlet, this type of appliance is no longer installed in new motorcaravans. Once again, room-sealed water heaters are preferred.

A large number of motorhomes are currently fitted with a Truma Ultrastore water heater.

After its introduction in the 1980s, the Carver Cascade gas-operated storage water heater was fitted by many caravan and motorhome manufacturers. Its storage vessel was well insulated, and later updates included 230V heating options and improvements to its notoriously slow drain-down mechanism. Many owners liked this unit, especially its compact design, which allowed it to be installed under a bed.

When Carver ceased manufacturing the Cascade in the late 1990s, another long-established storage-type water heater called the Truma Ulstrastore was fitted in a large number of motorhomes. This product is similarly available in different capacities and has a 230V electric element to augment its gas operation. Ultrastore water heaters are reliable and efficient, although they lack the compact design of the Carver appliance; furthermore, they lack the generous layer of insulation material around the storage tank that was another good feature on the Carver Cascade.

After the demise of the Carver Cascade, a replica curiously named the 'Henry GE' was manufactured in the Far East. The fact that the Henry GE adopts the dimensions of its Carver predecessor means that a replacement appliance can be installed in the original compartment. The previous cut-out formed in the side of a vehicle doesn't need alteration either.

Another available storage heater with a well-established background is the Maxol Malaga. This has also been sold bearing a Belling Badge.

More recently, the manufacturers of Whale water supply products decided to introduce new water heaters, too. The angular shape of these appliances, together with their covering of insulating material, enables them to be fitted in confined spaces, such as under a single bed. The first model launched has a nominal 13L tank whereas a later, smaller, lighter version offers an 8L tank. The gas and mains heating

A Henry GE water heater can be easily fitted in the place formerly occupied by a Carver Crystal product.

287

Below left: The larger of Whale's water heaters has a 13L tank, good insulation and operates on both gas and 230V electricity.

Below: The self-explanatory design of this Whale water heater control panel offers five running options.

systems yield five running options namely; 1. Gas only setting, 2. Electric low setting, 3. Electric high setting, 4. Gas and electric low setting, and 5. Gas and electric high setting. A universal wall adaptor plate is also available, which creates a tidy finish if one of these products is required to occupy a location hitherto used by an earlier type of heater.

So a surprising number of different types of water heater are installed in motorcaravans, but there is one feature common to them all. That is the importance of draining them down before the arrival of frosty weather. Frost damage was described in Chapter Ten and water heaters may be irreparably damaged if precautionary measures are ignored.

Payload considerations

Water is heavy and some motorcaravanners drain down a water heater before taking to the road. This might seem over-cautious but it is not a misplaced strategy if your vehicle is running close to its Maximum Technically Permitted Laden Mass (MTPLM). A Carver Cascade holds 9 litres (2 gallons), thereby taking up 9kg (19.8lb) of payload. A Truma Ultrastore has either a 10- or 14-litre capacity, which will add 10kg (22lb) or 14kg (30.9lb) to your load. *Note: If you do drain down a storage heater prior to leaving a site, be aware that very hot water is likely to badly burn grass. Bald patches are often found where a thoughtless owner has released the contents of a water heater.*

SAFETY

System safety checks

When you buy a new motorcaravan, its gas appliances will comply with the European regulations applicable to LPG appliances in leisure vehicles. In addition to a CE marking on the label, documents provided with your purchase will confirm their compliance with European Norms/British Standards and the fact that a qualified gas engineer has inspected and approved their installation.

Things are seldom as straightforward when you purchase a pre-owned motorcaravan. Ideally, a pre-owned van would be supplied with a recently signed and dated certificate to confirm the integrity of its supply system and appliances. If that is not available, a good service centre can arrange for a safety inspection to be carried out and will issue signed/dated documents to verify that the gas system is in safe working order.

This checking procedure should always be carried out before putting a pre-owned motorcaravan into commission. It only needs an appliance's gas and air

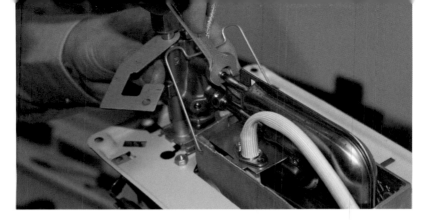

mixture to be incorrect and there's a risk that carbon monoxide could be emitted. For peace of mind, many owners also fit a carbon monoxide alarm – see Chapter Fourteen, Safety Tip on page 253.

Also bear in mind that a motorcaravan's gas appliances are not used regularly throughout the year. During periods of inactivity it is not unusual for insects, moths and spiders to get into the air intakes or flues. In some instances this can upset the delicate air/gas balance; it can also upset the ignition process. For example, a pilot flame on a space heater might ignite successfully but you subsequently find that the main burner then doesn't fire-up as it should. These problems are usually caused by obstructions, and even a spider's web spun around the cowl on a roof-mounted flue can upset a heater's ignition process.

There is no doubt that routine and regular servicing of all gas appliances is essential and owners should check their manufacturers' advice for information about the nature and frequency of these operations.

However, it must be kept in mind that within a four-hour standard habitation service, appliances are only checked to see that they are working correctly. This is often described as a 'functionality check' and a standard service will not involve dismantling work.

Modern gas heating appliances are complex products and DIY repairs should not be attempted.

 289

(i) Safety Tip

Operating pressures

Appliances are built to operate at specific gas pressures and the 2003 change in standards and the labelling of products was discussed in Chapter Fourteen. This earlier chapter describes the purpose of gas regulators and the fact that today's products, which are designed to run at 30mbar, must not be fitted into older motorcaravans built with different systems.

Both the igniter and flame-failure device on a gas burner need cleaning and resetting periodically by a trained fitter.

In consequence, servicing work doesn't involve the cleaning of burners in heating appliances or any other internal maintenance operations. These tasks are usually regarded as additional service operations.

Note, too, that the designs of modern heaters are complex and an unqualified person should never tackle servicing work. Furthermore, if you don't have work carried out by a competent, trained gas specialist, elements like the gas ignition might not operate correctly.

DIESEL AND PETROL HEATING

Pleasure boats and the cabs of long-distance lorries have been fitted with diesel-fuelled heating systems for many years, but it wasn't until 1998 that Murvi Motorcaravans started working with Eberspächer, a diesel heating specialist, to create a similar system for installation in Murvi van conversions. This subsequently drew interest from manufacturers of larger models, and in 2000 the author's self-built motorcaravan was the first UK coachbuilt to be equipped with an Eberspächer combined air and water heating system. Other manufacturers later installing Eberspächer diesel-powered heaters included Autocruise CH. In addition, Auto-Trail fitted diesel heating units manufactured by Webasto.

These heating systems normally run on diesel fuel drawn from the base vehicle's tank, but similar units are built to run on petrol.

Broadly speaking there are three levels of provision:

A Webasto fan-driven diesel heater is compact enough to be fitted under the seat in most commercial cabs.

1. Warm-air space heaters

Examples of compact, enclosed appliances include Webasto's Air Top 2000, 3500 and 5000 fan heaters. The fan-driven Air Top 2000S is sufficiently compact to fit under a cab seat and is used by several van converters, including Middlesex Motorcaravans.

Similar products include Eberspächer's Airtronic D2 (2.2kW) and D4 (4kW) models, which are often fitted under lounge seats in motorcaravans built by Auto-Sleepers and Romahome. More recently Eberspächer also launched a system that pairs-up an Airlectric 230V electric unit achieving a 1kW output with an Airtronic heater.

2. Combined water and space heater units

These are manufactured in several forms. The Eberspächer Combitronic Compact is enclosed in a casing that is usually mounted under the floor. This frees-up space in the living quarters and its components include a hot-water cylinder. The Combitronic has been installed in Autocruise CH coachbuilt motorhomes.

3. Combitronic Modular linked with base vehicle's cooling system

In this arrangement, the individual heating assemblies remain as separate modules for installation and are located wherever the designer thinks best. In some circumstances there can even be a link with the base vehicle, which affords additional benefits.

A coupled design extends a vehicle's water-cooling system so that hot-water pipes from the engine run through the living area too. Just as vehicle cabs have dash-mounted heaters distributing heat from the engine, an extended arrangement adds further small radiators with fans to distribute warm air in the living area.

In addition, piped hot water drawn from the engine runs through a coil in a copper cylinder to

The Eberspächer Airlectric 230V unit, which achieves a 1kW output, can be coupled to an Airtronic diesel heater.

In this Webasto installation, water heated by diesel fuel is taken to small radiators with fans mounted in the living area.

heat water for the shower, sink and washbasin. Effectively, this is a miniature version of the copper cylinders fitted in many people's homes, and, like the ones in houses, the small Eberspächer cylinder also has a 1kW immersion heater that runs using a 230V hook-up as well.

While a vehicle is being driven, the engine creates hot water, which circulates through both the copper cylinder and the fan-assisted space heaters. However, when the vehicle is parked and the engine is switched off, Eberspächer's compact Hydronic boiler – usually mounted out of sight near the sump – can then be activated to take over the heating duties.

An Eberspächer Hydronic heating system can be operated safely while you're driving, and that is a great help when the weather is cold.

The operation is controlled by a multi-function panel that can be manually activated, as well as programmed to operate for up to three different periods in 24 hours. The timing facility can also embrace a seven-day operating regime.

Remote control units are optional extras, as is a telephone activation feature.

Of course, some modular systems are fitted to

Hydronic diesel heaters from Eberspächer can be fitted in the engine compartment. They have an impressive output.

run wholly independently of the base vehicle, but if an Eberspächer installation is linked to a vehicle's cooling system, the owner can then use a Hydronic unit to pre-heat the engine in winter. It can also work in conjunction with a dashboard heater so that a snow-covered screen can be cleared when the system is manually switched or activated by remote control. These features are certainly useful.

Sheathed in insulation foam, Eberspächer's copper cylinder with an immersion heater stores very hot water.

Conclusion

Diesel heaters are remarkably economical and mean that you only need LPG to run your fridge, hob, grill and oven. In consequence, you can manage with small gas cylinders that, in turn, offer a weight-saving benefit. However, this is offset by the fact that a large Ah battery is needed to run the electric fans used in an elaborate Combitronic installation. Another point to remember is that some people find the noise of a diesel-fired system irritating.

In summary, gas appliances are undoubtedly the most common products used for heating motorcaravans, but diesel and electrical systems do have their advantages.

Panels with Eberspächer space- and water-heating systems offer an impressive array of control options.

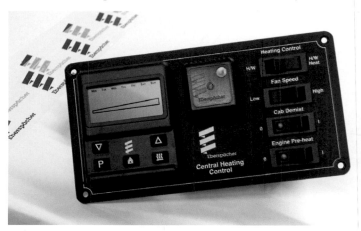

F I A T

ESS
MO

Service

GB

DI YMC

CHAPTER SIXTEEN

SERVICING AND
MOT TESTING

All motorists understand the importance of keeping a car serviced, safe, and MoT tested. However, in the case of a motorcaravan, there's another precautionary measure that owners have to take, and that is to have its conversion elements checked. The procedure is normally referred to as a 'habitation service', much of which relates to health, safety and functionality issues.

295

Some commercial vehicle workshops don't have sufficient access to accommodate large motorcaravans.

To conduct vehicle and habitation service operations, a ramp or inspection pit is an important facility.

The base on which a motorcaravan is built shares many features with other private passenger vehicles. For instance, it should be sold with an owner's manual, a service booklet and a list of approved service centres. But there's a snag. It is easy to be misled into thinking that an international address list of commercial dealers would be just what owners of motorcaravans need. Unfortunately that is not the case. Many commercial service centres are unable to accommodate motorcaravans because they're simply too large for their workshops.

A similar problem often occurs when a Ministry of Transport (MoT) test is needed. Legal matters relating to the MoT were set out in Chapter Six: the concerns here relate to practical issues. Approved test stations are sometimes unable to conduct an MoT test because large motorcaravans won't fit in the workshop. Similarly, unsuitable ramps, the position of a rolling road for brake testing and insufficient manoeuvring space also conspire to make things difficult. Unfortunately, issues like these are not always explained when you buy a motorcaravan.

In response to these difficulties, the magazine

Height nearly turned out to be a problem at this MoT station, which is otherwise able to test Class IV vehicles.

Base vehicle servicing and MoT

Further guidance about centres able to help motorcaravanners:
- In some areas, health authority ambulance servicing depots have started to carry out service operations and MoT tests on private vehicles. Check your local telephone directory.
- British Telecom (BT) motor transport workshops are sometimes able to service private vehicles.
- A local Road Transport Enforcement Department of the Vehicle Inspectorate is usually able to advise where heavy goods vehicles can be serviced and will give locations of MoT stations equipped to carry out Class IV MoT testing. Check your local telephone directory for Vehicle Inspectorate numbers. Additional information on the MoT test and the Vehicle and Operator Services Agency (VOSA) is given on pages 113–115.

The rollers for MoT brake testing aren't always positioned to accommodate the wheels on large motorcaravans.

Motorcaravan Motorhome Monthly (MMM) periodically publishes a list entitled 'Base Vehicle Servicing and MoT – Motorhome-friendly garages'. At the time of writing, this is a five-page compilation of readers' submissions listing 278 centres in 71 counties and major British cities. Each entry is accompanied by brief comments in which contributors describe their experiences.

Reprints of the latest *MMM* listing can be obtained by telephoning 01778 391187. This is an invaluable guide for owners of large motorcaravans in general and coachbuilt models in particular. The accompanying technical tip panel adds further advice to anyone searching for suitable servicing facilities.

VEHICLE SERVICING OPERATIONS

It would be impossible to list here all the servicing operations applicable to base vehicles used for motorcaravans. Detailed schedules are often available from franchised dealers and succinct guidance is normally included in the service packs included with new vehicles.

Elements such as oil and filter changes form part of the routine operations, as do precautionary measures such as changing a cam belt. In many vehicles this is carried out on the basis of mileage covered as well as years in use. However, unlike commercial users, motorcaravan owners don't usually notch up high annual mileages, so it is usually age rather than mileage that decides when a vehicle's cam belt needs replacing. On some vehicles this should be done every five years and it is an

Above right: Changing filters and lubricants is among the many tasks involved in a base vehicle service.

Above: Tiny cracks were just starting to appear on this Fiat Ducato cam belt after five years in use.

important requirement to note. If a cam belt breaks, considerable engine damage can occur, and the subsequent repair costs are often high.

Servicing work on a base vehicle's engine, transmission and running gear are important but some issues relate to the conversion itself. So, essentially, there are two areas of attention:

1 Work on the base vehicle
2 Work on the conversion, referred to as 'habitation servicing'.

Motorcaravans built on AL-KO Kober chassis

Although a large number of coachbuilt models are built on Fiat's base vehicles, it was pointed out in Chapter Three that on many Ducatos and Peugeot Boxers the original chassis is sometimes removed before building a motorhome. An AL-KO Kober motorhome chassis is then fitted in its place, which means that the motorcaravan's rear axle runs on AL-KO's torsion bar suspension rather than its original springs.

Where there has been an alteration like this, it's understandable that a Fiat servicing centre is unlikely to carry out checks and greasing operations on a product made by a different manufacturer. So who carries out these important operations?

To assist motorcaravanners, AL-KO Kober has a national network of service centres to assist owners of vehicles fitted with their chassis. Alternatively, this part of a vehicle's servicing work can be carried out if you have a habitation service performed by a dealer who is a member of the Approved Workshop scheme. In fact, the first area of attention on an Approved Workshop service schedule sheet is often described as 'underbody' issues.

Whether work on an AL-KO chassis and suspension is included in a habitation service conducted by a dealer that isn't a member of the Approved Workshop scheme is something a customer would need to check. A habitation service specialist might

AL-KO Kober has a network of approved service centres that's useful to note if your motorhome is built on an AL-KO chassis.

reasonably claim that servicing suspension elements is hardly a 'living area' issue and should logically be included when base vehicle servicing is carried out. Either way, it is an area of attention that mustn't be overlooked. Nor, for that matter, are checks of body-to-chassis mountings.

Challenges linked with base vehicle service operations

Tasks like changing air filters in an engine compartment require good access and this is provided by base vehicle manufacturers when designing engine compartments and their bonnets. However, in the case of A-class motorcaravans, bonnet lids form part of a glass reinforced plastic front panel designed by the converter rather than the vehicle manufacturer. Regrettably, there are some A-class models where apertures that are intended to provide access to the engine bay are impracticably small. Some service specialists claim that one recent A-class model yields insufficient space to replace an air filter when the bonnet is lifted.

Another access issue was also noted on a recent coachbuilt model that had been constructed using an AL-KO chassis. In this case, the installation of under-floor water tanks completely obscured the axle tube's greasing points, which lubricate the torsion bar suspension units. Routine lubrication is not

Access to the engine on this 1999 Fiat Ducato is sensibly designed and filters are quite easy to change.

Access to the engine is good on this Hymer A-class, but on some A-class vehicles changing an air filter is a nightmare.

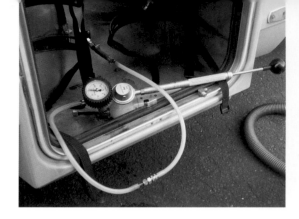

Carrying out an air pressure test on a gas supply system is an important safety element in a habitation service.

Flexible connecting hose can start to deteriorate over a period of years, and this is closely checked.

Low-level gas escape vents are checked to see that they're not obstructed; pipes are inspected as well.

only essential for torsion bar operation; it is also a warranty requirement.

So converting a vehicle into a motorcaravan sometimes introduces servicing issues that don't become evident until later. That is why some potential purchasers seek advice from service centre staff to ascertain if servicing work is straightforward on a model they are planning to buy. Magazine technical tests also highlight such issues.

HABITATION SERVICE WORK

As pointed out already, a habitation service isn't merely restricted to safety checks within the living area. So let's look closely at the scope of the work.

In a full habitation service, around 50 jobs need to be carried out, and this can take from three to four hours. In the schedules used by members of the Approved Workshop scheme, these normally fall into the following categories:

1 **Underbody** – chassis, running gear, suspension, tanks, spare wheel, corner steadies.
2 **Ventilation** – openings, roof lights, fixed and opening ventilators, freedom of airflow, heating fan operation.
3 **12V electrics** – road light operation, reflectors, fridge operation, interior lighting, leisure battery, wiring, fuses, pump, heater fans.
4 **Mains electrics** – inlet socket, connecting cable, earth bonding, RCD operation, domestic connections, visual and functionality check.
5 **Gas system and appliances** – leak test, regulator operation test, operation of appliances, pipe runs, flexible hose check/replacement, cylinder security, gas drop-out holes.
6 **Water system** – water pump, pressure/micro-switch operation, grit filter cleaning, tap operation, water filter, waste system, toilet seals, flush action, drain-down valves.

7 **Fire safety** – security alarms, gas alarms, smoke alarms, extinguisher type/expiry date, fire blanket location/fixing.

8 **Bodywork** – sealant, door locks, hinges, body attachments, racks, aerials, locker boxes, floor panel condition, cab-seat swivel, furniture condition, window seals, blinds, rising roof (where fitted), damp test.

Where fitted, rising roof mechanisms are checked along with the security of accessories fitted to a motorhome body.

Optional work

Absorption refrigerator service
In a standard service, checks are carried out to verify that an absorption refrigerator is working properly on its three sources of power (described in Chapter Eleven). However, a full service of an absorption fridge, as laid down by its manufacturers, includes replacing the gas jet (Dometic models only), realigning the igniter and cleaning the gas burner and flue. Checks also include confirmation that a flame failure device is operating correctly. To accomplish the various tasks, a service specialist normally has to remove a fridge from a motorhome and transfer it to a workbench. *Note: On some of the latest models it is claimed that service operations can be accomplished when the appliance is left in situ.* Either way, the full operation incurs an additional fee, and fridge removal/reinstallation is sometimes a significant factor when determining the charge.

Disassembly, cleaning and readjustment of gas heating appliances
When servicing is specified by the manufacturers of heating appliances, the work can also be included in a servicing operation for an additional fee. For instance, it was mentioned in the Safety Section in Chapter Fifteen that insects, dust and debris like leaves often get into the burner compartment or flue outlets and these need periodic removal. Burner assemblies and ignition items may need attention, too, but since these

A fridge service is normally an 'optional extra'. To clean a burner tube usually involves removing the appliance.

Inspection qualifications

Independent specialists who can verify and issue certificates relating to the integrity of mains electricity and gas supply systems in leisure vehicles must be qualified to carry this out.

Mains electricity

To establish that a 230V mains installation in a motorcaravan meets the latest technical requirements, an inspection can be carried out by an approved contractor of the National Inspection Council for Electrical Installation Contracting (NICEIC), or a member of the Electrical Contractors Association (ECA) or the Electrical Contractors' Association of Scotland (ECAS). When a successful, dated inspection certificate has been issued, this can be especially useful when selling a motorcaravan. Similarly when purchasing a pre-owned motorcaravan that carries no written statement about the safety of the mains supply system, its integrity can be verified by securing the services of an electrician who is a member of the NICEIC, the ECA, the ECAS or other approved regulatory body.

Gas

It is critically important that gas supply systems in motorcaravans achieve high standards of safety in respect of installation and use. For several years, manufacturers of motorcaravans have worked within British Standard (BS)/European Norm (EN) 1949:2002. However, in 2011 the British Standards Institute published a revised LPG installation standard; BS EN 1949:2011. The National Caravan Council (NCC) in conjunction with The Gas Safe Register decided to implement the new standard on 1 September 2012. In effect, this concerns motorcaravans designated as 2013 models.

Regarding work on existing, privately owned models built before that date, the inspection of a gas supply system and verification of its integrity should be carried out by an operator who is deemed 'competent'. You can achieve the necessary competence by attending a recognised training course and passing relevant examinations, such as ACS or ACoPs. Some motorcaravan owners, however, insist that repair, servicing and inspection work is undertaken by a CORGI (Council of Registered Gas Installers) engineer. However, CORGI no longer has gas registration scheme rights and since 1 April 2009, the Gas Safe Register™ has been officially recognised as carrying out gas safety inspections. To find if a gas engineer is registered with Gas Safe, call 0800 408 5500 or go to www.GasSafeRegister.co.uk

items are sealed from the living space, dismantling and service work of this nature does not get included in a standard habitation service. Like absorption refrigerators, heating appliances also need periodic attention, as their manufacturers point out.

Supply of Independent Certificates relating to the gas and electricity installations

At an Approved Workshop, a standard service is carried out by experienced staff. Moreover, certificates of the training courses they've attended have to be placed on display in the service reception. However, if you wish to be supplied with separate gas and electricity approval certificates, workshops can arrange for appropriate independent contractors (described in the accompanying panel) to undertake the inspections. This will incur a further fee unless a service centre is large enough to employ staff who hold these industry-specific qualifications.

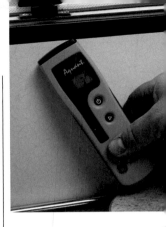

Damp checks

An operation of particular importance included in a habitation service is a damp check. Like many other tasks, this has to be carried out annually in order to comply with the conditions laid down in a motorcaravan's conversion warranty. Even in older models, having routine damp tests carried out is strongly recommended; and although they're included in a habitation service, dealers can often conduct them as a separate operation.

Some owners wish to carry out checks themselves and several types of DIY damp-check meter are on sale. Unfortunately some of the cheaper products are not always reliable, but few owners want to spend a three-figure sum on a professional tester with its all-important percentage meter.

Even professionally calibrated models, which express moisture content as a percentage, are not a lot of use in inexperienced hands. You need to know the conditions in which a meter will operate accurately and its results have to be interpreted correctly. For instance, in appropriate ambient temperatures, readings between 0–15% are considered acceptable. This is because there is natural moisture in some materials used in motorcaravan construction. However, readings between 16–20% signify that further investigation is required, while readings over 20 per cent indicate zones where remedial work is urgently needed.

Readings are typically taken in 40 to 50 areas, and the findings should be recorded on line drawings and given to the customer on completion of a test. Water ingress is always a matter of concern and the purpose of a damp check is to identify early signs of moisture in the fabric of a motorcaravan. If damp is detected, it is essential to take immediate action before it spreads. In fact, anyone purchasing a pre-owned motorcaravan should enquire if a recent damp test report is included in the package. If it isn't, buyers should insist that one is obtained before they proceed with the purchase.

Service schedule

Working to a strict job list is important, and when arranging to have your motorcaravan serviced, ask to see the centre's service schedule before confirming the booking. Similarly, when the work is completed you should be given a copy of the completed schedule, signed, stamped and dated. This document should include comments arising from the technicians' scrutiny. For instance, early signs of condensation forming within a double-

A professional calibrated damp meter is costly and several measures have to be taken to get meaningful readings.

(i) Useful Tip

Floor delamination

Where a bonded floor panel is fitted, a service check investigates if there is any sign of its plywood layers losing their bond with the insulation foam in the core. Composite 'sandwich' floors fitted in coachbuilt models are light, strong, and noted for good thermal insulation. However, their strength is badly compromised if the bonding adhesive fails and layers break away from each other. This is called 'delamination'. The problem can usually be solved if quick action is taken as soon as a fault is detected. For this reason, floor checking is included in habitation service work.

If a light bulb or an LED cluster like this is faulty, a replacement is usually fitted during a habitation service.

glazed window panel should be brought to an owner's attention.

These are standard procedures when a motorcaravan's habitation service is undertaken at an Approved Workshop. Unfortunately there have been incidences of non-accredited service 'specialists' completing the work but not providing customers with written documentation to confirm the operations they've carried out. This is wholly unsatisfactory.

Minor repairs and authorisations

When a service is carried out, it is not unusual for a technician to find faulty items. For example, an interior light might need a new bulb or a replacement fluorescent tube. Many centres will replace such small items as long as there is time to do the job within the allotted period for a service. And while the cost of small components will obviously be added to the invoice, most owners prefer small jobs like this to be carried out there and then.

Making more expensive replacements is a different matter and this is something to check when arranging a service. Get the dealer's assurance that a technician will not embark on costly repairs without gaining your permission first. Of course, 'costly' is a bit vague, so you might agree a cost limit, as well as asking the service receptionist what procedures are followed when a serious problem is encountered. And don't forget to leave the receptionist with your phone number.

Choosing a reliable service specialist

In the first few years of a motorcaravan's life, conversion elements will be covered by a warranty. However, converters of vans and manufacturers will clearly specify that habitation service work must be carried out in accordance with conditions set down in the owner's manual. When the need for a service approaches, you will also need to make sure that your chosen service centre receives the full approval of your motorcaravan's manufacturer. If there is any

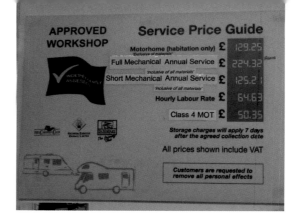

APPROVED WORKSHOP

Service Price Guide

Motorhome (habitation only)	£ 129.25
'Exclusive of materials'	
Full Mechanical Annual Service	£ 224.32
'Inclusive of all materials'	
Short Mechanical Annual Service	£ 125.21
'Inclusive of all materials'	
Hourly Labour Rate	£ 64.63
Class 4 MOT	£ 50.35

Storage charges will apply 7 days
after the agreed collection date

All prices shown include VAT

Customers are requested to
remove all personal effects

doubt, call the customer helpline and request that they approve, in writing, your nominated specialist.

Approved Workshop scheme

In the past there have been examples of poor standards of workmanship during habitation servicing. To resolve this, an initiative was launched by The Camping and Caravanning Club, The Caravan Club and The National Caravan Council (NCC).

Lengthy discussions followed and a nation-wide chain of Approved Caravan Workshops was established in 1999. The idea proved successful, and in 2003 centres specialising in motorcaravan servicing were also brought into the scheme. At that point the name was changed to Approved Workshop.

Before being accepted into the scheme, service centres have to undergo a lengthy and elaborate inspection conducted by an independent agency. A list of approved centres is also obtainable from the clubs and the NCC, all of whom have websites that provide the information. However, approvals are not valid indefinitely and re-examination inspections are conducted annually to ensure that standards are maintained.

The accompanying panel contains further information about the scheme. It provides owners with the assurance of high standards of workmanship, procedural consistency, a detailed invoice and a clear customer complaints procedure. Centres are also obliged to display a full tariff of charges in the service reception, and that is often something owners want to see before making a booking.

Conclusion

Having your motorcaravan's base vehicle and habitation elements serviced regularly is important. However, be aware of the seasonal nature of motorcaravanning and book your vehicle for servicing well in advance of busy spells. Service centres become extremely busy from early spring onwards.

Dealers who are members of the Approved Workshop scheme are required to display a tariff of service charges in their reception. Note: prices shown here were in force when the photo was taken and may have changed.

Useful Tip

Approved Workshops

The number of Approved Workshops is ever-increasing, although it should be noted that some specialise in touring caravans rather than motorhomes.

In one information leaflet, the Approved Workshop scheme is described as 'rigorous, uncompromising and designed to offer you, the customer, an assurance of first class service and value for money.'

Note: There is no implicit suggestion that workshops that are not members of the Approved Workshop scheme are unable to provide owners with a professional and high standard of service. Some most definitely do offer good service and workmanship; but there are others that don't.

CHAPTER SEVENTEEN

WINTER LAY-UP

Most modern motorcaravans are heated, well-insulated and able to provide comfortable accommodation during the cold months of the year. However, circumstances sometimes dictate that you don't have time to use your van in the winter. If it's going to be put into storage, there are some decommissioning tasks to be done.

If you're unable to use your motorhome in winter, some pre-storage work must be done.

If a vehicle is parked for long spells, fatigue cracks can develop on the tyres' sidewalls.

Since all but a few campervans are sold with heaters, many owners use their motorcaravans all year round. From a technical point of view this is ideal; mechanical equipment develops faults if it isn't used regularly.

Occasional driving

Even if you don't sleep in your motorcaravan during winter conditions, an occasional drive is strongly recommended. It helps prevent items from seizing-up, including components like brake mechanisms. Equally, if a vehicle isn't moved for months, the side walls of its tyres start to deteriorate. This is because the same sections are constantly bearing all the weight – and fatigue cracks will then appear later.

Relieving all the weight is achievable if a motorcaravan is fitted with four motorised or hydraulic levelling jacks. These offer security, too. However, robust lifting products like these are costly, and the cheapest way to preserve your tyres is to move a motorcaravan periodically half a metre one way or the other. A small rotation of the wheels then puts its weight on a different section of the tyres, although taking short drives is better still.

Understandably you wouldn't want to take a vehicle out for a routine drive when salt is liberally sprinkled on snow-covered roads. And even though winter enthusiasts sometimes use snow chains, these are tiresome to fit. That aside, it is best to keep a vehicle in use.

Winter breaks

If you do decide to drive your vehicle and use the living space, don't forget that some UK campsites are open most of the year. A few site owners even arrange Christmas and New Year celebrations, and these annual functions are so popular they have to be booked many months in advance.

Some retired motorcaravanners also use their vehicles as a 'second home', and when the weather turns cold, they book a ferry and head for the sun. Countries such as Portugal and Spain are especially popular.

Storage

Notwithstanding the advisability of keeping a vehicle in service, a large number of owners are obliged to park their motorhomes for extended periods. Some are able to keep their vehicle alongside the house; others use a secure storage compound.

Of course, some storage facilities are more secure than others. For instance, off-season pitches created in remote corners of campsites are seldom as secure as purpose-made compounds. Furthermore, before selecting a storage venue, always check the conditions

Snow chains are often used by winter motorcaravanners but they're not easy to fit.

of your insurance policy.

Unfortunately there have been incidents where motorcaravans have been stolen from insecure compounds, and in 1999 this prompted the inauguration of a trade organisation concerned with vehicle storage. A national register of inspected and secure sites was then compiled, and storage companies wishing to gain membership have to pass a rigorous inspection of the premises. Further information about this initiative is provided in the accompanying panel.

Alternatively, if you are a member of one of the national caravanning clubs, they usually keep address lists of storage specialists.

Vehicle security is enhanced when a storage specialist offers indoor parking facilities.

Several camping sites offer storage facilities, although some are less secure than purpose-made compounds.

Caravan Storage Site Owners' Association

Recognising the need to combat motorcaravan theft, a professional trade association was instituted in 1999 to represent caravan and motorhome storage owners. Known as CaSSOA (Caravan Storage Site Owners' Association), this professional body demands a high level of security at its storage centres.

The initiative is closely linked with insurance companies, many of which offer discounts on premiums if a motorcaravan is stored at one of the approved venues. The growing national chain of CaSSOA centres currently exceeds 600 members.

When a storage site owner applies for CaSSOA membership, an inspector checks the facility and successful applicants are issued with a gold, silver or bronze designation to reflect the level of security. Inspection criteria take note of features such as site location, protection from the elements, security, safety and control of access.

Your nearest CaSSOA-approved centre can be accessed through the organisation's website, www.cassoa.co.uk. Bear in mind that some storage sites only accommodate touring caravans; others impose limits on the size of vehicle. Also remember that there are many other secure storage sites located around Britain that are not members of the CaSSOA scheme.

LAYING-UP A MOTORCARAVAN

If you have to leave your motorcaravan unused for a long period, there are several decommissioning tasks you need to carry out. The following section provides basic guidance; more detailed information on water, gas, and refrigeration systems has been given in earlier chapters.

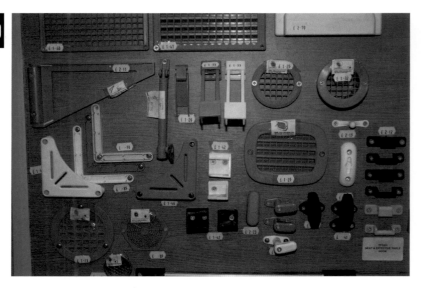

At the end of a season there are often components in need of repair. It's a good discipline to get these replaced before parking-up your vehicle.

All taps have to be opened and the lever on this type of mixer tap must be centralised. The reason for this is explained in Chapter Ten, page 184.

Freshwater tanks are drained down in different ways. In this Swift Sundance's inboard tank, a plug on a chain is merely withdrawn.

In this 2005 Dethleffs Esprit, the water system is drained down by lifting a yellow lever that is conspicuously installed under a bench seat.

A red manual control drains this Truma Combination heater, but it also works automatically and releases water when temperatures are low.

The water held captive in a taste filter cartridge can freeze, expand and split the casing. So remove the filter and buy a new one for installation later.

Even when drained, a waste tank's odour can creep up the pipes and enter the living area. So fit plugs in the sink, basin, and shower tray.

When all wastewater and toilet flush water has been drained, it's a good time to add cleansing chemicals. A variety of types are sold for different purposes.

There are different ways to drain flushing water from bench and swivel-bowl toilets. This picture shows one of Thetford's 1990s bench-type models.

Just in case someone overlooked their toilet emptying duties at the end of the last trip, always remove the cassette for inspection.

Spray the rubber seal and cassette closure blade with Thetford's maintenance spray. Alternatively, use olive oil, but avoid other types of lubricant.

When the cassette has been replaced, always leave the release blade wide open. If closed, dampness on the blade can cause it to stick to the seal.

Interiors get damp easily and inexpensive dehumidifiers are often available. Leaving some types of heaters running unattended is not wise.

When you've finished with an awning at the end of a season, check that it's totally dry before packing it away. Mildew stains are hard to shift.

Dilemma! Leaving blinds down prevents the sun from fading interior fabrics, but blind manufacturers state that it weakens the recoil springs.

During a long lay-up, many owners transfer upholstery to a warm room in a house. This also makes a vehicle less likely to be stolen.

Once a refrigerator has been emptied its door should be left slightly ajar. Guidance on cleaning the interior is given in Chapter Eleven, page 207.

Motorcaravanners often remove a leisure battery during a lay-up period. When transferred to a bench its charge condition is easily monitored.

Check the cells in a lead-acid leisure battery, and if the liquid electrolyte doesn't quite cover the plates, top them up with de-ionised water.

Engine batteries also need to be kept in good condition and the trickle chargers used for classic cars are useful for motorhomes in storage.

A modern gas supply system is fitted with control valves on branches that serve different appliances. These should all be turned off.

If it's to be in storage for a long time, it is strongly recommended that you remove gas cylinders. Important storage advice is given in Chapter Fourteen, page 255.

If you tow a trailer, spray an industrial lubricant like Tri-Flow on the plug and socket. Don't use WD40 here because it might react with this type of plastic.

Bear in mind security precautions; some storage centres disallow devices that prevent a vehicle from being moved.

Some manufacturers make breathable covers to order; both Specialised Accessories and Pro-Tec supply these products to motorhome owners.

Tip

Motorcaravan covers

If your motorcaravan is unused for extended spells, it might seem prudent to cover the roof with a large polythene sheet or plastic 'tarpaulin'. However, these materials sometimes attract damp, and condensation subsequently develops on the underside. In strong wind the flapping plastic can also damage paintwork and the surface of acrylic plastic windows.

Purpose-made motorcaravan covers manufactured using a breathable fabric are much better, even if a small amount of rain might penetrate some of the stitched seams. These products are also useful for keeping a vehicle free of green algae and bird droppings. However, you have to ensure that a motorcaravan is clean before fitting a cover because a film of dust acts as an abrasive when wind blows the fabric about. Some covers are costly, too, and can be quite a struggle to fit or remove – especially on large motorhomes with roof-mounted equipment.

Final notes

The above list of tasks doesn't claim to cover every procedure appropriate for all motorcaravans. Other jobs might also be identified in your owner's manual, so check this with care, because some of your appliances might be different from those discussed in this book.

If you've diligently carried out these close-of-season tasks, re-commissioning your motorhome shouldn't take long. Before leaving home once again you'll want to set up your water system and try it out. Equally, you'll want to check fridge operation, the gas cooker, and so on, especially if you haven't managed to get your motorhome serviced. Add to this a tyre pressure check – not forgetting the spare – and you'll soon be ready to leave. Enjoy your return to the open road and the pleasures that lie ahead.

Modern caravans and motorhomes are built to be used in winter as well as summer and many owners use them regardless of season.

CONTACT ADDRESSES

Note: This address list was correct at the time of going to press. It includes specialist suppliers and manufacturers whose products and services have been mentioned in the text. Several of the firms have websites that can be easily found using search engines.

The motorcaravan manufacturers listed here include specialists offering bespoke building services and individual fitting operations such as the installation of high-top roofs. To obtain a more complete list of motorcaravan manufacturers and importers, consult the monthly Buyers' Guides published in magazines such as

1. *MOTORCARAVAN, MOTORHOME MONTHLY*
2. *PRACTICAL MOTORHOME*
3. *WHICH MOTORHOME*

ABP Accessories,
27 Nether End, Great Dalby,
Leicestershire, LE14 2EY
Tel: 01664 561494
*(American RV Accessories
including Camco products)*

Adria Concessionaires,
Hall Street, Long Melford,
Sudbury, Suffolk, CO10 9JP
Tel: 0870 774 0007
(Importer of Adria motorhomes)

Adrian Bailey Classics,
Unit 1-1A Thornton Grove Works,
Thornton Grove,
Whingate, Leeds, LS12 3JB
Tel: 0113 263 4288
*(Supplier of obsolete and used
spares for Bedford CF vans)*

**Alan H. Schofield Classic
Volkswagen,**
Unit 14, Dinting Lane,
Glossop, Derbyshire, SK13 7NU
Tel: 01457 854267
*(Fabrication and supply of VW
panels and parts)*

Alde International (UK) Ltd,
14 Regent Park, Booth Drive,
Park Farm South,
Wellingborough,
Northamptonshire, NN8 6GR
Tel: 01933 677765
*(Central heating systems,
gas leak detector)*

AL-KO Kober Ltd,
South Warwickshire Business Park,
Kineton Road, Southam,
Warwickshire, CV47 0AL
Tel: 01926 818500
(AMC conversions)

Arc Systems,
13 Far Street, Bradmore,
Nottingham, NG11 6PF
Tel: 0115 921 3175
*(Service, repair and parts for
Carver heating products)*

Arnchem Valeting,
8A Victoria Road,
Tamworth,
Staffordshire, B79 7HL
Terl: 0787 7075605
*(Valeting products and motorhome
cleaning serice)*

Auto-Sleepers,
Orchard Works,
Willersey, Nr. Broadway,
Worcestershire,
WR12 7QF
Tel: 01386 853338
*(Wide range of van conversions
and coachbuilt models)*

Auto-Trail,
Trigano House,
Genesis Way,
Europarc,
Grimsby,
NE Lincolnshire, DN37 9TU
Tel: 01472 571000
*(Coachbuilt motorcaravans and
imported CI, Rollerteam and
Trigano models)*

Auto Glym,
Works Road,
Letchworth,
Hertfordshire, SG6 1LU
Tel: 01462 677766
*(Extensive range of automotive
cleaning products)*

Autovan Services Ltd,
32 Canford Bottom,
Wimborne,
Dorset, BH21 2HD
Tel: 01202 848414
*(Major body repair and rebuilding
work; inspection service)*

Bailey of Bristol,
South Liberty Lane,
Bristol,
BS3 2SS
Tel: 0117 966 5967
*(Approach SE Motorhomes using
Alu-Tech construction)*

Banner Batteries (GB) Ltd,
Units 5-8,
Canal View Business Park,
Wheelhouse Road, Rugeley,
Staffordshire, WS15 1UY
Tel: 01889 571100
*(Vehicle and leisure batteries,
AGM batteries)*

Bantam Trailers,
Units 5 & 6,
Wollaston Industrial Estate,
Raymond Close, Wollaston,
Northamptonshire, NN29 7RG
*(Trailers for small cars including
Smart for two)*

BeenyBox.co.uk,
Station Garage, Trevu Road,
Camborne,
Cornwall, TR14 7AE
Tel: 01209 711093
*(Underfloor sliding storage
locker system)*

Beetles UK Ltd, – see Danbury
Motorcaravans

Bentley Motorhomes,
Unit 3, Swinton Meadows
Industrial Estate,
Meadow Way, Swinton,
Mexborough,
South Yorkshire, S64 8AB
Tel: 01709 590079
(Motorcaravan manufacturer)

Bilbo's Design,
Eastbourne Road, (A22)
South Godstone,
Surrey, RH9 8JQ
Tel: 01342 892499
(Manufacturer of van conversions)

British Car Auctions Ltd,
Sales & Marketing Department,
Expedier House, Portsmouth Road,
Hindhead,
Surrey, GU26 6TJ
Tel: 01428 607440
(Motorcaravan auctions)

Bulldog Security Products Ltd,
Units 2, 3, & 4, Stretton Road,
Much Wenlock,
Shropshire, TF13 6DH
Tel: 01952-728171/3
*(Bulldog security devices
and posts)*

C.A.K. – see Caravan Accessories

Calor Gas Ltd,
Athena Drive, Tachbrook Park,
Warwick, CV34 6RL
Tel: 0800 626626
*(Supplier of butane, propane and
LPG products)*

CAMCO products – See ABP
Accessories

Campingaz
Coleman UK Inc.,
Gordano Gate, Portishead,
Bristol, BS20 7GG
Tel: 01275 845024
*(Supplier of Campingaz butane
and LPG appliances)*

**The Camping &
Caravanning Club,**
Greenfields House,
Westwood Way,
Coventry, CV4 8JH
Tel: 024 7647 5448

Car-A-Tow – see Pro-Tow

**Caravan Accessories
(C.A.K. Tanks) Ltd,**
10 Princes Drive Industrial Estate,
Kenilworth,
Warwickshire, CV8 2FD
Tel: 0870 757 2324
*(Water tanks, accessories,
components, mail order)*

The Caravan Club
East Grinstead House,
East Grinstead,
West Sussex, RH19 1UA
Tel: 01342 326944

The Caravan Centre,
Unit 3A, Gilchrist Thomas
Industrial Estate,
Blaenavon, NP4 9RL
Tel: 01495 792700
*(Specialist breakers supplying
caravan/motorcaravan products)*

The Caravan Panel Shop
Unit 7, Willacy Yard,
Bay Horse Lane,
Catforth, Preston,
Lancashire, PR4 0JD
Tel: 01772 691929
*(Copy GRP mouldings made from
damaged body parts)*

The Caravan Seat Cover Centre,
Cater Business Park,
Bishopsworth,
Bristol,
BS13 7TW
Tel: 0117 941 0222
*(Seat covers, new foam, new
upholstery, made-to-measure
curtains)*

Carver products – see Arc
Systems, Miriad Products and
Truma UK

**Caravan Storage Site Owners'
Association (CaSSOA),**
Market Square House,
St James Street,
Nottingham, NG1 6SG
Tel: 0115 934 9826
*(Register of approved
motorcaravan storage sites)*

Cave and Crag,
Market Place, Settle,
North Yorkshire, BD24 9ED
Tel: 01729 823877
*(Retailer stocking Khyam free-
standing awnings)*

Concept Multi-Car,
Unit 1, Pennypot Industrial Estate,
Hythe,
Kent, CT21 6PE
Tel: 01303 261062
*(High-top roof installation, Reimo
products, van conversions)*

Cramer UK – see Dometic

CRiS
Dolphin House, New Street,
Salisbury,
Wiltshire, SP1 2PH
Tel: 01722 413434
*(Motorcaravan Registration and
Identification Scheme)*

Crossleys,
Unit 33A, Comet Road,
Moss Side Industrial Estate,
Leyland,
Lancashire, PR26 7QN
Tel: 01772 623423
*(Major body repair and rebuilding
work)*

Customer Enquiries (Vehicles),
DVLA,
Swansea,
SA99 1BL
Tel: 0870 2400010
(Guidance on vehicle registration)

Danbury Motorcaravans,
Armstrong Way,
Great Western Business Park,
Yate,
Bristol, BS37 5NG
Tel: 01454 310000
*(VW Type 2 Campervans with
modern conversions, Type 2 VW
Brazilian imports, supply of retrofit
interiors)*

Design Developments,
24 Carbis Close,
Port Solent,
Portsmouth,
Hampshire, PO6 4TW
*(Barry Stimson design consultant
and motorcaravan manufacturer)*

Devon Conversions,
Mainsforth Road,
Ferryhill, Co Durham, DL17 9DE
Tel: 01740 655700
(Van conversion specialist)

Dometic Group,
Dometic House,
The Brewery,
Blandford St Mary,
Dorset, DT11 9LS
Tel: 0844 626 0133
*(Formerly Electrolux Leisure;
amalgamated with WAECO
in 2007: Air conditioners,
refrigerators, Seitz windows,
Cramer cookers)*

**Driver and Vehicle Licensing
Agency (DVLA),**
Swansea,
SA99 1BA
Tel: 0870 2400010
*(Guidance on vehicle registration;
notification of changes to a
vehicle)*

319

Driverite Air Assistance Systems,
*(Available through dealers - air
assistance units; NOT full air
suspension)*

Eberspächer (UK) Ltd,
10 Headlands Business Park,
Salisbury Road,
Ringwood,
Hampshire, BH24 3PB
Tel: 01425 480151
*(Petrol and diesel-fuelled space
and water heaters)*

E & P Hydraulics,
Unit 13,
Elder Court, Lions Drive,
Blackburn,
Lancashire, BB1 2EQ
Tel: 01254 297785
(Hydraulic leveling system)

E.E. Calver Ltd,
Woodlands Park, Bedford Road,
Clapham,
Bedford, MK41 6EJ
Tel: 01234 359584
(Indoor motorcaravan storage)

**Electrical Contractors Association
(ECA),**
3 Buenavista Gardens,
Glenholt,
Plymouth
Tel: 01752 700981
(Mains supply system checking)

Electrolux Leisure Appliances –
see Dometic

Elddis Motorhomes,
Explorer House,
Delves Lane,
Consett,
Co Durham, DH8 7PE
Tel: 01207 699000
*(Motorcaravan manufacturer;
formerly Explorer Group)*

Elsan,
Elsan House,
Bellbrook Park,
Uckfield,
East Sussex, TN22 1QF
Tel: 01825 748200
*(Manufacturers of toilets and
chemical treatments)*

Essanjay Motohomes,
Unit 2, Sovereign Business Park,
48 Willis Way,
Poole,
Dorset, BH15 3TB
Tel: 01202 683608
*(Motorhome and habitation
servicing, components)*

Exhaust Ejector Co,
Wade House Road,
Shelf, Nr. Halifax,
West Yorkshire, HX3 7PE
Tel: 01274 679524
*(Replacement acrylic windows
made to order)*

Exide Leisure Batteries,
Customer Services (Until 2012)
Unit 2, Pisces,
Moseley Road,
Trafford Industrial Estate,
Manchester, M17 1PF
Tel: 0845 4502400
*(Exide base vehicle and leisure
batteries)*

Farécla Products Ltd,
Broadmeads,
Ware,
Hertfordshire, SG12 9HS
Tel: 01920 465041
*(Caravan Pride G3 acrylic
window scratch remover,
GRP surface renovator,
Mer cleaning products)*

The Farnborough VW Centre,
10 Farnborough Road,
Farnborough,
Hampshire, GU14 6AY
Tel: 01252 521152
(VW campervan restorations)

Fiamma accessories – Contact
your motorcaravan dealer

Fenwicks Superior Products,
Fir Tree Farm, Nantwich,
Cheshire, CW5 8JR
Tel: 01270 524111
*(Cleaning products, window
scratch remover)*

Fifth Wheel Co,
Holywell Road, Rhuallt,
Denbighshire, LL17 0AW
Tel: 01745 583000
(Fifth Wheel leisure vehicles)

Filtapac,
2, Highcliffe, Wellingore,
Lincoln, LN5 0HG
Tel: 01522 810340
*(Water filters, refills and
purification products)*

F. L. Hitchman,
46, The Trading Estate,
Ditton Priors,
Bridgnorth,
Shropshire, WV16 6SS
Tel: 01746 712242
*(Portable water containers and
Superclean tank cleaner)*

Foam for Comfort,
Unit 2,
Wyther Lane Trading Estate,
Wyther Lane, Kirkstall,
Leeds, LS5 3BT
Tel: 0113-274 8100
*(Synthetic foam, latex, composite
bonded foam)*

Gaslow International,
Castle Business Park,
Pavilion Way,
Loughborough,
Leicestershire, LE11 5GW
Tel: 0845 4000 600
*(Refillable gas systems,
Gaslow gauges, regulators, and
components)*

Gas Safe Register™,
PO BOX 6804,
Basingstoke, RG24 4NB
Tel: 0800 408 5500
*(Information about Gas Safety
Checks, formerly conducted
by CORGI)*

GB-Sol,
Unit 2,
Glan-y-Llyn Industrial Estate,
Cardiff Road, Taff's Well,
Cardiff, CF15 7JD
Tel: 02920 820910
*(Semi-flexible lightweight solar
panels)*

General Ecology Europe Ltd,
St. Andrews House,
26 Brighton Road,
Crawley, RH10 6AA
Tel: 01293 400644
*(Nature Pure Ultrafine
water purifier)*

Grade UK Ltd,
3 Central Court,
Finch Close,
Lenton Lane Industrial Estate,
Nottingham, NG7 2NN
Tel: 0115 986 7151
*(Status TV aerials, portable TVs
and accessories)*

Grip-Track Mail Order
Tel: 01522 778905 and 07774
604843
www.griptrak.co.uk
*(Portable trackway for
motorcaravans in muddy fields)*

Hawke House Marine Ltd,
Unit E1, Heritage Business Park,
Gosport,
Hampshire, PO12 4BG
Tel: 02392 588588
*(Cut-from-roll Vent Air-Mat anti-
condensation underlay)*

Hella Ltd,
Wildmere Industrial Estate,
Banbury,
Oxfordshire,
OX16 3JU Tel: 01295 272233
*(Hella Towing electrical
equipment)*

IMP,
RO24 3-4 Jarman Way,
Royston,
Hertfordshire,
SG8 5FE
Tel: 01763 241300
*(Zwaardvis high stability table
pillars and sliding mechanisms)*

International Tool Co,
Interlink Way South,
Bardon Hill,
Coalville,
Leicestershire,
LE67 1PH
Tel: 01530 278480
(Mail order precision tyre gauges)

Isabella International Camping,
Isabella House, Drakes Drive,
Long Crendon,
Buckinghamshire,
HP18 9BA
Tel: 01844 202099
*(Awnings and free-standing
structures)*

JC Leisure,
Strand Garage,
Winchelsea,
East Sussex, TN36 4JT
Tel: 01797 227337
*(Van conversions on various base
vehicles)*

Jenste,
The Stables, Pashley Farm,
Ninfield Road,
Bexhill-on-Sea,
East Sussex, TN39 5JS
Tel: 01424 893880
*(RYD live/neutral polarity
changeover unit)*

John Guest Speedfit Ltd,
Horton Road,
West Drayton,
Middlesex, UB7 8JL
Tel: 01895 449233
*(Push-fit plumbing couplings
and pipe)*

Johnnie Longden Ltd,
Unit 24, Dawkins Road
Industrial Estate, Poole,
Dorset, BH15 4JD
Tel: 01202 679121
*(Accessory wholesaler supplying
Henry GE water heaters)*

Jonic,
Eastgate,
White Lund Industrial Estate,
Morecombe, LA3 3DY
Tel: 01524 844106
*(Bedding and fabric accessories
specific for motorcaravans)*

Just Kampers,
Unit 1, Stapeley Manor,
Long Lane, Odiham,
Hampshire, RG29 1JE
Tel: 01256 862288
*(VW Camper and Transporter parts
1968–2004; accessories)*

Labcraft Ltd,
Sunderley Barns, Thaxted Road,
Wimbish
Nr. Saffron Walden,
Essex, CB10 2UT
Tel: 01799 513434
(Lighting and 12V products)

Leisure Accessories,
Britannia Works,
Hurricane Way,
Airport Industrial Estate,
Norwich, NR6 6EY
Tel: 01603 414551
*(Diaphragm pump repairs and
sales)*

Leisure-Serve UK,
8 The Buntings,
Bicester,
Oxfordshire,
OX26 6WE
Tel: 01869 247936
*(Supplier of refrigerator
components and accessories)*

Khyam
See Cave and Crag
*(Free-standing quick erect
awnings)*

**Magnum Mobiles and Caravan
Surplus,**
Unit 9A, Cosalt Industrial Estate,
Convamore Road,
Grimsby,
DN32 9JL
Tel: 01472 353520
*(Caravan/motorcaravan surplus
stock; bespoke building services)*

Marlec Engineering,
Rutland House, Trevithick Road,
Corby,
Northamptonshire, NN17 5XY
Tel: 01536 201588
(Wind and solar systems)

Maxview,
Common Lane, Setchey,
King's Lynn,
Norfolk, PE33 0AT
Tel: 01553 813300
*(TV aerials, satellite TV products,
free guidebooks)*

Merlin Equipment,
Unit 1, Hithercroft Court,
Lupton Road,
Wallingford,
Oxfordshire, OX10 9BT
Tel: 01491 824333
(PROwatt inverters)

Mer Products, See Farécla

Middlesex Motorcaravans,
22 Station Parade.
Whitchurch Lane,
Edgware,
Middlesex, HA8 6RW
Tel: 020 8952 4045
*(Complete and part-build panel
van conversions; VW T5 roof
installations)*

Miriad Products,
Park Lane,
Dove Valley Park,
Foston,
South Derbyshire,
DE65 5BG
Tel: 01283 586060
(UK Distributor of Truma parts)

**The Motor
Caravanners' Club,**
Wood Farm Estate,
Marlbank Road,
Welland,
Malvern, WR13 6NA
Tel: 01684 311677

**Munster Simms
Engineering Ltd,**
Old Belfast Road,
Bangor,
Co. Down,
Northern Ireland,
BT19 1LT
Tel: 02891 270531
*(Whale heaters, semi-rigid
pipework, pumps, taps and water
accessories)*

Murvi,
4 East Way,
Lee Mill Industrial Estate,
Ivybridge,
Devon, PL21 9GE
Tel: 01752 892200
(Van conversion specialist)

**The National
Caravan Council,**
Catherine House,
Victoria Road,
Aldershot,
Hampshire, GU11 1SS
Tel: 01252 318251
*(Trade association for caravans and
motorhomes)*

**National Inspection Council for
Electrical Installation Contracting,
(NICEIC)**
Warwick House,
Houghton Hall Park,
Houghton Regis,
Dunstable, LU5 5ZX
Tel: 01582 539000
*(Certification to confirm a
motorcaravan is correctly wired for
mains electricity)*

The Natural Mat Company,
99 Talbot Road,
London, W11 2AT
Tel: 0207 9850474
*(Slatted sprung beech bed
systems, anti-condensation
underlay)*

**National Trailer and
Towing Association,**
1, Alveston Place,
Leamington Spa,
Warwickshire, CV32 4SN
Tel: 01926 335445
*(Trade association for all aspects of
towing equipment)*

**Noise Killer Acoustics
(UK) Ltd,**
103 Denbydale Way,
Royton,
Oldham,
OL2 5UH
Tel: 0161 643 8070
*(Noise reduction systems
for motorcaravans)*

North East Truck+Van,
Cowpen Bewley Road,
Haverton Hill,
Billingham,
Cleveland,
TS23 4EX
Tel: 01642 370555
*(Major chassis alterations:
air suspension installations)*

Nu Venture Campers,
Unit 7,
Actons Walk,
Wood Street,
Wigan,
Lancashire, WN3 4HN
Tel: 01942 238560
*(Motorcaravans built to customer
specification)*

Nu Venture Motor Homes,
Unit 2,
Seven Stars Road,
Wallgate,
Wigan,
Lancashire, WN3 5AT
Tel: 01942 494090
*(Motorcaravans built to customer
specification)*

O'Leary Spares and Accessories,
314 Plaxton Bridge Road,
Woodmansey,
Nr Beverley,
East Yorkshire, HU17 0RS
Tel: 01482 868632
*(Caravan/motorcaravan
surplus stock)*

Osma rainwater products
– sold through builders' merchants
*(Osma weld adhesive used for
waste pipes and tank connections)*

Parma Industries,
34-36 Carlton Park
Industrial Estate,
Saxmundham,
Suffolk, IP17 2NL
Tel: 01728 745700
*(Wheel trims, dashboard
plastic veneer, general accessories)*

Pennine Leisure Supplies,
Unit G9, Lock View,
Elland,
West Yorkshire, HX5 9HD
Tel: 01422 313455
*(Wholesaler of accessories and
BCA Powerpart products)*

Plug-In-Systems – Contact your
motorcaravan dealer
*(12V control components, water
level sensors, gauges)*

Powerpart 230v accessories – see
Pennine Leisure

Propex Heat Source Ltd.,
Unit 5,
Second Avenue Business Park,
Millbrook,
Southampton,
SO15 0LP
Tel: 023 8052 8555
www.propexheatsource.co.uk
*(Propex compact blown air gas
heaters: Malaga Mk II water
heater)*

Pro-Tow
Unit 1, 565 Blandford Road,
Hamworthy, Poole,
Dorset, BH16 5BW
Tel: 01202 632488
*(Car-a-Tow towing frames; Solar
Solutions solar panels)*

PWS,
Unit 5,
Chalwyn Industrial Estate,
Old Wareham Road,
Parkstone, Dorset,
BH12 4PE
Tel: 01202 746851
*(Racks, protector bars, custom-
made tow bars)*

Rainbow Conversions,
Unit 1, Algores Way,
Wisbech,
Cambridgeshire, PE13 2TQ
Tel: 01945 585931
*(Van conversions built to order;
Vöhringer ply and accessories)*

Regal Furnishings,
Unit 4, Merlin Way,
Quarry Hill Industrial Estate,
Ilkeston,
Derbyshire,
DE7 4RA
Tel: 01159 329988
*(Upholstery, foam, bespoke
curtains)*

Remis UK, – through accessory
dealers
*(Remis blinds, flyscreens, roof
windows)*

RoadPro Ltd,
Stephenson Close,
Drayton Fields,
Daventry,
Northamptonshire,
NN11 5RF
Tel: 01327 312233
*(Accessories, chargers,
reversing aids, TVs)*

Russek Publications,
Unit 6,
29a Ardler Road,
Caversham,
Reading,
Berkshire, RG4 5AE
Tel: 0845 0942130
*(Vehicle repair manuals including
Talbot Express models)*

Ryder Towing Equipment Ltd,
Alvanley House,
Alvanley Industrial Estate,
Stockport Road East,
Bredbury,
Stockport,
SK6 2DJ
Tel: 0161 430 1120
(Electrical towing equipment)

RYD,
Live/neutral polarity changeover
unit – see Jenste.

Sargent Electrical Services, Ltd,
Unit 39,
Tokenspire Business Park,
Woodmansey,
Beverley,
HU17 0TB
Tel: 01452 678987
(12V controls and panels)

Seitz Windows – see Dometic
Group

**The Self Build Motorcaravanners
Club,**
PO BOX 3345,
Littlehampton,
BN16 9FU
www.sbmcc.co.uk
*(Web-based club serving
motorcaravan self-builders)*

Sew 'n' Sos
Tel: 01775 767633
*(Storage bags, covers and blinds
made from heavy-duty fabrics)*

SF Detection,
Hatch Pond House,
4 Stinsford Road,
Poole,
Dorset,
BH17 0RZ
Tel: 01202 645577
*(Carbon monoxide detectors,
LP Gas alarms)*

Shield Total Insurance,
Floor 9,
Market Square House,
St James's Street,
Nottingham, NG1 6FG
Freephone 0800 39 30 33
*(Motorcaravan insurance including
self-builds)*

Ship Shape Bedding,
Turners Farm,
Crowgate Street,
Tunstead,
Norfolk, NR12 8RD
Tel: 08704 464233
*(Cut-from-roll DRY Mat™
anti-condensation mattress
underlay)*

SHURflo Ltd,
Unit 5, Sterling Park,
Gatwick Road,
Crawley, RH10 9QT
Tel: 01293 424000
(Water pumps)

Sika Ltd,
Watchmead,
Welwyn Garden City,
Hertfordshire, AL7 1BQ
Tel: 01707 394444
*(Sikaflex cartridge sealants
and adhesive sealants)*

Silver Screens,
P.O. Box 9, Cleckheaton,
West Yorkshire, BD19 5YR
Tel: 01274-872151
(Insulated window covers)

Smart Tow
Tel: 07950 968348
*(Dual sensing vacuum-assisted
braking system for A-frame towing)*

**The Society of Motor
Manufacturers and Traders,**
71 Great Peter Street,
London, SW1P 2BN
Tel: 020 7235 7000
*(Trade association with sub
committee concerned with
motorhomes)*

Sold Secure Trust,
5c Great Central Way,
Woodford Halse, Daventry,
Northamptonshire, NN11 3PZ
Tel: 01327 264687
*(Test house conducting security
device testing)*

Spinflo – see Thetford (UK)
Sterling Power Products,
Unit 8, Wassage Way,
Droitwich, WR9 0NX
Tel: 01905 771771
*(Chargers, inverters and
related products)*

Stoves plc,
Company name changed to:

Glen Dimplex Cooking Ltd,
Stoney Lane, Prescot,
Merseyside, L35 2XW
Tel: 0151 426 6551
(Grills, hobs, ovens)

SvTech,
Chandler House, Talbot Road,
Leyland, Lancashire, PR25 2ZF
Tel: 01772 621800
*(Specialist consultants on weight
upgrades and official weight plate
alterations)*

Swift Group,
Dunswell Road, Cottingham,
East Yorkshire, HU16 4JX
Tel: 01482 847332
*(Manufacturer of Ace, Autocruise,
Bessacarr, and Swift motorhomes)*

Symonspeed Ltd,
Cleveland Garage,
1 Cleveland Road,
Torquay,
Devon, TQ2 5BD
Tel: 01803 214620
(SOG toilet system)

TEK Seating Ltd,
Unit 32, Pate Road,
Leicester Road Industrial Estate,
Melton Mowbray,
Leicestershire,
LE13 0RG
Tel: 01664 480689
(Cab seating, seat swivels, seat
bases and upholstery)

Thetford (UK),
Unit 19,
Parkwood Industrial Estate,
Oakham Drive,
Sheffield,
S3 9QX
Tel: 01142 738157
(Norcold refrigerators, toilets
and treatments, Spinflo cooking
appliances)

Towsure Products,
151-183 Holme Lane,
Hillsborough, Sheffield,
South Yorkshire,
S6 4JR
Tel: 0870 60 900 70
(Retailing and mail order
accessories)

TOWtal,
Grove Road,
Stoke-on-Trent,
ST4 4LN
Tel: 01782 333422
('A' Frames, electric brake
actuators, trailers, scooter
racks, tow bars)

Truma UK,
Truma House,
Beeches Park,
Eastern Avenue,
Burton-upon-Trent,
Staffordshire,
DE13 0BB
Tel: 01283 511092
(Space and water heating systems,
gas components, Carver spares)

Trylon Ltd,
Unit J,
Higham Business Park,
Bury Close,
Higham Ferrers,
Northamptonshire,
NN10 8HQ
Tel: 01933 411724
(Resins, glass and guidance
on glass reinforced plastics)

The 12Volt Shop,
9 Lostwood Road, St Austell,
Cornwall, PL25 4 JN
Tel: 01726 69102
(Mail order of 12V electrical
components)

Tyron Safety Bands,
Castle Business Park,
Pavilion Way, Loughborough,
Leicestershire, LE11 5GW
Tel: 0845 4000 600
(Safety bands for filling
wheel wells)

Van Bitz,
Cornish Farm,
Shoreditch,
Taunton,
Somerset,
TA3 7BS
Tel: 01823-321992
(Strikeback T Thatcham-Approved
security, gas alarm, Battery
Master)

Van Window Specialists,
Unit 4,
Riverside Works,
Methley Road,
Castleford,
West Yorkshire,
WF10 1PW
Tel: 01977 552929
(Made-to-measure windows,
supply and fit, VW van
conversions)

Varta Automotive Batteries,
Broadwater Park,
North Orbital Road,
Denham,
Uxbridge,
Middlesex,
UB9 5HR
Tel: 01895 838989
(Leisure batteries, including
gel batteries)

VB Air Suspension,
Unit 13,
Elder Court,
Lions Drive,
Shadsworth Business Park,
Blackburn,
Lancashire, BB1 2EQ
Tel: 01254 848010
(Full air suspension systems, air
assistance and jacking products)

**The Vehicle and
Operator Service Agency,**
91/92 The Strand,
Swansea, SA1 2DH
Tel: 0870 60 60 440
www.vosa.gov.uk/
(Vehicle legislation and
general enquiries)

V & G Caravans,
107 Benwick Road,
Whittlesey,
Peterborough,
Cambridgeshire,
PE7 2HD
Tel: 01733 350580
(Replacement replica
panels in GRP)

WAECO UK products
– see Dometic Group

Watling Engineers Ltd,
88 Park Street Village,
nr. St. Albans,
Hertfordshire,
AL2 2LR
Tel: 01727 873661
(Specially designed towing
brackets)

Webasto Products UK Ltd,
Webasto House, White Rose Way,
Doncaster Carr,
South Yorkshire, DN4 5JH
Tel: 01302 322232
(Diesel-fuelled heaters,
water evaporative air conditioners)

Whale – see Munster Simms
(Water accessories)
Wheelhome,
Tip's Cross, Blackmore Road,
Hook End,
Brentwood,
Essex, CM 15 0DX
Tel: 01277 822208
(Specialist building compact
motorcaravans from MPVs)

Witter Towbars,
Drome Road,
Deeside Industrial Park,
Deeside,
Chester, CH5 2NY
Tel: 01244 284500
(Towbars and cycle carriers)

W4 Ltd,
Unit B,
Ford Lane Industrial Estate,
Arundel,
West Sussex, BN18 0DF
Tel: 01243 553355
(Mains 230V kits, socket testers,
ribbon sealants)

Young Conversions,
Unit 47, Barton Road,
Water Eaton, Bletchley,
Milton Keynes,
Buckinghamshire, MK2 3BD
Tel: 01908 639 936
(Full or part conversions on any
base vehicle, stage payment
conversion, one-off designs)

ZIG Electronics, Ltd,
Saxon Business Park,
Hanbury Road,
Stoke Prior, Bromsgrove,
Worcestershire, B60 4AD
Tel: 01527 556715
(12V controls, chargers, water
level sensors and gauges)

Zippo UK,
Unit 27,
Grand Union Centre,
336B Ladbroke Grove,
London W10 5AS
Tel: 020 8964 0666
(General purpose large-size
gas lighters)

Zwaardvis – see IMP
(High quality table support
systems and accessories)

3M Co,
(Minnesota Mining and
Manufacturing Co.)
To find local supplier
Tel: 0161 237 6130 or
(Manufacturer of Thinsulate
thermal insulation)

INDEX